Value Based Management

VALUE BASED MANAGEMENT

AN INTRODUCTION

Edited by

E Mrudula

2010

Icfai Books

The Icfai University Press

Value Based Management – An Introduction

Editor: E Mrudula

First Edition: 2010
Printed in India

Published by

The Icfai University Press
52, Nagarjuna Hills, Punjagutta
Hyderabad, India – 500 082
Phone: (+91) (040) 23430–368, 369, 370, 372, 373, 374
Fax: (+91) (040) 23352521, 23435386
E-mail: info@icfaibooks.com, icfaibooks@icfai.org, ssd@icfai.org

ISBN: 9788131405062

Editorial Team: Bala K, K Bindu and S Sreedar

Contents

Overview

Senior managers, corporate finance personnel and operating managers are looking for a new management approach that would help them in creating and enhancing the value of their company as well as shareholders. It is often viewed that the major goal of any business is to create and enhance the shareholder value. In today's competitive world, the traditional financial management tools that are already available are no longer sufficient to create or maximize the value of the company. It was, therefore, necessary for organizations to introduce a new approach. This is known as 'Value Based Management' (VBM). It is usually defined as a management approach that is used in maximizing the value of shareholders. It also helps in evaluating how the decision making process will affect value creation and its impact on the organization. The main aim of VBM is to make the stakeholders (shareholders, community, customers, employees and others) profit from the value the company creates.

The company must create a higher return on the capital it employed than any other alternative investment. This can be made possible by making use of certain performance measures like EVA (Economic Value Added), CVA (Cash Value added), MVA (Market Value Added), CFROI (Cash Flow Return on Investment), SVA (Shareholder Value Added), and BSC (Balanced Scorecard). All these performance measures are discussed in detail in this book.

The book is divided into two sections. The first section, titled "Introduction," discusses the history, pros and cons, various performance measures and other aspects of VBM. The second section, titled "Experiences", consists of the experiences of industries and companies that have implemented VBM and are successful in creating and increasing or maximizing the value of their companies as well as shareholders.

The first article titled "**Understanding Value Based Management**" by *E Mrudula* discusses the history of VBM, the three elements, and the benefits and pitfalls of VBM. It also explains the various tools of VBM and also how efficiently VBM works.

The second article titled "**Value Based Performance Measures: A Comparative Study**" by *A Lakshminarasimha* and *R Harish* discusses performance measurement techniques like EVA, MVA, CFROI, TSR, and SVA that are used by various consultants like Stern Stewart, BCG, Alcar, Marakon and McKinsey. The authors arrive at the conclusion that smaller companies may use comparatively simple measures such as EVA and MVA. Larger companies may benefit by using more complex metrics. The extent to which one makes the adjustments and refinements to improve accuracy can also be decided based on the relative importance and sensitivity of making very refined calculations and it is not the metric that one uses that determines the final result, but how one actually performs.

The third article titled "**Facets of 'Shareholder Value Creation'**" by *V V Gopal* discusses the two approaches of measuring shareholder value—single and multi-period metrics—along with examples of companies like Cadbury Schweepes and Electrolux, which have adopted these two approaches for maximizing their shareholder value.

The article also discusses the role of intangible assets and employees in creating shareholder value. It cites the example of Allied Plywood Corporation, an employee-owned company which focused on its unique incentive systems. As a result of this, the company was able to improve its quality of products and maximize shareholder returns. How shareholder value can be created during economic downturn and divestiture is explained through the example of Infosys.

A review of the book **"Value Based Management: Developing a Systematic Approach to Creating Shareholder Value"** by *Niranjan Swain, Nupur Hetamsaria* and *Gina George* is about developing an effective and tested model for establishing and managing a firm's value and shows managers how to measure value, understand the differences between internal and external value, and identify and implement activities that contribute to value. It concludes by saying that value management is a powerful tool which, if used correctly, can drive dramatic improvements in decision-making. However, care should be taken to see that this tool is not misused and organizations should be aware of what they are trying to achieve and how their business issues should drive a customized approach to value management.

The fifth article titled **"New Concepts in Value-Based Management: TRS Mapping and Total Economic Profit"** by *John J Ballow, Brian F McCarthy* and *Michael J Molnar* suggests two new tools—TRS mapping methodology and Total economic profit—by which forward looking executives can focus on what really matters in creating a high performance business. According to Accenture's research of high performance business, those organizations that can manage for both today and tomorrow will be the most successful.

The sixth article titled **"Contemporary Value Based Management: Fallacies of Today's Value Based Management and its Impact on Corporate Investment Behavior"** by *Achim Seisreiner* and *Sebastian Träger* argues that the multidimensionality of value helps the VBM to return to the right track. As today's VBM is restricted to the logic of shareholder satisfaction, corporate decision-making is mainly influenced by the future prospects of adding value to the invested capital. The authors say that there exists an immense variety of value sources that need to be included to fully assess corporate value added. They also suggest that VBM can secure corporate sustainability only by broadening its value.

The second section deals with experiences of different organizations that practiced value based management.

"**Implementing Value Based Management**" by *Samuel C Weaver* and *J Fred Weston* cites the case of Hershey Foods which is a leading snack food company and the largest North American manufacturer of quality chocolate and non-chocolate confectionery products to overcome the problem of diversification. It has used two methods to overcome the problem of diversification—calculate averages over long periods of time and compound annual returns to shareholders. As a result of these methods, the company was able to enhance its domestic market share to 26.8% compared to Mars at 17.0% domestic market share.

"**Concept and Usage of EVA by Two Indian Leaders: Infosys and HLL**" by *T R Shastri* discusses the implementation of EVA by two Indian companies who are leaders in their own area—service and manufacturing sectors. The author, after comparing the economic profits of both these leaders, concludes that economic value addition as a percentage of capital deployed is always higher in HLL than in Infosys.

"**Empowerment and Growth: The EVA Story at TCS**" by *S Mahalingam* discusses the TCS way in stepping towards institutionalising leading edge practices in hiring, training, and people care, with an innovative EVA-based compensation model that offers high growth, high performance internal environment to empower, proactive, high-brand consultants operating in a dynamic external environment, to become a truly global organization. This article outlines the evolution of EVA, the EVA model, strategic benefits and a comprehensive EVA-based Incentive Compensation Plan in TCS.

The tenth article titled "**Value Based Management Concepts: Suitable Tools for Airline Management?**" by *Carsten Homburg, Andrea Theissen* and *Alexander Knigge* discusses the level of implementation of VBM concepts in the major global airlines. A survey was conducted from May to July 2004 based on the number of transported passengers during 2003 in 80 private airlines. The survey examined the importance of value based key performance indicators for both the perennially operative business plan and strategically subordinated business plan, which made the airlines consider VBM as an important strategic planning instrument.

The survey revealed that the importance of these concepts for airline management was lower than in other industries.

"**PKN ORLEN: Polish Energy Giant's Growth Strategies**" is a case study written by *Shalini*. It discusses Poland's largest oil refining and fuel retailing company, PKN (Polski Koncern Naftowy) ORLEN, which has grown rapidly since its establishment in 1999. Aiming to become a major oil company in Europe, the company has forayed into foreign markets through acquisitions. The case offers scope to discuss the growth strategies of PKN ORLEN in western and central Europe's energy markets through a 'value based management project' that would consolidate its various business operations.

The last article titled "**Shareholder Value Creation of Microsoft and GE**" by *Pablo Fernández* defines and analyzes shareholder value creation. To help understand the concept better, the example of two listed companies, General Electric and Microsoft between 1992 and 2003, are used. Equity market value, the shareholder value added, the shareholder return, and the required return to equity are defined to obtain the created shareholder value. The created shareholder value of 400 American companies during the eleven-year period, 1992-2003, is also calculated in the article.

SECTION I

INTRODUCTION

1

Understanding Value Based Management

E Mrudula

Corporate managers in today's competitive world are looking for an enhanced financial performance tool—Value Based Management. It is used to increase the value of the company and, thereby, maximize the value of the shareholders. It is also used to monitor, plan, and control the firm's operations which help in enhancing shareholder value. Different financial measures are used in measuring and creating value to the company. Some of the most popular measures include Free Cash Flow method, EVA, MVA, and CFROI. Various consulting firms serve as promoters of these financial measures. This article discusses what is VBM, explains the various tools of VBM and also how well does VBM work.

"The value of a principle is the number of things it will explain; and there is no good theory of disease which does not at once suggest a cure."

– Ralph Waldo Emerson[1]

[1] VBM & The EVA Metric: A Way to Add Value!, Vidhya S R, Bharathidasan Institute of Management, http://www.indiainfoline.com/bisc/ari/valu.pdf

Introduction

Today's competitive world is putting greater focus on value creation than anything else. It has become the core task of the management. In order to achieve this, traditional financial management systems are no longer sufficient. Companies are striving to create a new and enhanced financial management control to create value and maximize the value of shareholders—Value based management. It is a new management buzz word that ensures that corporations are able to maximize the value of the company, and they're by the shareholders. It is used for improving organizational performance and, there by, creating value for the company. The three essentials of VBM are to create value, manage the value and measure it. It is simple to create and manage but complex to measure. The basic idea of VBM is to maximize the value of the shareholders and also to make employees, customers and others, profit from the value the company creates. The main difference between VBM and traditional financial system is in the importance given to cash flow and growth potential. VBM generally aims to provide corporate governance, corporate culture, corporate mission, decision system and reward systems.

According to the research made and given on www.valuebasedmanagement.com before industrial revolution the companies were small and were able to create value. But by the end of the 19th century, corporations had become big and complex and it was difficult for them to create value. At the beginning of the 20th century due to the Internet bubble bursts and the Enron scandal stakeholders were blamed for all the scandals and the companies were forced to develop a new management tool apart from the traditional financial management measures and this tool was called value-based management.

VBM as a management system or a strategy which helps to maximize value creation, increases corporate transparency, internal communication, decision-making process, allocation of resources, planning and budgeting. It also helps in preventing takeovers; yet VBM is not without pitfalls. Creating value may seem to be simple, but it isn't. Implementing and measuring the value of the company using various performance measures, especially like balanced scorecard, is a complex process. An effective VBM method requires effective support from the top managements. Though, adopting a performance measure creates value to the company as well as to the stakeholders, implementing them is quite costly.

Generally, it is a well-known fact that the value of any organization is determined by cash flows that are expected in the future. The value of a company is created when it invests a certain amount of capital at returns that exceed the cost of that capital. It focuses on better decision-making among all the levels of the organization. Once VBM is implemented in an organization it brings tremendous benefits to the organization by way of improving the performance as well as by creating value. It is obvious that a manager, called value based manager would be handling the operations of VBM. It is the VBM manager to decide how he uses this management approach in creating value and as a decision-making tool.

The first step in implementing VBM is maximizing the value of the company as well as that of the shareholders. The traditional financial performance measures like earnings growth, earnings per share and return on investment were not enough for creating value. Therefore, today's companies concentrate more on future cash flows. VBM, apart from looking at the financial perspective is also used in satisfying the customer, product innovation and the employee who, thereby, also creates value as well as increase it.

Performance Measuring Tools

Some of the important performance measuring tools include economic value added/market value added, cash flow return on investment, total return to shareholders and shareholder value added and cash value added. Organizations use these measures to create and maximize shareholder's value, thereby, also increasing the value of the company. It is implemented globally. Barclays, the biggest and fifth largest bank in assets in Britain, has implemented VBM in order to increase its financial performance. Some of the above mentioned performance measures are briefly discussed. Various consultants have promoted the use of each of these tools. Like the free cash flow by McKinsey & Co., EVA by Stern Stewart & Co and CFROI/TSR by Boston Consulting Group promoted method.

Economic Value Added (EVA) is one of the most important financial performance measures that is used to measure the true economic profit of an organization. It is generally calculated as the difference between the net profit after tax and capital charges. Bennett Stewart explains that Stern Stewart has introduced EVA to help managers incorporate two basic principles of finance into their decision-making. The first is that the primary financial objective of any company should be to maximize the wealth of its shareholders. The second is that the value of a company depends on the extent to which investors expect future profits to exceed or fall short of the cost of capital. Stern Stewart has worked with 300 companies to make them aware of EVA and to make them become EVA companies. Their clients include virtually every type of company, public and private, from banks to heavy manufacturers and even government agencies, including the US Postal Service[2]. The list of the companies Stern Stewart has worked with is given on http://www.sternstewart.com/evaabout/evacomp.php.

Value Based Management Framework

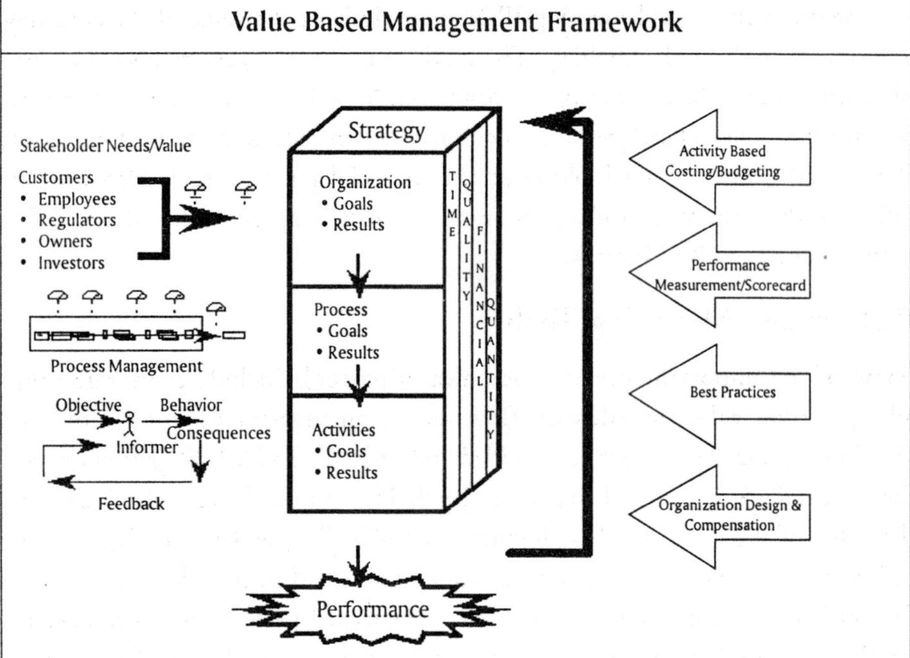

VBM provides an integrated measurement and management framework defined by three levels of performance, in an almost mechanical structure in the above figure. The levels represent different depths of measurement detail, namely:

1. **Organization** – describes the organization entity in a highly aggregate fashion. Organization performance is equal to the sum of the performance of all of the processes. Strategy is developed at the organization level. Execution of strategy is accomplished

Contd...

[2] http://www.sternstewart.com/evaabout/whatis.php

Contd...
by taking actions and performing activities. Organization level measures include such things as ROE, Profit Margin, Customer Satisfaction and Service Level. Decisions and measures at the organization level define process measures and change in activities. There is a very clear relationship or linkage between each of the levels. 2. **Process** – describes groupings of related activities. Activities in a process usually occur in a number of departments, where the output of an activity becomes the input to the next activity in sequence, across the organization. Process performance is equal to the sum of the performance of each of the activities within a process. All organization activities fit within a process of some kind, whether it be operational, administrative or management. Process measures include process capacity, number of errors produced, and cycle time, from the beginning of the process to completion. Processes consist of sub-processes, aided by support processes. Support processes facilitate or enable primary processes. Examples of support processes include: – acquisition of appropriately skilled personnel – provision of proper training programs – provision of appropriate computing and communications technology – change management/human resources management 3. **Activity** – describes the work done by people or machines within the context of a department. An activity consists of a set of tasks, which have a common activity driver. An activity is a meaningful level of analysis for which to measure performance. At this level, it is possible to capture information in all key dimensions of time, quality, cost (resources consumed and capacity (quantity)). Because activities are performed and managed within functional departments, they provide a meaningful mechanism with which to analyze job and organization design, as well as to provide a mechanism to perform activity based budgeting.
Source: Performance Measurement and Value Based Management, by Paul Sharman, Focused Management Information Inc, www.focusmag.com, 2000.

Market Value Added (MVA) is the difference between the market value of the company and the invested capital. There is a direct relation between MVA and shareholder value. Higher value of MVA means the company has created substantial wealth to its shareholders and vice-versa. Cash Flow Return on Investment (CFROI) is originally developed by HOLT value associates. It is calculated annually. It is mainly used by portfolio managers and corporations. It is calculated as cash flow divided by market value of capital employed. Shareholder Value Added (SVA) is a value-based performance measure of a company's worth to shareholders. The basic calculation is Net Operating Profit After Tax (NOPAT) minus the cost of capital from the issuance of debt and equity, based on the company's Weighted Average Cost of Capital (WACC).

As John D Martin and J William Petty in their book "Value Based Management—The Corporate Response to the Shareholder Revolution" says for any VBM program to be successful it is essential for an organization to have three primary elements—support of top executives of the company, link between behavior and compensation and finally understanding of the concept of VBM thoroughly by the employees to implement it in their day-to-day work. They also mention that the accounting information that is prepared taking into account the generally accepted accounting principles which come from a number of sources has certain limitations like accounting earning not being equal to cash flow, accounting number not reflecting risk, not including opportunity cost of equity, accounting practices varying from firm to firm and finally they reflecting considering time value of money.

Conclusion

It has been now a decade since companies have been using VBM. Firms have customized, adopted and made various modifications to it and have found that VBM is a management tool which if used properly, leads to increase in shareholder value. Many companies like HP, Tisco, Infosys, and HLL have implemented it and are successful in creating and enhancing shareholder value.

(E Mrudula is Consulting Editor at Icfai Books, Hyderabad.)

References

1. "What Is Value Based Management", www.valuebasedmanagement.com
2. "Some Thinking about Value Based Management", www.squarewheels.com/articles2/vbm.html
3. "Value Based Management: Focusing On Creating Wealth for Shareholders", www.sas.com
4. "Value-Based Management: An Integrated Approach to Value Creation a Literature Review", by Anne Ameels, Dr Werner Bruggeman and Geert Scheipers.
5. "Value Based Management – The Corporate Response to the Shareholder Revolution", by John D Martin and J William Petty, Harvard Business School Press, 2000.
6. What is Value-Based Management? An Excerpt from Valuation: Measuring and Managing the Value of Companies, Second Edition, Timothy Koller, http://www.exinfm.com/pdffiles/whba94.pdf, The McKinsey Quarterly 1994 Number 3.

7. "Value Based Management", http://www.sca.com/default.asp?/investors/value.asp
8. "Value Based Management", http://www.allianz.com/azcom/dp/cda/0,186870-44,00.html
9. "Value Based Management: Economic Value Added or Cash Value Added?" by Fredrik Weissenrieder, Weissenrieder Consulting AB December 1, 1997
10. "Value-Based Management Control Processes to Create Value through Integration: A Literature Review", by Anne Ameels, Werner Bruggeman and Geert Scheipers, Vlerick Leuven Gent Management School, http://www.vlerick.b ... vlgms-wp-2002-17.pdf
11. "A Unifying Theory of Value Based Management" by Samuel C. Weaver and J. F. Weston, Anderson Graduate School of Management Finance (University of California, Los Angeles), 2003.

2

Value Based Performance Measures: A Comparative Study

A Lakshminarasimha and R Harish

From the smallest business entity to the largest one, businesses and businessmen are continuously improving their total income and wealth. If all strategic decisions of a firm are made using a suitable measurement technique, which has an orientation on value creation, it would be more beneficial to all the stakeholders concerned. In this article, an attempt is made to summarize the various value-based performance measurement techniques (such as EVA, MVA, CVA, CFROI, SVA and others), and tie them up to the degree of sophistication required, depending on the size and complexity of the companies and their operations. Reference is also made to the Balanced Score Card technique, as it monitors performance across diverse dimensions in an integrated manner. Adopting the appropriate performance measure would enable all organizations from the tiny to the large to measure and then strategise.

"Commerce is a game of skill which many men play, but which few play well".

– Ralph Waldo Emerson

Source: www.pes.edu, June 2006. The article was originally published as "Organizational Performance Measures: A Review".

Introduction

The strategic purpose of a firm is to create value that meets the needs of its shareholders. Value Based Management is central to Strategic Management. Value consists of the performance characteristics and attributes provided by companies in the form of goods and services for which the companies' customers are willing to pay. The financial goal of a profitable business is to produce returns in excess of its weighted average cost of capital from lenders and investors.

At this point we may reflect on why this is so. In larger companies it is the basic need of the Institutional Investors. The Business Press also emphasizes the objective of creation of value for the share holders. In large companies Top Management Compensation is being linked to creation of share holder value. Leading major companies have already adopted the use of better measures like EVA.

Now addressing Management Process linkages, Business Strategy consists of the management process of discovering, defining and implementing business activities that will result in a value-enhanced future of the firm. Having said this, this is invariably linked to the Performance Measurement System, which is a management process that is used to monitor business activities and facilitate achievement of the firm's objectives. These two form two nodes of the triangle, the third node being Shareholder value propositions. All of them are interconnected by the Business Processes—which is a collection of Linked Business Activities.

The above concept can be best illustrated by the diagram below:

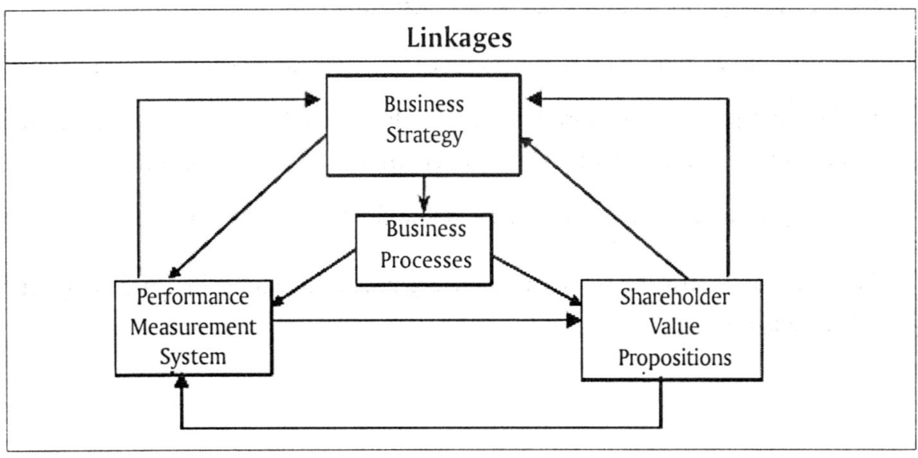

Business Strategy: Management process to ensure that the business produces value for the firm.

Performance Measurement System: Process of measurement to monitor the progress of the firm towards value addition.

Business Process: Activities within a firm which are linked to each other, and add value to the company's product/service.

Shareholder Value Propositions: Relationships between the firm and its stakeholders, relative to other options.

In the diagram, "Linkages" assuming business strategy, the processes and shareholder value propositions are fairly well defined, what is left to be defined is the performance measurement system.

The Principles of Performance Measurement are:

- Performance measurement should be systematic.
- The measurement method proposed supports business strategy.
- Each performance measure has a good logic behind it.
- The measurement method measures at least 80% of the inputs required for achieving a given level of performance.
- Measures performance of both business and management processes.
- Performance standards should be laid by the external environment.
- The company or organisation should already have a measurement culture and subjective elements in the measurement system are minimal.
- The proposed measurement system should be simple to use.

The type of metric to be used in an organization would be guided by the following diagram.

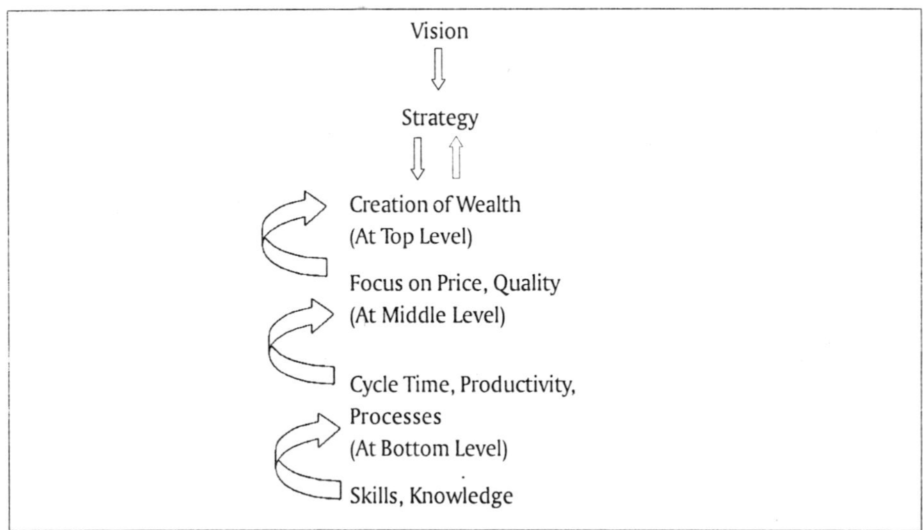

At the bottom level, simple methods may be okay. As one progresses towards the top where creation of real wealth is the prime concern, the metrics have to be examined a little carefully to determine the one which fits the organization.

It may be noted that this article would be discussing such methods which are of importance for strategic decision making and not those which are useful at the operational level, such as skills, knowledge, productivity, quality, etc.

Review of Some Measurement Methods Currently Available

We have traditional accounting based measures such as earnings per share and return on investment. But these do not reflect the risk or the opportunity cost of investment. We need a measuring yardstick or a metric which can measure value creation.

In recent years, many companies the world-over have taken to 'value based' performance measures, which are superior to the accounting based metrics, in that they provide a more realistic and practical insight into a company's performance and also help in making better choices when faced with alternative business projects and investment plans. The 'value' referred to in 'value based' performance measures is shareholder value. The emphasis on shareholder value emerges from the premise that the ultimate aim of all businesses is to maximize the long term wealth of their owners, i.e., their shareholders. Also, maximizing shareholder value acts as an overarching objective that helps to resolve conflicts and take trade-off decisions in a consistent manner.

1. Stern Stewart Approach – EVA & MVA

a) Economic Value Added (EVA)

The most popular and simplest value based performance measure is Economic Value Added (EVA). EVA is in fact a registered trade mark of Stern Stewart & Co., a New York based consulting firm, which introduced this concept in 1982. EVA is an estimate of a company's 'economic profit' or 'residual income', which is the amount by which the earnings exceed or fall short of the return that investors could get by investing in other businesses of comparable risk. EVA is defined in monetary terms and is a period-based measure.

In equation form, EVA = NOPAT – {WACC x CI}

where,

NOPAT = Net Operating Profit After Tax

(In simple terms, NOPAT is essentially net profit after tax + interest. Interest is added back as it is considered under cost of capital.)

WACC = Weighted Average Cost of Capital or Capital Cost Rate

(= Charge rate on equity x proportion of equity in total capital + cost of interest bearing debt x proportion of debt in total capital x (1 – tax rate). Charge rate on equity is the opportunity rate of return from an equity investment of comparable risk.)

CI = Total Capital Invested at the beginning, or the average capital during the period

(This is primarily book value of common equity & preferred stock plus interest bearing short-term & long-term debt.)

EVA is considered superior to several commonly used financial performance yardsticks. For example, maximizing rates of return on investment, capital employed or net assets (i.e., ROI, ROCE, RONA), do not necessarily maximize the absolute value of return to shareholders, which is in fact more important. Further, these measures ignore the requirement that the rate of return should at least be equal to the rate of capital cost.

Likewise, Return On Equity (ROE) too does not consider the capital cost rate, and hence, it does not tell whether the company is creating wealth for shareholders or destroying it. More important is the fact that ROE can be enhanced by increasing leverage, which is not advisable, as it would increase the company's financial risk. Both earnings and earnings per share (EPS) can be increased by investing more into the business and scaling up operations, even if the rate of return is not up to the mark.

EVA has become a popular performance measure among many of the world's renowned and admired companies, because of its simplicity and clear and direct linkage with shareholder value creation. Around 250 major corporates across the world (with total annual revenue exceeding $400 billion) have implemented EVA by engaging the services of Stern Stewart & Co. Coca Cola, Siemens, Whirlpool and Eli Lilly are among the globally well known users of EVA. Among leading Indian companies, Infosys, Tata Steel and Tata Consultancy Services are examples of those that have adopted EVA.

EVA is measured for each period with the objective of progressively increasing the same. The methods available for improving EVA are to achieve better returns on existing operations, reduce the cost of capital, use less capital to realize the same returns, invest in projects that provide higher returns, liquidate capital or curtail investments in operations with inadequate returns. In order to realize its full potential, EVA has to be integrated into the strategy development process, backed by a sources and drivers of value creation.

The main limitation is that as EVA is in monetary terms, it is heavily influenced by business size. Further, it is based on financial accounting methods which can be manipulated by managers. It focuses on immediate results and is weak as a long term performance metric. It is also not adjusted for inflation-induced biases.

It may be noted that going by the tenets of basic economic theory, if product and factor markets are perfectly competitive, there should be no excess profits and consequently no economic value addition. This brings us to an important practical reality that sources of value addition such as first mover advantage, ability to realize better prices, etc., could erode over time due to increasing competition. Thereafter, companies would have to look for more attractive alternatives to maintain their performance levels.

b) Market Value Added (MVA)

MVA is a companion measure to EVA, advocated by Stern Stewart & Co. MVA of a firm is defined as the difference between total market value of capital and the actual capital invested by way of common equity, preferred stock and all forms of debt. In terms of a formula,

MVA = Market value of capital – Book value of capital

The principle behind MVA is that if the difference between market value and book value of capital is positive and increasing, shareholders' wealth would increase.

However, in case the market value of a company's equity increases at a slower rate than the equities of other comparable firms with similar risk profile, then the company in question would in fact be destroying value for its shareholders in a comparative sense, though in absolute terms it may be creating value. The primary disadvantage with MVA therefore is that it does not consider the opportunity cost of the capital invested in the company. The other limitations of MVA are that it does not take account of interim returns to shareholders (by way of dividends) and cannot be applied to privately held firms or to business divisions within a company.

The concept of Excess Return (ER) overcomes the first disadvantage associated with MVA as pointed out above. ER is defined as the difference between the actual value and the expected value at the end of the measurement period. In other words, it amounts to redefining MVA with a minor adjustment as follows:

MVA = Market value of capital – book value of capital – increase capital value that would have been achieved through investments in other alternative avenues of comparable risk

Going back once again to the basic concept of MVA, in theory, market value of equity should reflect the capital market's expectations of future free cash flows, discounted at the cost of capital. However, actual market value could be influenced from time to time to varying degrees by several extraneous factors, short term speculative pressures, etc., as a result of which MVA is subject to fluctuations and distortions.

c) EVA Projection and MVA

Though its opponents criticize that EVA is primarily a financial measure that reports past performance, it can be projected into the future and used for comparing investment options. If one forecasts the capital, NOPAT and capital charge of future years, one can project a future EVA stream and also calculate the present value of the EVA stream. In theory, this should be the same as MVA, because conceptually, MVA reflects the present value of all future EVAs., Therefore, in principle,

$$MVA = EVA_1/(1 + c)^1 + EVA_2/(1 + c)^2 + EVA_3/(1 + c)^3 + \dots\dots\dots$$

where, c = weighted average cost of capital.

Figure 1: EVA and MVA

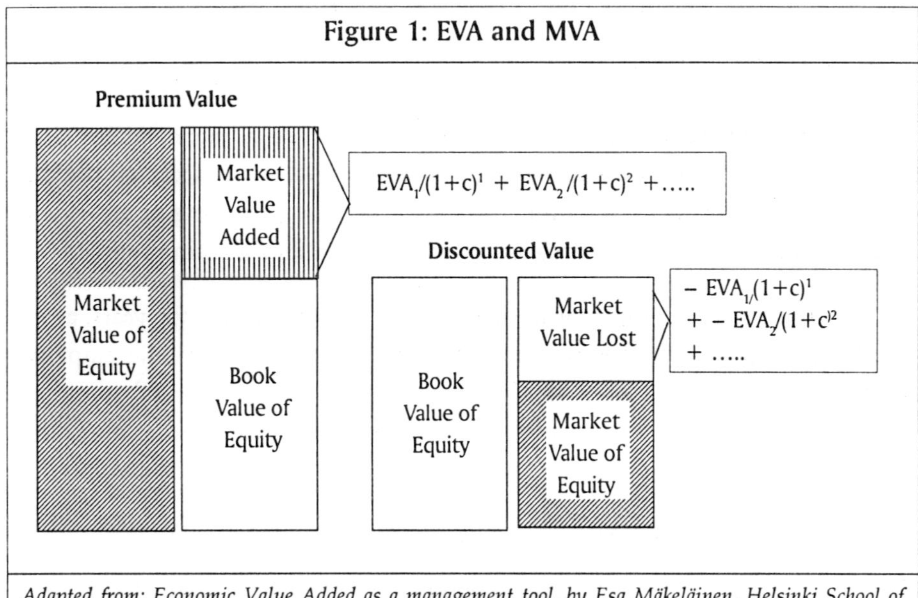

Adapted from: Economic Value Added as a management tool, by Esa Mäkeläinen, Helsinki School of Economics, Finland, http://www.evanomics.com/evastudy.shtmla

2. BCG Approach – CFROI, CVA, TSR and TBR

The central elements of BCG's approach are Cash Flow Return on Investment (CFROI) and Cash Value Added (CVA). The concepts of Total Shareholder Return (TSR) and Total Business Return (TBR) form the foundation of this method. Over 100 global corporate majors have engaged BCG to implement the CFROI program. Procter & Gamble is the best known user of CFROI and TBR. These concepts were originally developed by HOLT Value Associates.

a) **Cash Flow Return on Investment (CFROI)**

In simple terms, CFROI is the equivalent of ROI computed based on cash flows, instead of profits. CFROI compares the sustainable cash flow generated by a firm with the total cash invested (towards both fixed assets and working capital) to generate these inflows. Sustainable cash flow is defined as cash flow less economic depreciation. Economic depreciation is the annuity required for replacing the productive assets at the end of their economic life, calculated as amount required to replace the productive assets divided by future value interest factors of annuity (FVIFA), calculated over the economic life of the assets at the average cost of capital. For a single period, CFROI can be calculated as follows:

CFROI = [Cash Flow – Economic Depreciation]/Cash Invested

For multiple periods, CFROI is computed as the internal rate of return (IRR) that equates the gross investment made by the capital owners to the periodic cash flows by recognizing the finite economic life of depreciating assets and the residual value of non-depreciating assets such as land and working capital.

CFROI for a given project or business plan is the same for all the years, as it is calculated based on the IRR principle. In contrast, return on capital employed (ROCE), which is calculated as NOPAT divided by Book Capital, shows an upward trend. It is less than CFROI during the initial years and is more than CFROI during the later years.

b) **Cash Value Added (CVA)**

CVA is BCG's metric for measuring economic profit. It is conceptually similar to EVA, but is based mainly on cash items.

CVA = OCF – ED – CCOGI

where, OCF = Operating Cash Flow

ED = Economic Depreciation

CCOGI = Capital Charge on Gross Investment

CCOGI is the average capital cost per year (in absolute terms) that meets the investors' financial requirements. It is constant over the investment period.

It is claimed that CVA is superior to EVA, as it is not affected by accounting distortions. Further, when the rate of return equals cost of capital, while CVA is zero for each year, EVA shows an upward trend with negative figures in the initial years and positive figures during later years. This is because CVA considers capital charge on gross investment, which is constant; while EVA considers charge on book capital, which reduces over time.

c) Total Shareholder Return (TSR)

TSR represents the change in capital value of a company's shares plus dividends over a given period, divided by the shares' value at the beginning of the period. For a single holding period, TSR is defined as follows:

TSR = [(End Market Value – Beginning Market Value)/Beginning Market Value] + [Dividend/Beginning Market Value]

For multiple holding periods, TSR is computed as the long-term internal rate of return (IRR) that shareholders earn by investing in a company's stocks.

$$\text{Beginning Market Value} = \text{Dividend}_1/(1+\text{TSR})^1 + \text{Dividend}_2/(1+\text{TSR})^2 + \ldots + \text{End Market Value}_n/(1+\text{TSR})^n$$

BCG considers TSR as the most useful measure of value creation because it takes into account both dividends and capital gains, is not biased by size and is difficult to manipulate. But TSR cannot be calculated for a privately held firm or for the division of a company. (It may be noted here that MVA does not consider dividends and is biased by size, as it computes absolute figures).

d) Total Business Return (TBR)

TBR is the internal counterpart of TSR. It can be applied for private companies or business units whose shares are not publicly traded. Definition of TBR is quite similar to that of TSR, with the difference being that free cash flows from operations are considered in place of dividends. For a single period, TBR is computed as follows:

TBR = [(End Business Value – Beginning Business Value)/Beginning Business Value] + [Free Cash Flow/Beginning Business Value]

The beginning and end values are estimates of business value of the firm at the beginning and end of the period. These may be estimated as Free Cash Flow divided by Cost of Capital or NPV of expected Cash Flows.

TBR for multiple periods is measured through the IRR approach as indicated below:

$$\textbf{Beginning Value} = \textbf{Free Cash Flow}_1/(1+\textbf{TBR})^1 + \textbf{Free Cash Flow}_2/(1+\textbf{TBR})^2 + \ldots + \textbf{End Value}_n/(1+\textbf{TBR})^n$$

TBR is moderated using a time fade model, which considers that a company's return on investment and its growth rate would reduce over time towards a global average due to competitive pressures from new entrants.

As TBR incorporates cash flow returns on both existing assets and assets to be added in future, it is significantly influenced by CFROI. BCG recommends combining of CFROI with TBR to take resource allocation decisions. If current CFROI vs cost of capital and TBR of business plan vs target TBR are both positive, such projects would receive the highest priority for investment.

Figure 2: BCG Approach – TSR, TBR, CFROI and CVA

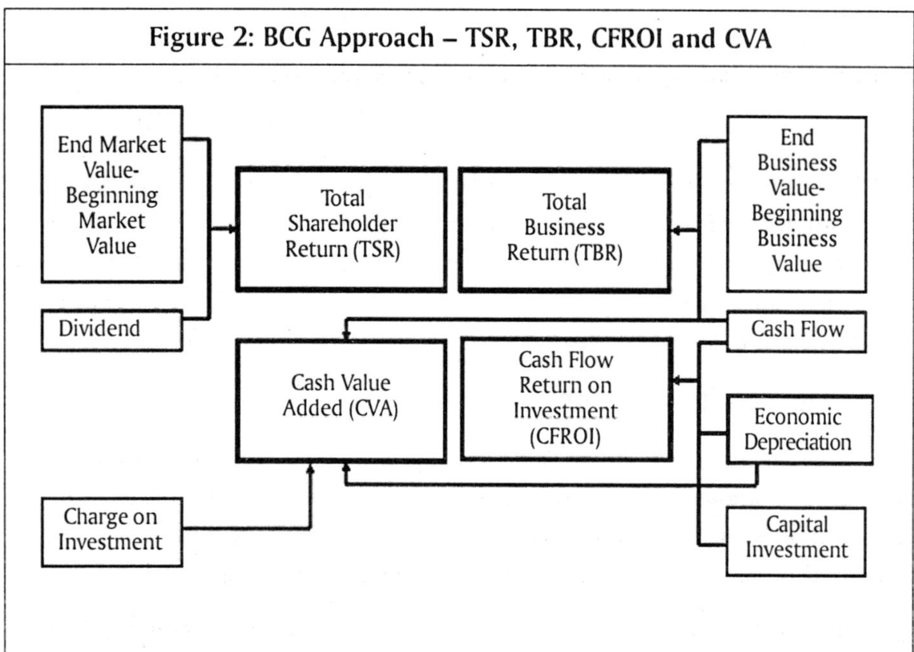

Detractors of the BCG Approach criticize that CFROI and CVA defer most of the depreciation to later years in order to achieve even distribution of returns and capital cost through the project's life time. CFROI also includes salvage value of assets in its calculations. These features make the performance measures more subjective, as part of the future profit is brought into the present. It is said that CFROI is a long term subjective measure, while EVA is a short term objective measure.

3. ALCAR Approach – Shareholder Value Added (SVA)

Shareholder Value Added (SVA) is authored by Dr. Alfred Rappaport, co-founder of LEK/Alcar Consulting Group, and is based on the Discounted Cash Flow (DCF) methodology. One of the drivers of Shareholder Value is said to be value growth duration, which represents the period over which investments are expected to earn returns in excess of the cost of capital. Thereafter, the competitive edge would be lost, and the rate of return would reduce to the cost of capital.

SVA is far less used than EVA or CFROI. The idea of SVA is to discount the estimated future cash flows to the present and hence continuously calculate the value of the firm.

SVA is calculated as follows: Forecast profit after tax and depreciation for the value growth duration; then subtract capital expenditure and increase in current assets during each year to arrive at the annual net cash flows. Discount the cash flow stream using weighted average cost of capital. Estimate the residual value of the business and find its present value. Thereafter, calculate total shareholder value (TSV) as below:

TSV = Present value of operating cash flow stream + present value of residual value – market value of debt

Pre-strategy value = [Cash flow stream before new investment discounted at weighted average cost of capital] – market value of debt

Shareholder Value Added (SVA) by the strategy = TSV – Pre-strategy Value

The SVA approach suggests that firms should select strategies that maximize SVA, find highest valued use for all assets, link performance evaluation and managerial incentives to SVA and return cash to shareholders if the investment options are not attractive.

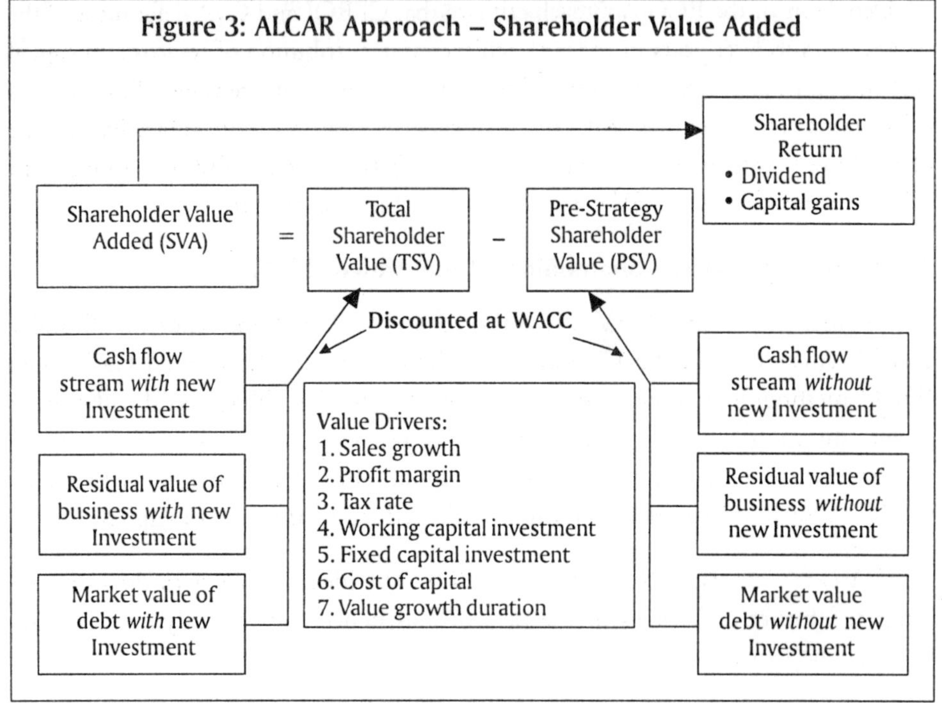

4. MARAKON Approach

The Marakon Approach to value based performance measure is developed by Marakon Associates, an internationally renowned management consulting firm. Here, shareholder value creation is measured as the ratio of market value (M) and book value (B) of a firm's equity, where market value is the value in the stock market, while book value is the sum invested by the shareholders. Shareholder wealth is positive and increasing if M/B is greater than 1 and increasing. In effect, this is MVA expressed in terms of a ratio instead of in monetary terms. Value creation is determined by two value drivers—'market economics' and 'competitive position'.

Market economics reflects the attractiveness of the market in which the company operates. It is evaluated as the total economic profit (EP) or equity spread (difference between return on equity and cost of equity) generated by all companies in the applicable product-market context. If the aggregate EP is positive, the market economics is considered as attractive. The basic principle behind Market Economics is thus similar to that of EVA, though it is applied to the industry in this case and not to the company.

Market economics is, in turn, said to be determined by two direct and four limiting forces. The direct forces are intensity of direct competition and customer pressure. The four limiting factors are intensity of indirect competition (substitutes), threat of entry, supplier pressures and regulatory pressures. EP projections have therefore to be made with a fair degree of accuracy by objectively determining the impact of these factors.

Competitive position indicates a company's competitive advantage over its rivals. It is defined as the quantum of EP generated per unit product by a business, relative to the average EP per unit earned by all competitors in the market. This is influenced by two factors—product differentiation (price premium due product superiority) and economic cost position (due to lower economic cost of production). Here again, the concept of Economic Profit is applied, which is the fundamental principle behind EVA as well.

Figure 4: MARAKON Approach – Strategic Determinants of Value Creation

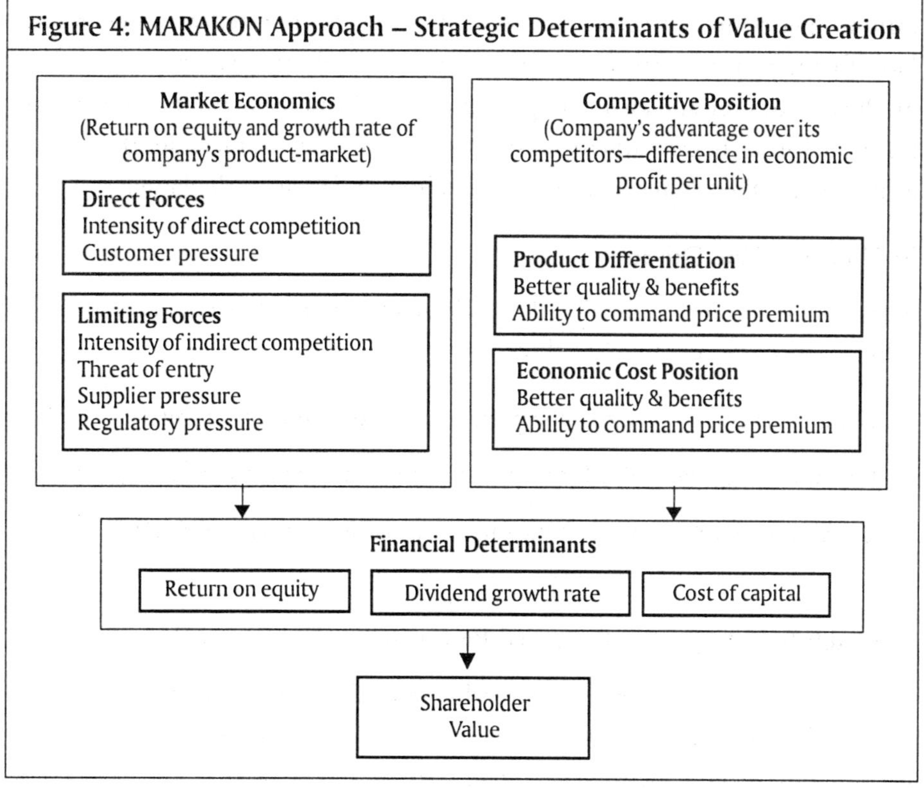

Various strategic options can be arrived at by considering the impact of the underlying parameters affecting market economics and competitive position, thereby producing more credible and accurate forecasts than that generated by using only a financial model.

5. McKinsey Approach

McKinsey & Co's approach is based on the economic profit concept. McKinsey distinguishes itself by way of an overall framework and principles for value based management. The four steps advocated by McKinsey are explained briefly below:

a) Ensure the Supremacy of Value Management

Top management should take on embrace value maximization as the ultimate financial objective by focusing on discounted cash flow (the most direct method of value creation) and avoid traditional measures like accounting rates of return, earnings per share and profit growth as they do not truly reflect value creation. Non-financial goals such as productivity, market share, customer satisfaction, product innovation and quality improvement should motivate employees in various functional areas. In cases where non-financial goals are in conflict with the financial goals, the conflict should normally be resolved in favour of the latter.

b) Find the Value Drivers

The key drivers that influence the performance of the business and hence its value, need to be identified at three levels:

Generic level	e.g., Operating margin & return on capital
Business unit level	Product mix, customer mix, operating leverage, etc.
Grass roots level	Operating value drivers like capacity utilization, cost per delivery.

c) Establish Appropriate Managerial Processes

The principal message here is that value maximization objective should drive strategy formulation and evaluation, target setting, budgets, action plans and performance measurement & incentive systems.

d) Implement VBM Properly

Implementing value based management is a complex process and requires a change in the mindset of the decision makers. Six conditions are necessary for excellent value based management: being performance driven, value-based, managed bottom up as well as top down, two-way communications, strong self-reinforcement process and low cost.

6. Balanced Scorecard

Kaplan and Norton feel that financial measures are inadequate for guiding and evaluating organizations' trajectories through competitive environments. In effect, they feel that organizations should have leading indicators to create future financial value. The Balanced Scorecard, which is their creation, provides for a comprehensive fame-work that translates a company's strategy and vision into a coherent set of performance measures.

The Balanced Scorecard Links Performance Measures

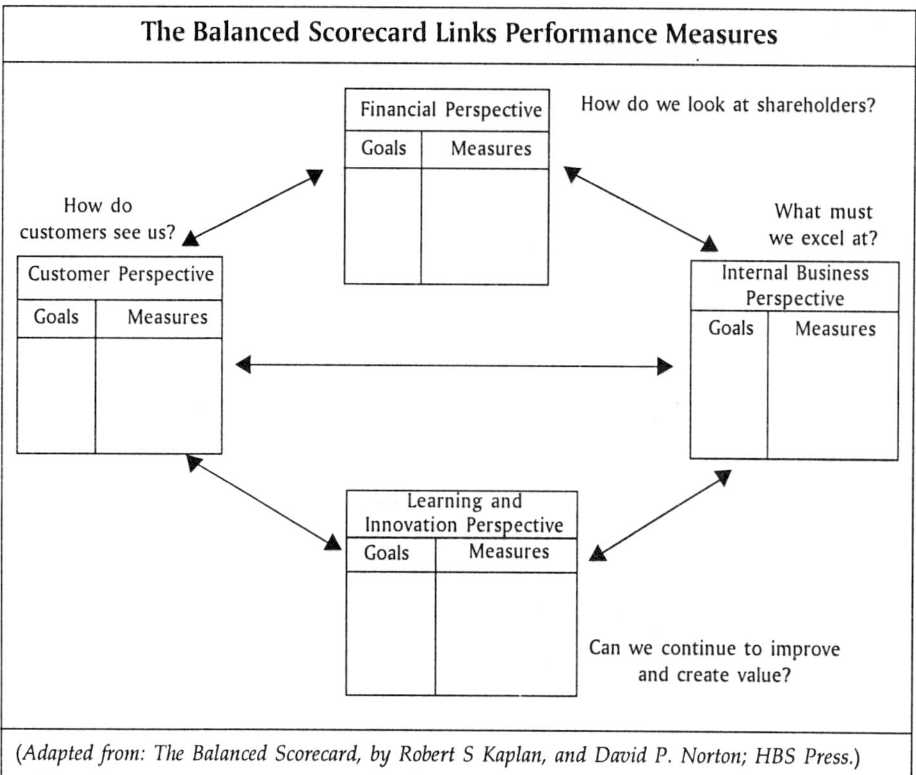

(Adapted from: The Balanced Scorecard, by Robert S Kaplan, and David P. Norton; HBS Press.)

Financial Perspective

The Balanced Scorecard retains the financial perspective. Financial measures indicate whether a company's strategy, implementation and execution are contributing to profitability.

Customer Perspective

The measures include customer satisfaction, customer retention, new customer acquisition, customer profitability and market share.

Internal-Business-Process

In this the company's managers identify the critical internal processes in which the organisation must excel. The processes must enable deliver value propositions that will attract and retain target customers, while satisfying shareholder expectations of excellent financial returns.

Learning and Growth Perspective

This perspective focuses on building infrastructure for long-term growth and improvement.

Increasing Popularity of the Balanced Scorecard

The increasing popularity of the balanced scorecard is due to:

- Performance measurement is connected to strategic success.
- Places emphasis on the importance of all stakeholders, not just investors.
- Encourages consideration of linkages among performance measures in all areas of the firm.
- The need for some measures which comment of preparedness for future success is recognized.

The problems with the balanced scorecard are:

- Measurement set is not systematic in nature.
- Connection between the measures and achievement of shareholder value is not clear.

- Difficult and costly to capture the data required to measure what is needed.
- Focus is on the present.
- The key to strategic success is preparing for the future.
- Difficult to identify gaps, conflicts and redundancies in the measurement system.

Discussion

The various value-based performance measures have emerged from the need to find a more realistic and practical alternative to traditional accounting based measures. They have several commonalities and also differences. They fall into two broad categories—(1) those that arrive at a measure of economic profit or return on investment and (2) those which directly capture shareholder return. Some measures are expressed in terms of absolute values and others in terms of a ratio or percentage. There are measures which are more suited for inter-period comparisons and those that provide an integrated multi-period result by using the IRR or DCF approach. A statement comparing the major value based measures along these is tabulated below.

Performance Measure	Principle	Nature of Measure	Methodology & Application
1. EVA	Economic profit	Monetary value	Inter-period comparison
2. CVA	Economic profit – cash	Monetary value	Inter-period comparison
3. CFROI	Cash return on investment grain from markets	Ratio/percentage	IRR from multi-year projections
4. MVA	Shareholder return – capital Gain from markets	Monetary value	Inter-period comparison
5. SVA	Shareholder value – calculated from performance projections	Monetary value	DCF from future projections
6. TSR	Shareholder return – capital gain + dividend	Ratio/percentage	IRR from multi-year projections
7. TBR	Investor return – business gain + dividend	Ratio/percentage	IRR from multi-year projections
8. Marakon	Shareholder return – equality of calculations & market reality	Ratio/percentage	Inter-period comparison

All the principal value-based performance measures are propounded by internationally renowned management consultants. There is strident marketing spiel from the consultants exhorting that their method is superior to that of the others, which has led to what is referred to as 'the war of metrics.'

Though the different methods profess the use of alternative parameters and claim superiority over each other, when looked at in broader terms, the extent of divergence in terms of the ultimate conclusions would not be all that significant. While making strategic business decisions, the subjectivity in projecting future profits/cash flows and discounting rates is likely to be a greater source of error/differences in judgment than that caused by the differing approaches of the various metrics.

The activities in the Balanced Scorecard approach, takes around four months for a firm to develop and the consultant's involvement is heavy. The complexity involved at each stage, viz: Measurement program design, Definition of strategic objectives, Selection of strategic measures, and building the implementation plans; is high. The firm has to deploy considerable resources and time to capture the data required.

As stated, there is a definite need to measure and strategise and the comments below would relate the measures discussed to the size of the company.

Normally, in large organizations (Rs.1000 crores and above of sales) many initiatives would be under way e.g., Business process re-engineering, Total quality management, Lean initiatives, SCM programs etc., These may not be linked to targeted improvement of strategic objectives. Each of the initiatives is pushed by different champions in the organisation and compete for scarce resources. Managers, in a variety of manufacturing and service organizations, who have tried to build balanced scorecards for their organizations, have found that it is not as simple as it seems. The factors which have contributed the failed experiences include, defects in the structure, errors in the choice of measure etc.

In small companies, the scene is that the alternatives would be chosen based on simple ROI measures; the other factors (considered intangible) being evaluated at the management level on a subjective basis.

In mid-size companies quoted in the stock market such measures as MVA could be used. An attempt is made to put the above diagrammatically.

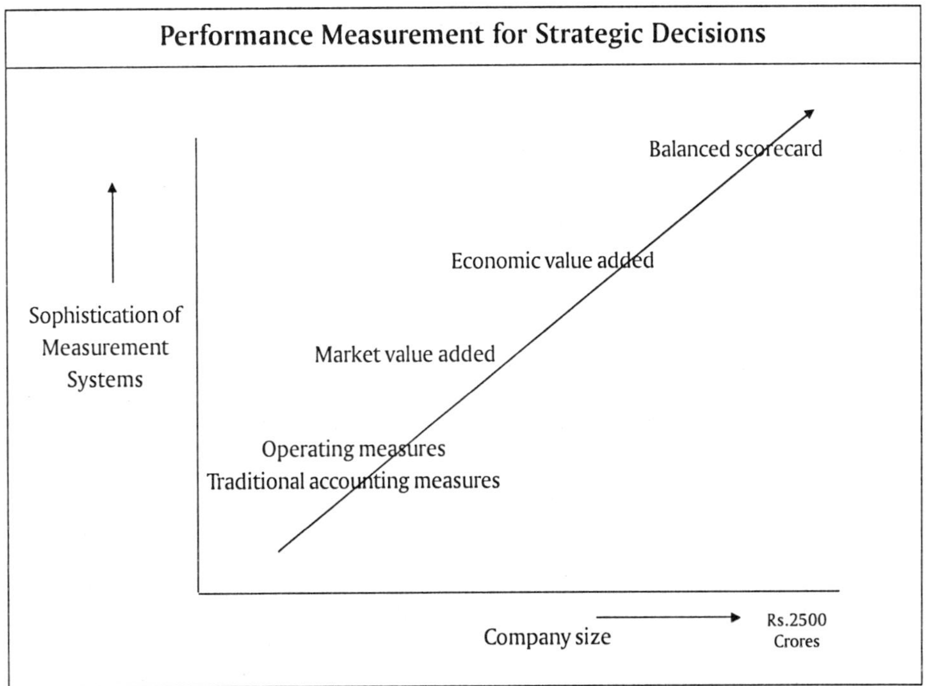

Conclusions

Companies have to grow in a competitive environment, in order to survive. To grow the companies need to strategise. However, to this end it is necessary for the managers to take risks, and experiment so that the company can learn and grow. Suitable metrics need to be chosen. The incentive compensation of the executives must be linked to the performance as indicated by the chosen metric so that the senior executives keep focused on long-term achievements as well as the short term.

In conclusion, while the merit of value-based metrics as such is not in doubt, the choice of metric should very well be decided based on one's convenience and objectives. Smaller companies may use comparatively simple measures such as EVA and MVA. Larger companies may benefit by using more complex metrics. The extent to which one makes the adjustments and refinements to improve accuracy can also be decided based on the relative importance and sensitivity of making very refined calculations. It may also be prudent where necessary to compare the results arrived at from more than one metric. Ultimately, it is not the metric that one uses that determines the final result, but how one actually performs.

(A Lakshminarasimha, Faculty Member, Icfai Business School, Bangalore. He can be reached at lnarsimha@ibsindia.org

R Harish, Faculty Member, Icfai Business School, Bangalore. He can be reached at harish@ibsindia.org).

References

1. "What is EVA?", http://www.sternstewart.com
2. "Economic Value Added (EVA)", http://pages.stern.nyu.edu/~adamodar/New_Home_Page/lectures/eva.html
3. "Alfred Rappaport – Creating Shareholder Value", http://www.valuebasedmanagement.net/books_rappaport_creating.html
4. "Creating Shareholder Value A Guide for Managers and Investors" by Alfred Rappaport http://www.simonsays.com/content/book.cfm?sid=33&pid=408386
5. "Economic Value Added", http://www.5paisa.com/scho/ch09.html
6. "Metric Wars—Marketing battles erupt as Stern Stewart and rivals seek your hearts, minds, & dollars". http://instruction.bus.wisc.edu/mcarpenter/readings/metric.htm
7. "Measuring Long Term Performance", http://www.tataryerson.com/knowledge/Mckinsey%20Business%20Forecast.pdf
8. "Value-Added Measures of Performance—Notes prepared" by Pamela Peterson, Florida State University, http://wise.fau.edu/~ppeter/value/notes.htm
9. "The Balanced Scorecard", by Robert S. Kaplan and David P. Norton (1996), Harvard Business school Press, Boston, Massachusetts.

3

Facets of 'Shareholder Value Creation'

V V Gopal

Creation of shareholders' value now lies at the core of every business. Any negligence in this area makes a firm succumb to crisis, curtailing its very existence. With so much importance associated to value creation, all the firms these days are competing with one another in their own ways, either through employee-oriented performance measurement, effective brand management techniques or divestment of loss making units, to attain the maxims of consumer value and satisfaction and mark their success in the long run.

"Shareholder value is a modern business cliché: A mantra intoned with solemnity at every Annual General Meeting and in every Annual Report. But for all the words, few people have clear idea of what shareholder value comprises".

– The Sunday Times[1]

Creating shareholder value is a fundamental requirement for all companies. Any company that fails to do so either risks being starved of capital, having its senior management replaced or being acquired. The necessity to put shareholder

1 http://www.competetowin.co.uk.

value creation at the top of corporate agenda is the result of myriad factors such as increased pressure to deliver assured rate of return and perform better year after year. Therefore, most of the world's leading companies are vying with one another to adopt the mantra of shareholder value to meet the increasing expectations of their shareholders.

There are many dimensions to creating and defining shareholder value based on various functional perspectives such as finance, human resources, branding and more importantly during unfavorable economic conditions. Corporate houses are now striving to create, sustain and enhance value to their shareholders more as a conscious governing objective rather than a mere ideal to be achieved in some distant future. It has assumed, and rightly so, the importance it deserves in the present day competitive business environment amidst the clamor for socially responsible behavior.

While most of the companies are involved in the process of creating value for their shareholders, a few of them are involved in not just creating value but maximizing value for their shareholders. Value is said to be created when a company earns a return over and above the cost of capital. Maximizing value therefore requires a continuous search for corporate and business strategies that will translate into tangible returns for the shareholders.

Understanding Shareholder Value

The term 'shareholder value' refers to the financial worth of shareholders in the company. There are three important perspectives for assessing the value of the shareholders. The first is based on the balance sheet perspective, the second on stock market perspective and the third on the economic perspective. In the first instance, shareholder value is the summation of share capital, and reserves and surplus. The stock market perspective defines shareholder value as market capitalization (i.e., market price multiplied by number of shares issued) of the shares issued by the company. The economic perspective views shareholder value as economic value minus the company's borrowings i.e. bank loans and corporate bonds. A plethora of new measures for value creation have emerged which provide a more accurate estimate of value creation rather than the traditional accounting measures. These new measures include, Total Shareholder Returns (TSR),

Cash Flow Return on Investment (CFROI), Economic Value Added (EVA), Market Value Added (MVA) and Cash Value Added (CVA).

Shareholder Value: Creation and Measurement

The key to success for corporate houses lies in identifying those specific areas of product, services and prices that would provide shareholders the maximum return for their investment. There are two approaches of measuring shareholder value, based on single or multi-period metrics. While the single-period metrics include EVA and MVA, the multi-period metrics include CFROI and CVA.

Single Period Value

EVA has been defined as a measure of the after-tax cash flow generated by the company's operations minus the cost of capital employed to generate that cash flow. This concept has gained tremendous popularity, chiefly because it allows the shareholder to determine how much money is left over and above the cost of capital. However, it has certain drawbacks, as it does not capture the investor's perception with respect to the management's ability to generate positive EVAs in future years. In order to assess how the markets are viewing the EVA generation ability of the organization, the concept of MVA came into being. MVA is the difference between a company's market value and the capital invested. Alternatively, MVA is the premium the market awards a company over and above the amount investors have invested in it. This is on the basis of market expectations of future EVAs. Caselets on Cadbury Schweppes and Electrolux discuss the initiatives taken towards generating shareholder value.

Multi-Period Metrics

CFROI is defined as the cash flow divided by the market value of capital employed. The CFROI model avoids the use of accounting book capital in valuing the firm's existing assets and thus provides an accurate estimate in determining shareholder value. Based on a simplified CFROI, Boston Consulting Group developed an alternate economic profit measure called CVA. CVA is based on cash flows and not on earnings and is the spread between CFROI and the real cost of capital, multiplied with the investment in fixed assets plus working capital.[2]

---

2 "Value-based Management: An Integrated Approach to Value Creation, A Literature Review" by Anne Ameels, Prof. Werner Bruggeman and Geert Scheipers.

Business Design: A Source of Shareholder Value

The focus of management in modern businesses is to formulate a business design with explicit focus on shareholder value and a thrust on challenging requirements in the marketplace. Business design differs from the traditional strategy framework as it facilitates in making complex balance sheet decisions. The emerging dimensions of business design that create shareholder value are customer selection and value

Cadbury Schweepes – Managing for Value

Cadbury Schweppes is one of the biggest international beverage and confectionery companies in the world with a market capitalization of £10 bn (December 2004). To double shareholder value within five years, the company adopted the Economic Profit approach. The strategy involved a unique approach called the Managing for Value (MFV) program, consisting of five different elements all covered under the scope of shareholder value creation. These elements included raising financial performance, value based management, rewards, sharpening the culture and leadership capability.

Raising Financial Performance and Value-based Management

Shareholder Value objectives were translated into specific financial targets. Earnings Per Share targets were fixed at 10% per year and a target of generating free cash flows to the extent of £150 mn was set. Economic profit was used as a viable measure instead of accounting profits. The implementation of value-based management increased the strategic thinking capabilities of the entire firm.

Leadership Capability and Sharpening the Culture

The idea was to develop an outstanding management team possessing a specific set of strong leadership capabilities who can lead teams through the process of value-based management and execute ambitious strategies. The MFV program also focused on the importance of cultural changes to nurture three behavioral traits—accountability, aggressiveness and adaptability.

Rewards

The MFV initiative was based on the understanding that value for the shareholders will be created when the interest of the employees are closely aligned with that of the shareholders. To address this objective, the company adopted the system of reward recognition wherein the top 30 managers became eligible to participate in a long-term investment plan that linked rewards with the performance of the company shares. Further, the top 150 managers were eligible to receive stock options.

With the adoption of MFV program, the company developed immense benefits in terms of increase in economic profit, brand sales and average shareholder returns as shown below:

- Increase in economic profit by 46% during 1997-98.
- Increase in brand sales by 4% during 1997-98.
- Increase in average shareholder returns from 8.8% in 1990-96 to 23.6% in 1996-99.

proposition. Strategic control of the profit stream, identifying the scope of critical activities, product and service offerings that make the organizations function effectively are the various business designs that facilitate shareholder value creation.

Role of Intangible Assets in Creating Shareholder Value

CFOs leverage their knowledge of finance to formulate strategies for understanding the links between tangible and intangible value drivers, their value generating capacity and methods to measure it. The major component among the intangible assets being intellectual capital which will go a long way in generating value to the organization. Intellectual capital which contributes to shareholder value are human capital, organizational capital and relational capital. Human capital includes attributes such as intellect, skill, creativity and the way the manpower in the organization works. Organizational capital includes company-owned items such as systems, processes,·databases and the value and culture surrounding the organization. Relational capital includes external relations with customers, suppliers, partners, networks and regulators.

Electrolux

Electrolux, a Swedish-based company, is the world's largest producer of indoor and outdoor home appliances, with 123 manufacturing facilities in 24 countries. Financial results for 1999 showed enhanced performance, with operating income increasing by 22%. Earnings per share increased by 29% and EPS increased to 17.2% from the 1998 figure of 14.8%. To further improve its financial performance, Electrolux adopted value creation as a key performance measure. Prior to this measure, the company had initiated a restructuring exercise in 1997 and the whole process was completed in 1999. The value creation process adopted by the company was targeted towards delivering shareholder value.

Within the company, value creation was measured as earning before interest and taxes less the weighted average cost of capital on net assets. Value creation was measured on a regular basis by sector, product line and region. The company used the concept of ID cards, by means of which the hurdle rates for the organization were depicted with a clear explanation on how the company is going to remove the financial hurdles. With the value creation process being implemented, significant changes to managerial compensation system took place with the aim of aligning the managerial performance to the value creation concept. Bonuses of the top 350 managers were linked to value creation within their own business sector, while for some it was linked both to the business sector and group level performance. Secondly, an annual share option program was introduced for top 100 managers. The company took environmental issues seriously. In appreciation of the same, many Socially Responsible Funds in Sweden picked up the company's shares.

Contd...

Contd...
The company also introduced environmental performance indicators for each of its business sectors and has allocated a separate section in the balance sheet to highlight the environmental activities and performance. The environmental performance indicators included CO_2 per value added, energy cost percentage per value added and water per value added. All these environmental indicators showed increased reduction from base year figures. Finally, the company has evolved as a value creating organization, a performance developer on which it can build its shareholder value for years.

Management and Measurement of Intangible Assets

With the development of modern business, the value creation process has moved to center stage. Intellectual capital has transcended from physical capital domination to organizational capital and then onto human capital. Various management models have evolved but there are wide disparities in the transition to knowledge economy. One obvious approach to measuring shareholder value is to try and retain the rigor of conventional accounting by adjusting its traditional instruments. The alternative is to abandon traditional accounting and adopt the method of value-based accounting. An approach that has helped to a major extent in creating value, has been the adoption of the concept of Holistic Value Added (HVA). HVA is a measure aimed at integrating the financial and intangible parameters to provide comprehensive information to shareholders. Another important achievement of the HVA model is delivering improved economic profit relative to the expectations of the shareholders.

Role of Employees in Creating Shareholder Value

Value creation for shareholders from an employee-oriented perspective, is the number of employees multiplied by the difference between employee productivity and cost per employee. A new approach in measuring employee oriented performance has been the adoption of the workonomics model developed by the Boston Consulting Group. The model describes the competence levels and experience of the company's managers and employees. These employee-oriented measures can generate powerful insights, foster more efficient behavior and create more value for investors. Initiatives taken by Allied Plywood Corporation are in tandem with the above.

Allied Plywood Corporation

Allied Plywood Corporation, a 100% employee-owned company headquartered at Virginia, USA is the manufacturer of a wide array of furniture products. The company focuses on a unique incentive system where profits are shared by employees on a monthly as well as annual basis. The company introduced a unique justice-based system christened "The Allied Way" wherein 77% of the employees' paypack is variable. At the core of the justice system is the Management Council, a representative body comprising employees from the grassroot level to top management that takes all major decisions relating to the day-to-day affairs in running the company. This system ensured two-way accountability for the company. Primarily, it helps in improving the quality of the product and maximizing the returns of the shareholders (i.e., employees). The company derived these benefits on account of strategic planning, empowerment, delivering economic justice and improved cash flow. All these benefits were attributed to the employees, management and the company.

Brand as a Source of Shareholder Value

Companies like Procter & Gamble, Unilever, Xerox, Heinz, Apple and Gillette possess tremendous brand management competencies, yet they failed in their attempts to generate shareholder value. The learning is that merely having strong brands, which generate consumer value, is not enough. What is important is the markets in which they operate and the strategies that their managers pursue. By failing to understand shareholder value dynamics, marketing managers run the risk of misallocating resources and restraining the firm's ability to move into emerging markets and effect profitable new growth strategies. The attractiveness and profitability of the market depends on the intensity of competition and the extent of pressure from customers.

A market faced by intense competition will not be able to deliver returns above the cost of capital. Factors that act as catalysts in propelling the intensity of competition are the degree of product standardization, the gap in the production capacity, number of competitors and growth in the market. Customer pressure arises on account of two important determinants: First, the price sensitivity and second, the negotiating leverage. Another way in which the brand contributes to shareholder value is by increasing the level of cash flow. A brand's cash flow is determined by four factors: Its price, growth, costs and investment. Finally, strong brands can lower investment levels because of their potential leverage over the supply chain. An example of how a company used brand management competencies to deliver shareholder value is explained in the case relating to the motorcycle giant – Harley Davidson.

Creating Shareholder Value During Divestiture

With acquisitions failing to provide the right kind of fuel for corporations, managements are reframing their priorities and are looking to divest non-core business units. New challenges are cropping up both for the buyers as well as sellers. In fact, divestitures are being increasingly identified as a preferred route to creating and preserving shareholder value. Eliminating underperforming assets permits management to concentrate on its core competencies and business. Having chosen the divestiture route, management needs to set up priorities for the divesting process. The issues to be taken care of are maximizing the purchase price, maintaining the support of the board and senior management, managing tax consequences and minimizing disturbance to other operations and personnel. Towards this end, a systematic divestiture process on the following lines would be appropriate.

- **Strategic Assessment:** Management must be fully aware of the value that divestiture will bring for prospective buyers.
- **Preparation:** Sellers should be ready to resolve the issues that will crop up from the buyer's perspective during divestiture.
- **Value Preservation:** Sellers need to protect assets, maintain workforce consistency and communicate activities and plans clearly.
- **Completion:** Pitfalls during completion of the transaction and misleading statements in the divestiture transaction need to be weeded away.
- **Transition and Separation:** If the divested business is integrated closely into the parent company, a separation can be a formidable and expensive pre-close effort for the seller.
- **Measurement:** Without appropriate measurement mechanism in place, management may not know whether the deal aligns with organizational perspective or if goals need to be adjusted to match with the emerging scenario.

Value Creation at Harley–Davidson

On August 31, 2003 Harley-Davidson, the only major American player in the global motorcycle market, celebrated its 100th anniversary. Schoolmates Arthur Davidson and William S Harley founded the company in 1903. Both of them shared a passion for bikes. By 1904, Harley-Davidson bikes began participating in the motorcycle races and were driven by biggest racers of that period, such as Ralph Hepburn, Eddie Brink, Joe Petreli and Red Parkhurst. The bikes served in all the major wars fought by the country. The company received four Navy 'E' awards for excellence in wartime production. The soldiers returning from war brought the bike culture to America and the bikes carried national pride. Pictures of rock stars like Elvis Presley seated on these bikes further cemented its brand image.

Till then, the company had been creating value for its shareholders by positioning the brand as a lifestyle product by lowering buyer's price sensitivity, synchronizing operating processes and through its enterprise risk management capability. Harley considered premium cash flow as the most significant factor for determining shareholder value. To overcome its competitors, the company created a perception of value over price in the minds of the customers. All its spare parts were made of quality steel as compared to plastic parts supplied by many other competitors. By maintaining a disciplined approach to meeting the risks with respect to finance, human, operational and concentration, the company was able to sustain sufficient profits.

Creating Shareholder Value During Economic Downturn

Another challenge confronting corporates is the manner in which shareholder value can be created when the company focuses on profit growth rather than on revenue growth. To gear up to the task, the competence that owners must demonstrate is two-fold, both of which are equally important i.e., rational allocation of capital and reduction (or elimination) of the fundamental business risks. While shareholders are suppliers and owners of invested capital, corporate managers are stewards of the invested capital. With the economy undergoing a metamorphosis and organizations moving from the traditional manufacturing turf to knowledge and service related activities there is a compelling need for a dramatic change in the organizational structure. In this context, valuing information and knowledge will be of paramount importance to value creation. To have a clear perspective of the entire economy, shareholder value should address the technical, regulatory and financial changes in the global economy.

A company can be called profitable and hence value-creating when it generates revenues that not only cover the normal production and operating expenses of running a business, but also provide a sufficient and fair return on the owners' capital, including a required return, to debt and equity suppliers of financial capital. The caselet below highlights how Infosys, despite economic ups and downs was able to successfully deliver shareholder value.

Infosys – Sustaining Shareholder Value

Infosys Technologies was founded on July 2, 1981 with a capital of Rs.10000. Today, the company has a revenue of more than $1 bn and is one of the most admired companies, not only in India but also globally. The company was able to leverage on opportunities and moved from body shopping to Offshore Development Centers (ODC). Infosys was one of the frontrunners in successfully tapping ODC opportunities before perfecting its Global Delivery Model (GDM). GDM was a mixture of body shopping and ODC models. In addition, the company ran Proximity Development Centers (PDC) comprising employee teams working in close proximity with the clients in areas of implementation and marketing. The GDM model paved the way for Infosys to position itself from a purely offshore development firm to a global IT based problem-solver. Business process improvements, derisking and corporate governance enabled Infosys to create sustainable and predictable revenue streams and value for its shareholders. The company's founders set high standards at a time when corporate malpractices were rampant. The company demonstrated strong corporate governance standards and business ethics as the cornerstone for its success.

Shareholder value creation is increasingly gaining importance and a number of organizations are embracing this philosophy. The debate surrounding the relevance of shareholder value creation has moved from the classroom to the boardroom, signifying its importance. Some important factors, which have induced managements to adopt the concept of shareholder value creation are, a relatively large ownership position, compensation tied to shareholder return performance and threat of takeover by predators. In the ultimate analysis creating shareholder value requires more than just the will to succeed. It requires concrete plans and real action from the macro perspective. Planning, target setting, performance management and incentive system must work in tandem to effectively link value creation with strategy. This again will involve the entire organization and will help to focus all employees on a common goal.

(V V Gopal, Faculty Member, the Icfai Business School, Hyderabad. He can be reached at vvgopal@icfai.org).

4

BOOK REVIEW

Value Based Management: Developing a Systematic Approach to Creating Shareholder Value

Niranjan Swain, Nupur Hetamsaria and Gina George

This book discusses the creation and implementation of a managerial mindset focused on value creation. It provides a back-to-basics approach by outlining key concepts and providing examples, explanations, diagrams and case histories on how every decision a management team makes can consistently create shareholder value. Value-based management instils a mindset where everyone in the organization learns to prioritize decisions based on their understanding of how those decisions contribute to corporate world. This book is organized into four key groups and includes a wide-ranging discussion of the concepts underlying the definition of value. It introduces the concepts primarily dealing with value-based decision-making. The book also outlines key issues involved in implementing value management.

Source: The Icfai Journal of Applied Finance, January 2003, Vol. 9 No 1. This is a review of the book titled "Value Based Management: Developing a Systematic Approach to Creating Shareholder Value" authored by James A Knight and published by McGraw-Hill.

Today's managers are confused by deferring priorities as they receive conflicting signals from the performance measures used in each of the management processes, including strategic planning, budgeting, reporting and compensation. Managers are skeptical about new initiatives and don't understand how to prioritize them. Managing for value addresses the conflicts by prioritizing each of the initiatives in the context of the company's goal to consistently create shareholder value. But the mindset of managing for value is not enough in itself. To achieve maximum value it must be translated into reality, that is, using it in frontline decision-making. Successful value management requires that a mindset of managing for value be integrated into the way the decisions are made.

James A Knight discusses the issue of value management in five categories viz., goal, strategy, measures, processes and decisions. Making value management a reality requires management to agree that value maximization is the company's goal and managing a company for value requires delivering maximum return to the investors while balancing the interest of other important constituents including customers and employees. Management must then develop a business strategy to achieve the goal of maximizing value creation.

The company's strategy development effort answers questions like "how will the company achieve its objective?" Strategy defines the company's targeted markets and customers by answering the question "how will the company differentiate itself?" With the right strategy in place, the management must then implement the strategy and measure progress to achieve the strategy. Performance measures need to reflect the company's business strategy and shift the focus of managers to decisions that create value. Performance measures do not replace strategy; rather they capture the results of the strategy. They will do little, if anything, to improve management decision-making. To affect the decision-making, performance measures must be integrated into the management process.

There are four key management processes to be considered when installing value management into any company. They are strategic planning, budgeting, reporting and incentives. Finally, value is created in a company through the operating and investment decisions the company makes. Value management becomes a reality when the value management mindset is embedded in the operating and investment decisions the company is making.

What is Value Creation?

Value creation is the wealth created for a company's stockholders through price appreciation and dividends. Value created can be calculated in a variety of ways wherever the information on stock price and dividends is readily available. Calculating value is a trivial exercise because value in the future is not easy to calculate and such calculations are subjective in nature. Value is therefore an imprecise term whose analysis is more an art than a science. The author here limits the discussion on value to stock market value, which is, the net present value of the expected sequence of future cash flows the company will generate for the equity holders of the company.

Value is subjective: Value lies in the eyes of the beholder, which is why, value has a variety of meanings and people can have very different views of what the value of a company is at any given point in time. The past value appears objective; however, with respect to present and future value the value judgment becomes non-observable and subjective. A variety of factors contribute to these perspectives including an individual's quality of information, perception of control, time horizon, uncertainty and tolerance of risk.

Types of values: Value in the present and the future is subjective and when value is quantified it is based on beliefs about a number of factors. The beliefs may change and if they do, so will the value. Different types of value represent investors' views of value under different circumstances and assumptions. The stock market incorporates these different views of value into the market price through individual's actions to buy or sell based on their beliefs about future cash flows. Book value for instance represents the investors' equity contribution to the business. This perspective on value is limited by what has happened in the past as it is the reflection of all past investments, financing and operating decisions and provides a view of value as the cumulative effect of prior events while remaining mute on future prospects.

Information controls value: Value is always based on expectations of the future and is difficult to quantify. However, on any given day, market price is an indicator of what people's beliefs are, because at any given time the value as quoted by the offered price of shares represents the lowest marginal value a holder is willing to accept in return for a share of the company's stock. The bid price represents the converse, the highest marginal value an investor is willing to pay for shares in the company stock. Investors indicate their beliefs in their decision to buy or sell because these decisions represent their beliefs about the company's prospects.

The role of management: The role of the management is to create value for the shareholders. Creating value for the shareholders means creating value that meets or exceeds their expectations for value creation. If management can beat the investors' expectations, so much the better. But, sometimes the management may find itself in a position where the probability of beating the investors' expectations is low. In such situations, the management's role is to maximize true value or what the market would find to be true if it had access to all information about the company's operations. In addition, management needs to manage the expectations of investors so they don't go ahead of the company's ability to deliver results and also do a thorough analysis of the holders of the company's stock to determine what the investors really want.

The slippery slope of value creation: Creating value for shareholders operates under three rules viz., level of profitability has nothing to do with value creation, all management teams start on a level playing field for creating value and different companies face different challenges in creating value. These three rules are the slippery slope of value creation. No matter how good a company is at creating value, investors will price it accordingly. By increasing the stock price, investors give management credit for their performance to date. At the same time this also increases the degree of difficulty in creating future value.

Why Manage Value?

Apart from growing shareholders' influence, there are numerous reasons to manage for value; like, to prevent undervaluation of the stock, to encourage value-creating investments, to improve resource allocation etc. Some companies create much more value for their shareholders than others because they consistently outperform their peers in the industry. The message here is that, over time, consistency is more important and beneficial to shareholders than one-time value-creating events such as restructuring, financial engineering, and reengineering. One reason they consistently outperform their peers is that they are managed differently because they focus on creating value for investors by improving the operations of their business, becoming more competitive and by growing. In a sample of 750 companies, one-time value creators created, on an average, 62% of value relative to their peers. The consistent value creators, on the other hand, created 400% of the value of their peers.

Challenges in value creation: Today's companies confront four daunting challenges as they attempt to consistently create value. They are increased complexity, greater uncertainty and risk, time compression, and conflicting priorities. Managers are being asked to reduce uncertainty and risk, speed up decision-making and balance conflicting priorities. With increased pressure to show short-term results, managers can easily be misled into believing that investments will destroy value and the growth is bad. In reality, there is good growth and bad growth. Good growth adds value, while bad growth destroys value. The trick is to identify good growth opportunities.

Lessons from the consistent performers: Consistent value creators do three important things that distinguish them from others. They capture the business strategy in their performance measures, pay management for value creating performance and focus managers on the business strategy. It is these value-creating strategies that separate excellent companies from typical companies. Excellent companies don't just measure results; they look beyond the results to the key drivers of their strategy and then include these drivers in the performance measures and calibrate them. Focusing management by linking performance to the business strategy is more difficult to assess than the other two because a company is not required in any disclosure to investors to explain how well they focus on their business strategy. But two tests can be used to discern if management is focused on their strategy: (1) Can management articulate their strategy? and (2) Are they describing a business strategy or a financial results strategy? These tests aim at finding out what management plans to do and how they plan to do it.

Investors' Expectations and Strategy

Investors invest capital with the expectation of receiving a return on their investment. Management has the task of earning the return expected by those investors and in doing so management has to maximize value. To do this job, management must accept and invest in projects with positive returns (good growth) and reject projects with negative returns (bad growth). Investors expect to see that the management has a strategy that will continue to produce returns in both the short-term and long-term. Knight here discusses what drives investor expectations and how to measure those expectations and how to determine if the company's strategy will deliver enough value to meet the investor's expectations.

What returns are investors looking for? There is no single perspective that defines investor expectations. The data must be gathered to support multipoint points of view and construct a composite of expectations. Data sources include the following—historical market returns, historical peer and company returns, macroeconomic data and industry, and economic forecasts. Historical returns should be adjusted for macroeconomic factors such as interest rates and tax. This is important as it gives a more accurate picture of future expectations. The next step is to examine the historical returns earned by comparable companies and the company's own historical returns to investors. When combined with the market prices, cost of capital, and interest rates, these three data points allow us to isolate the investor's expectations today.

What level of risk? Trying to answer a question like what level of risk investors are willing to accept in a company's stock is simultaneously complex and simple. It is complex because investors have their own beliefs about risk, which they have assessed implicitly or explicitly in setting a value on the company's stock. The simple answer is that the return the investors expect to earn is risk-adjusted. This means the issue of risk for assessing investor's expectations is a non-issue; whatever risk they expect or have assessed is already included in the stock price at the starting time.

Will your strategy meet expectations? Do you know how much value your company's strategy will create? What is the strategy's objective? Is the level of planned value creation enough to satisfy investors? Will the strategy satisfy investors? Companies that can answer these questions have a clearer road map to meeting investor expectations and creating value. Knowing how much value you plan to create is better than not knowing. Management should always prefer to know whether or not the plan they have would meet investor's expectations. Knowing the value of the strategic plan helps to answer the questions, "Are we going to meet our investors' expectations?" and "Is the strategy good enough?" Very few companies go through the process of valuing their strategic plan. Yet, unless you know the value of your strategic plan, you are flying blind in uncertain weather. Valuing the plan is meant to tell us what we expect will happen, not what actually will happen. What actually happens will be different from what we expected. The purpose, then, is to compare our expectations relative to investors' expectations and to make sure the differences can be explained and resolved.

What is Value Management?

Managing for value is nothing new. Yet, today few companies are realizing the maximum value they could create. Managing for value can play an important role in investment and operating decision. A focused approach on value can help management make trade-offs between different opportunities and conflicting priorities. Value management is a way of focusing managers on the company's strategy to achieve better alignment and create value. It means using the right combination of capital and other resources to generate cash flow from the business. Value management is not an event that occurs once a year but is an ongoing process of investing and operating decision-making that includes a focus on value creation. Each decision has an opportunity to create value and it depends on the quality of decision taken. Decision-making has three elements namely objectives, alternatives and information.

Value-based decision-making: The objective of any decision is to create value, but often, an organization has conflicting objectives that require managers to make trade-offs between objectives, which is difficult to do without a single, overriding objective that provides guidance in making the trade-offs. Managing for value provides a weighing scale to help managers balance different considerations, make trade-offs, and come to decisions that maximize value for the organization. Managing for value also improves the quality of decision-making by increasing the number of alternatives under consideration. Quality information is the third and most critical element for decision-making. Companies that have better information can use it to gain insights that will enable them to achieve competitive advantages over their rivals.

Managing for value focuses on managers and provides insights into the trade-offs that managers are implicitly making, generating a broader set of alternatives, and improving the information used to make decisions. Value managed companies focus on value oriented decision-making in the four key management processes of planning, budgeting, compensation, and management reporting. When taken together, the results of value management can help the company build and maintain competitive advantage.

The goal of management is to maximize value by executing the company's strategy. However, successfully achieving this goal is difficult as business issues become more complex, organizations grow, industries consolidate and the speed of competition increases. Today, managers are challenged to develop strategies that respond to changing circumstances and to execute those strategies to maintain and build value.

Roadblocks: There are various roadblocks which keep the strategy from being executed and this prevents the company from attaining its goals. These roadblocks create a lack of focus and ambiguity of direction. Today many large organizations suffer from semi-permanent roadblocks, which have become self-fulfilling prophecies and can challenge even the most innovative management teams and therefore the value of breaking down the roadblocks to effective strategy execution is enormous.

The greatest roadblock to successful strategy execution in today's organizations is lack of focus. This occurs due to lack of coherent strategy to provide direction to the company as in case of companies like IBM and AT&T that lacked a coherent strategy in 1990s. Also, the push and pull of conflicting priorities where each priority may be well intentioned, but together they are pointing the company in different directions makes the company lose focus. Incrementalization is another factor that offers greater risks than benefits in industries where the pace of change is rapid. Thus a successful strategy implementation is all about identifying and overcoming the roadblocks.

Overcoming the roadblocks: Overcoming the roadblocks to strategy execution is a four-step process. The first step involves identifying the performance measures, developing compensation systems and defining the pay for performance.

The second step is identifying the value drivers. The third step is using these value drivers to build a strategic/operating managerial reporting system that can be used for decision-making, improving the strategy development and execution process. Finally, improved communication is required for the successful execution of strategy. Linking the value drivers, the performance measures, compensation and how they are related to one another and the signals they send for management decision-making is a crucial building block to strategy execution.

Performance Measures

Performance measures are one of the most misused management tools in business. Poorly chosen measures create wrong signals for managers, leading to poor decisions and hence poor results. The three myths surrounding the misuse of performance measures are growing. Quarterly earnings per share is all that matters, accounting measures tell the whole story and one can manage with financial reporting.

Performance measures are helpful in managing the business when they actually capture the issues influencing the decisions that managers are being asked to make. At the same time two conflicting measures could confuse and potentially paralyze the manager into inaction. Particularly, financial performance measures can be very confusing when the mangers are asked to make a choice between "return measures and quarterly income results".

Ways to measure performance: There are numerous ways of measuring financial performance like incomes, cash, return and value measures but choosing a measure that is right for the company is an i.nportant activity that can make enormous difference in the way decisions are made. The alternative is a structured approach that captures all the issues the company wants to include in the measure and focuses on maximizing the value of the measure to the organization.

Constructing and implementing a structured process: Construction and implementation of a structured process require understanding various related issues; like, in order to determine whether a single measure would suffice or if multiple measures would be more effective involves determining the accuracy of the proposed measure. This requires an understanding of the important business issues. Also, complexity with regard to company's difficulty in assembling the information required in calculating the measure and then using it as a measure for decision-making, is another important issue to be addressed.

Analyzing the performance measures from the standpoint of the shareholder is a necessary ingredient in developing a performance measurement system that addresses the long-term, wealth creating interests of the shareholders. That is why correlation makes a difference when it comes to judging performance using various measures. Since different companies have different characteristics like the competitive economic situation, industry economics, number of competitors, asset intensity, intellectual content and product life cycle. A combination of financial and strategic measures should address these issues of strategic, industry and company fit to ensure that the selected performance measures serve management purpose.

Limitations: But financial performance does not tell the whole story and therefore we need to consider strategic performance measures like customer relationships, employees relationships and capability enhancement. Such measures can add substantially to the communication and shared understanding of the organization about the importance and relative priorities of different programs across business and functions while improving the decision-making.

Compensation Strategy

There is currently a serious lack of original thought in the area of incentive compensation. Today's compensation programs are designed to be competitive with peer companies within the industry but they miss the main focus of management, which is on achieving the business strategy. Due to this, companies suffer from problems like the compensation doesn't support their business strategy; on excellent performance is worth little more than average performance and the pay packages are designed as one-size-fits-all. The success of the compensation and incentive programs depends on the design and the attitude of the individuals towards compensation strategy. These two factors determine the strategy effectiveness.

Incentive strategy designing: The various factors involved in designing an incentive strategy include, opportunity design which addresses the question of what could be earned and consists of four issues i.e., participation which draws the line in determining who will, and will not, participate in the opportunity. The expected opportunity size that determines the amount of expected incentive payment. Maximum payments or caps are an issue because they influence the upper end of the opportunity and are a way of protecting the company from over paying for performance and balancing short- and long-term goals and performance. Also, the time horizon for the incentives should match the company's business strategy as well as the needs of the individual.

The second factor affecting incentive strategy design is performance design that addresses how the incentives are earned. It includes deciding what measures are to be used. This involves selection of financial and strategic measures of performance, the weight of the measures to assess the relative importance of each measure in order to determine the performance on which the incentive award will be based, the degree of difficulty of goals and targets for the measures as it affects the behavior of the individuals and finally the choice of the targeted or sharing approach.

Another interesting area of performance design involves the use of risk. Because of the differences in the individual's attitudes towards risk, individual risk tolerance is another important element of incentive design and therefore understanding the risk tolerance of individuals and matching them to the risk tolerance of others within the organization as well as the risk tolerance of organization is essential for an effective compensation strategy.

Leverage design is another factor that influences the relationship between incentives and performance in an organization. The higher the leverage the more incentives are paid per incremental improvement in performance. Leverage provides the opportunity to modify the incentive to both alter the risk/reward ratio and increase the focus on performance measure at different levels.

Finally, delivery design addresses the type of payment, use of stock (real, phantom and restricted), options (at the money, in the money and out of the money), tax consequences to the company and the individual, mix of payment, timing of the payment and the restrictions affecting the delivery of incentives to participants. Delivery mechanisms must reflect the strategies that minimize the after tax cost to the company while maximizing the after tax benefit to the participants.

Thus incentives represent a strategic tool that drives performance and when included in the value management program of the company they help to achieve the full potential of the company's strategy to create value.

Implementing Value-based Management

Value management can only be successful in a company if the decision-makers understand what it is and how they can affect value creation through their decisions. To achieve success in value management, the company needs to integrate value-based decision-making throughout the organization by translating the principles, concepts and practices of value-based decision-making into the language of the business at the same time managing several critical variables like senior management leadership and commitment where senior management needs to address a combination of issues to ensure successful implementation of value based decision-making. The management must be aware of the program and acknowledge its importance among company's other priorities. It also needs to demonstrate its commitment by showing interest in the program and ensuring the availability of sufficient resources for the program to be successful.

The program should fit in with the management processes and the decision-making environment should reinforce the value-based decisions from all directions and the management processes (planning, budgeting, incentives and reporting) ideally should reinforce the same messages. Establishing clear messages and consistent signals are very important for the success of the value program and for the execution of business strategy.

A combination of training and education programs needs to be developed so as to build awareness of the value concepts and to integrate them into the day-to-day decisions management makes. To be effective, the education and training programs should be introduced to both line and staff managers, must fulfill the need for baseline as well as technical education, has to be upfront and ongoing, mandatory for everyone and related closely to the business issues facing the company.

Communication is another important variable that is essential for people to understand value creation and discover how the decisions they make influence the amount of value created. A successful communication program requires repeated delivery of messages, their periodic reinforcement, effective translation of the language of value into language of operations and redundancy that helps to enhance the communication effort by increasing the number of times the manager is exposed to value concepts and their application.

Time horizon and task sequencing are other important considerations and therefore it is necessary that organizations must choose realistic time horizon and correct sequencing of tasks which could otherwise be the death knell of an implementation program. Because, when the expectations are not met, managers view the program as a failure, which leads to reprioritization of the implementation program. Finally, the respected managers in the company who carry the torch for the implementation program, referred to as champions, are the most critical variables to the success of a value program. They could be content champions and process champions each integral to the success of implementation process. The role of the content champion is to understand the company's business issues and their implications on decision-making, performance measurement and incentive design. It becomes the resource for the company and an internal arbiter regarding the application of value concepts. While the role of a process champion is to manage the implementation process, the focus should be on organizational buy-in and the level of commitment to value in the organization.

Why does Value Management Fail?

Various value-creating companies have used value-based decision-making and seen the advantages of it for so long, but all of them are not using this approach. This is because many of them have not tried managing for value seriously while the others have failed to implement value-based decision-making. There are various myths that prevent the companies from trying value management.

The first is a belief that the business they are running is different from other businesses. They believe that the business needs to be managed through their knowledge and expertise and that value management would get in the way of their judgment. The second is an abiding faith in the power of earnings per share and that all management has to do is take care of earnings, and the value creation will take care of itself.

Now looking at the companies that have tried value management and failed we see that they break down into five traps. The first one is "flying by the seat of pants". Those companies that fell into this trap lacked a true commitment to value-based decision-making as in the case of Quaker Oats. The second one relates to "unrealistic expectations" that easily derail the value management program.

When the implementation suffers lack of understanding and buy-in by the people at the same time not taking sufficient time to lay the foundation of implementation it runs the risk of derailing. The third reason for failure to implement value-based management into the organization lies in over-focusing on the measure itself. The most common mistake is to assume that the measure of value is the management of value. It makes sense to have a measure that accurately represents the underlying business economics but companies with highly analytical staffs run the risk of allowing the measure to overwhelm the implementation.

The risk of value management program withering from "analysis paralysis" is another trap to which organizations fall as a prey. This is because many-a-times the staff is too concerned about perfecting the measure and analyzing potential consequences and not concerned enough about demonstrating the real value of the program. Line managers of an organization think in terms of operating results not in terms of value creation. This difference in the way operating mangers and financial mangers think leads to many companies falling in trap assuming that "everyone does speak finance" or try to train a large group of managers in finance or accounting. But a little good planning can go a long way in avoiding these traps.

Conclusion

Thus value management is a powerful tool. When used correctly to focus managers, it will drive dramatic improvements in decision-making. However, like any other tool, it can be misused. Therefore, organizations should take time to understand what they are trying to achieve and how their business issues should drive a customized approach to value management. Also, they must take adequate time to customize the measures they use and the way they are integrated into the company.

(James A Knight is the managing partner of SCA ConsultingÕs Value Management and Performance Measurement Practice. SCA, an international management consulting firm, combines its strategy, finance, and compensation expertise to assist leading companies in establishing and achieving effective strategies. Knight was formerly a leader of The Boston Consulting GroupÕs Value Management Practice.

Dr. Niranjan Swain is a Faculty Member at Icfai Business School, Hyderabad, Nupur Hetamsaria and Gina George are fellow students at Icfai Institute for Management Teachers [IIMT]).

5

New Concepts in Value-Based Management: TRS Mapping and Total Economic Profit

John J Ballow, Brian F McCarthy and Michael J Molnar

This article discusses two new concepts in Value Based Management—TRS Mapping and Total Economic Profit. TRS mapping methodology intends to do two critical things: a) Explain 100% of a company's valuation by linking TRS all the way through to the income statement and balance sheet; b) Make communicating company performance to insiders and outsiders much simpler. The Total Economic Profit Measurement tool is used to measure annual performance in Accenture. It provides a flexible metric to measure, manage and motivate organizational performance tying it back directly to shareholder return.

No one gets paid for being half right. But when it comes to creating shareholder value, half right is about as good as most companies get. Although managers make diligent efforts to raise returns to shareholders by focusing on current

Source: www.accenture.com/institute. Intangible Assets and Future Value, Issue 2, May 2004.

operations metrics, such as earnings per share, net income, economic profit or return on invested capital, empirical studies reveal that these measures have only a modest impact. Even the most favorable studies only show an explanatory power of approximately 50 percent of shareholder return-hardly impressive.[1]

Sustained high performance flows from many factors, but key among them is management's ability to consistently discern the drivers of current and future value. The Accenture Institute for High Performance Business has joined with the Accenture Finance & Performance Management and Strategy & Business Architecture service lines to develop a methodology to understand and drive Total Return to Shareholders (TRS). We refer to it as the Accenture TRS Mapping methodology. The Accenture TRS Mapping methodology is intended to do two critical things: (1) explain 100 percent of a company's valuation by linking TRS all the way through to the income statement and balance sheet and (2) make communicating company performance to insiders and outsiders much simpler. We also have in hand an annual measure of performance, the Accenture Total Economic Profit Measurement tool, which provides a flexible metric to measure, manage and motivate organizational performance, tying it back directly to shareholder return. With these two tools, forward-looking executives can focus their organization on what really matters in creating a high-performance business.

Current Value is Just a Piece of the Puzzle – TRS Mapping Brings it all Together

Most companies use current performance metrics, such as earnings per share or economic profit, to direct their allocations of resources for maximizing total returns to shareholders. However, in our work with many companies across industries, we have found that successfully boosting earnings per share or economic profit can have little effect, or even a negative effect, on returns to shareholders. With TRS Mapping, by contrast, executives have the total picture and necessary metrics for understanding and improving shareholder return.

---

1 For example, see Peter D Easton, Travis S Harris, and James A Ohlson, "Aggregate Accounting Returns can Explain Most of Security Returns," *Journal of Accounting and Economics* (1992); Gary C Biddle, Robert M Bowen, and James S Wallace, "Does E\A® Beat Earnings? Evidence on Associations with Stock Returns and Firm Values", *Journal of Accounting and Economics (*1997); Stephen O'Byrne, "E\A and Its Critics," *Journal of Applied Corporate Finance* (1997).

Accenture's goal with TRS Mapping is to map the connections among the various drivers of TRS itself. Starting at the top, we derive the TRS in each period by adding the dividends received to the change in the market value of the equity, then dividing by the original market value of the equity. For the sake of simplicity, if I buy a share for $100, receive $5 in dividends and the share appreciates to $110 during the year, the TRS is 15 percent—a $15 return on a $100 investment. (See Figure 1 for a graphical representation of the key components of TRS).

Figure 1: Key Components of Total Return to Shareholders (TRS)

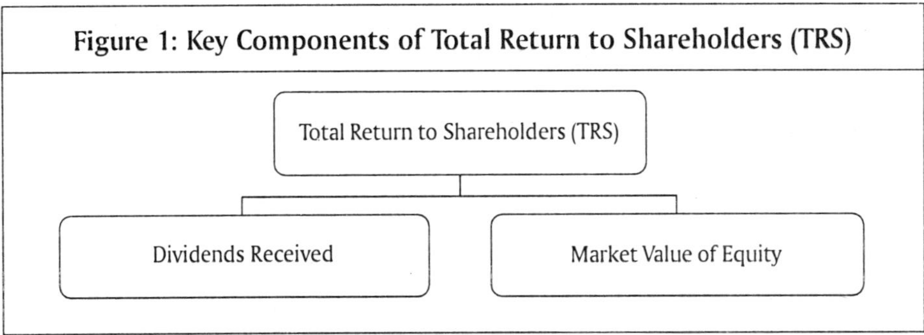

You cannot get to TRS from traditional accounting metrics. For example, while you can divide the sum of the dividends and the market value of equity by earnings to get a multiple similar to the price to earnings ratio, the only action it will recommend is the very general one of increasing earnings. However, many ways of increasing earnings will actually lower the multiple and leave a company with the same or lower value, e.g., increasing earnings in the current period by starving investment and limiting future growth prospects.

Economic profit calculations are a step forward in that the cost of capital is subtracted from a net earnings figure, net operating profit after taxes, adjusted to better reflect economic rather than accounting principles. While some studies have suggested that economic profit has more explanatory power than pure accounting measures, economic profit methodology estimates usually rely on a complex multifactor regression model. In other words, when economic profit methodology predictions are inaccurate, as they often are, they do not provide clear targets for correcting the model or improving organizational performance. This can leave companies in the lurch: For example, in 1996 AT&T achieved its EP target but saw its stock price decline 9 percent while the broad market rose 20 percent. Because it could not figure out how to fix the problem, the next year it dropped the program altogether and returned to accounting measures like earnings per share.[2]

The Accenture TRS Mapping methodology provides the complete set of linkages between TRS and its drivers. (See Figure 2) As in many economic profit methodologies, we calculate the economic profit by subtracting the cost of capital from the net operating profit after taxes (with some adjustments).[3] Dividing that

Figure 2: The Accenture TRS Mapping Methodology Shows a Complete Mapping of Value Creation

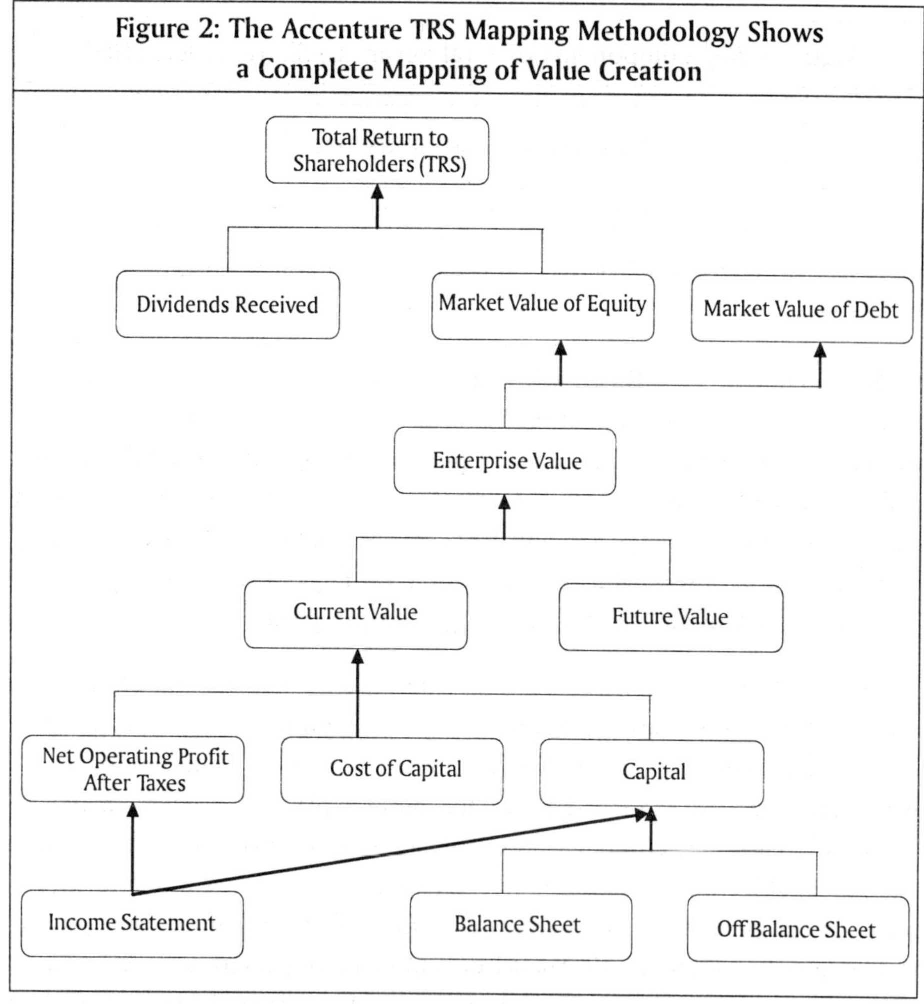

[2] For more detail, see John D Martin and J William Petty, *Value Based Management: The Corporate Response to the Shareholder Revolution* (Boston: Harvard Business School, 2000), 205-208.

[3] TRS Mapping™ can accommodate both simplified EP and highly adjusted EP calculations.

economic profit by the cost of capital and then adding back total capital gives us an estimate for the market's valuation of the company's current operations, what we call current value. To calculate what we call the future value, the expectations embedded into company enterprise value, we subtract current value from the enterprise value.[4] By subtracting the market value of debt from the enterprise value, we get the market value of equity. Assessing the market value of equity change from one time period to another along with the dividends received gives us the ability to calculate TRS. The TRS map shows all the linkages to current and future value, with a clarity that makes it easy for employees to drive value in the future.

Total Economic Profit – Current Year Annual View Plus Subsequent Year Targeting

Annualizing TRS Mapping gives this concept operational life by linking a company's annual activities with its market-determined enterprise value. As we can see from Figure 3, between traditional accounting metrics such as earnings ($300), total capital ($950) or enterprise value ($5,000), there is a wide gap, conventionally covered with a multiple. An economic profit methodology charts some of that distance. By deducting the opportunity cost of capital from the net operating profit after taxes, we get an economic profit of $85. By assuming that profit indefinitely (discounted back to the present) and adding back total capital, we get a current value of $1,800, an estimate of the market's valuation of the company's current operations. By subtracting current value from enterprise value we get the future value of $3,200.

However, while current and future values add up to enterprise value (and then it is just a short step to TRS), they do not show the way back to annual operations. Therefore, economic profit programs build complicated multi-factor regression models to make some of the necessary linkages, for example, between current value and market value, to arrive at an adjusted annual economic profit. However, these bridges, although useful, still hang in the air.

---

4 Note that these calculations are based on the ground breaking work of Merton Miller and Franco Modigliani. See Merton H Miller and Franco Modigliani, "Dividend policy, growth and the valuation of shares." *Journal of Business*, 34, 411-433, 1961. In this journal article they present an equation of the value of the firm as the current and expected future cash flows of the firm.

Figure 3: Economic Profit Calculations Provide Additional Insight but Still Inadequate

	Annual Operating Value	Enterprise Value View
Sales	$ 1,000	
Cost of Goods Sold (COGS)	$ 600	
S&GA Costs (SGA)	$ 100	
Earnings Before Interest and Taxes (EBIT)	$ 300	
Taxes (40%)	$ 120	
Net Operating Profit After Tax (NOPAT)	$ 180	
Cash	$ 100	
Net Working Capital	$ 300	
Property, Plant and Equipment	$ 500	
Other Assets	$ 50	
Total Capital	$ 950	
Cost of Capital (WACC)	10%	
Capital Charge	$ 95	
Current Value[1]		**$ 1,800**
Economic Profit of Current Value[2]	$ 85	
Future Value[3]	?	**$ 3,200**
Enterprise Value[4]		**$ 5,000**

Notes:

1. Current Value = (Economic Profit/WACC) + Capital
2. Economic Profit of Current Value = NOPAT – Capital Charge
3. Future Value = Enterprise Value – Current Value
4. Enterprise Value = Market Value of Equity + Market Value of Debt

Our link back to TRS Mapping is provided by decapitalizing future value to obtain an annual view of future value, the Economic Profit of Future Value.[5] Turning to Figure 4, decapitalizing the future value of $3,200 (that is, multiplying by the cost of capital) gives us $320, the amount of economic profit from future value. The combination of the economic profits of current ($85) and future value ($320) gives us the total economic profit ($405) for that year.

[5] It should be noted that all the concepts presented in this paper, including TRS Mapping, Total Economic Profit, and the Economic Profit of Future Value, are patent pending. All rights reserved.

Figure 4: Total Economic Profit Provides the Missing Linkage to Value

	Annual Operating Value	Enterprise Value View
Sales	$1,000	
Cost of Goods Sold (COGS)	$ 600	
S&GA Costs (SGA)	$ 100	
Earnings Before Interest and Taxes (EBIT)	$ 300	
Taxes (40%)	$ 120	
Net Operating Profit After Tax (NOPAT)	$ 180	
Cash	$ 100	
Net Working Capital	$ 300	
Property, Plant and Equipment	$ 500	
Other Assets	$ 50	
Total Capital	$ 950	
Cost of Capital (WACC)	10%	
Capital Charge	$ 95	
Current Value[1]		**$ 1,800**
Economic Profit of Current Value[2]	$ 85	
Future Value[3]		**$ 3,200**
Economic Profit of Future Value[4]	$ 320	
Enterprise Value[5]		**$ 5,000**
Total Economic Profit[6]	$ 405	

Notes:

1. Current Value = (Economic Profit/WACC) + Capital
2. Economic Profit of Current Value = NOPAT – Capital Charge
3. Future Value = Enterprise Value – Current Value
4. Economic Profit of Future Value = Future Value *WACC
5. Enterprise Value = Market Value of Equity + Market Value of Debt
6. Total Economic Profit = Economic Profit of Current Value + Economic Profit of Future Value

Figure 5, shows how we can use these concepts to target performance going forward. In order to earn our weighted cost of capital, we need to aim at the total economic profit targeted, here $437. This is the sum of the economic profit of current value ($85) and the economic profit of future value ($352).[6] Of course, we need not aim at merely maintaining value—a higher TRS figure will imply higher current and future value targets.

6 Because we are targeting a year ahead, we have multiplied the Future Value number from Figure 5, $320, by the WACC, 10%, to get the Future Value target, $352.

Figure 5: Total Economic Profit Targeting Providing a WACC Rate of Return

	Year 0	Year 1	Year 2	Year 3	Year 4	Year 5
Actual Current Year Performance						
Net Operating Profit After Taxes (NOPAT)	180.00	198.00	217.80	239.58	263.54	289.89
Capital Charge[1]	95.00	113.00	132.80	154.58	178.54	204.89
Economic Profit of Current Value	85.00	85.00	85.00	85.00	85.00	85.00
Economic Profit of Future Value[2]	320.00	352.00	387.20	425.92	468.51	515.36
Targeted Performance for Next Year						
Economic Profit of Current Value[3]	85.00	85.00	85.00	85.00	85.00	N/A
Economic Profit of Future Value[4]	352.00	387.20	425.92	468.51	515.36	N/A
Total Economic Profit Targeted	437.00	472.20	510.92	553.51	600.36	N/A
Capital Balance at End of Year						
Cost of Capital (WACC)	10%	10%	10%	10%	10%	10%
Capital[5]	1,130.00	1,328.00	1,545.80	1,785.38	2,048.92	2,338.81
Actual Value at End of Year						
Enterprise Value	5,000.00	5,500.00	6,050.00	6,655.00	7,320.50	8,052.56
Current Value[6]	1,800.00	1,980.00	2,178.00	2,395.80	2,635.38	2,898.92
Future Value[7]	3,200.00	3,520.00	3,872.00	4,259.20	4,685.12	5,153.63
Expected Value at End of Year						
Investment[8]		5,500.00	6,050.00	6,655.00	7,320.50	8,052.56
Current Value[8]		1,980.00	2,178.00	2,395.80	2,635.38	2,898.92
Future Value[8]		3,520.00	3,872.00	4,259.20	4,685.12	5,153.63
Difference (Actual – Expected)						
Investment		-	-	-	-	-
Current Value		-	-	-	-	-
Future Value		-	-	-	-	-

Notes:

1 Beginning capital balance times WACC. First year assumed to have a beginning capital balance of $950 with 10% cost of capital

2 Economic Profit of Future Value = future value x WACC

3 Target EPCV equal to EP as that will provide a WACC rate of return for current value

4 Target EPCV equal to WACC x expected FV for next period

5 Prior year NOPAT assumed to be reinvested and therefore added to capital balance (i.e. 180 + 950 = 1130)

6 Current Value = (Economic Profit/WACC) + Capital

7 Future Value = Enterprise Value – Current Value

8 Expected return is a WACC return on initial investment

We, then, must provide $437 in total economic profit to our shareholders in the upcoming year, but how much of this is drawn from current or future value is a matter of indifference to the market. We might, for a number of reasons, elect to concentrate on current value, drawing more than $85 from it, or we might elect to focus on the sort of long-term investments that depress current cash flow but boost long-term growth expectations. Total economic profit aligns organizational aims with shareholder interests while preserving a measure of flexibility in investment choices. Managers have the flexibility to make the investments they want—with the market being the ultimate judge of whether it believes those investments are good ones. As Accenture's research of high-performance businesses shows, those organizations that can manage for both today and tomorrow will be the most successful.

Making it Work – Aligning Incentives

These concepts are more than a financial exercise: they are meant to guide organizational and individual behavior. To do so they must be extended into the incentive plan. While a detailed discussion of the incentive plan is beyond the scope of this research note, we do want to make some key points about how incentives are to be structured in a total economic profit program.

First, how the target is set matters. In conventional incentive plans, management sets a floor, a target and a ceiling (see Figure 6). Employees are rewarded incrementally once they have surpassed the floor and until they have reached the ceiling. However, there is far too much arbitrariness in the setting of targets based on metrics that do not link to total return to shareholders (TRS) and can be massaged into actuals. As a result rewards too often go not to those who have performed the best, but to those who have devoted the most time and effort to politicking—a misuse of resources. In addition, there is a marked tendency to reflexively raise the bar for top performers and lower the bar for underperformers, which discourages top performance and mistakenly encourages poor performance.[7]

---

[7] Michael C Jensen, "Paying People to Lie: The Truth about the Budgeting Process," *European Financial Management* 9, no. 3 (September 2003): 379.

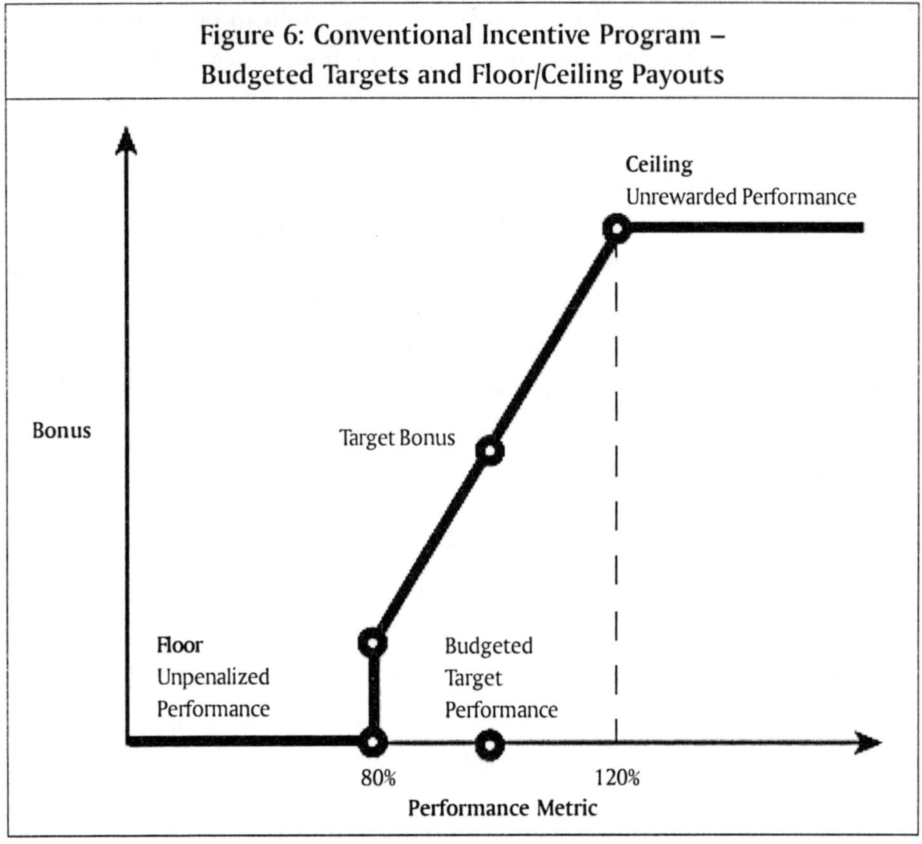

Figure 6: Conventional Incentive Program – Budgeted Targets and Floor/Ceiling Payouts

A total economic profit incentive plan eliminates much of the arbitrariness and thus the opportunity for politicking. The target bonus is derived from the total economic profit (see Figure 7). Corporate and the business units work together to allocate the economic profit of current and future value to the individual business units, but they work with enough hard numbers to constrain capriciousness. Conventional incentive plans work only with current value, leaving future value—which is often the larger amount—up for grabs. Our concepts start with the whole and provide a rigorous method for allocating to the parts.

Second, the conventional plan's 80 percent floor and 120 percent ceiling are prone to distorting incentives for both poor and good performers. Take, for example, an underperforming division that may finish out of the money, perhaps at only 60 percent of its target. If management decides to make a dash for the 80 percent level, it may do so by declining investments with long-term paybacks but no

Figure 7: Characteristics of a Total Economic Profit Incentive Plan

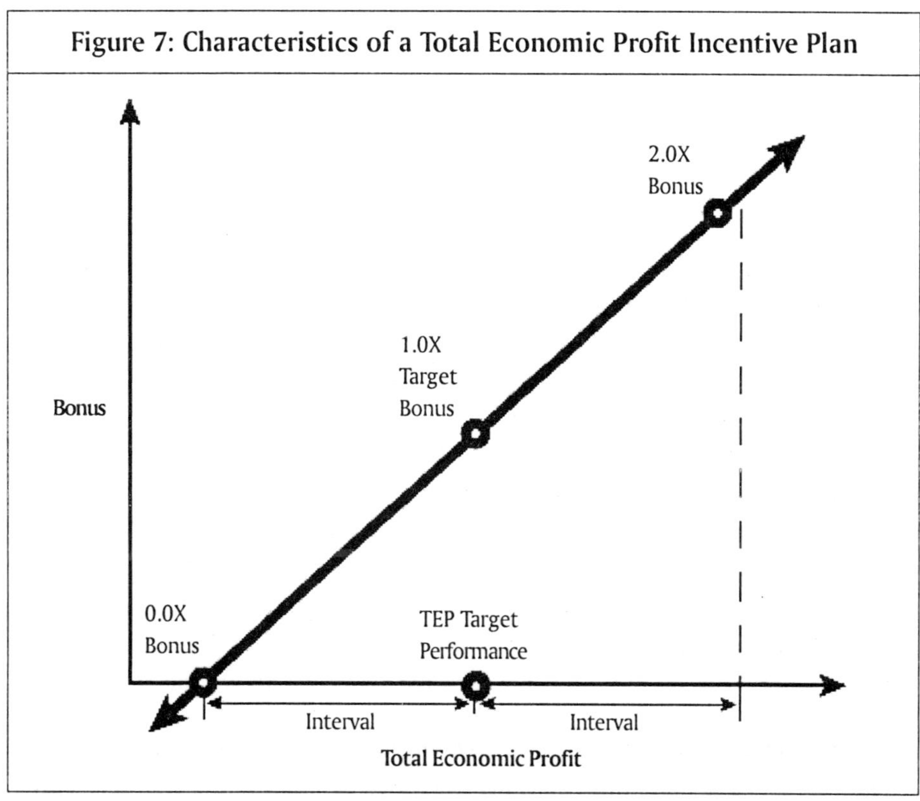

current paybacks, or by bleeding reserves and making accounting adjustments, or both. If management decides instead to give up, it has a great incentive to miss big, taking a large restructuring charge in the current year, setting up reserves to bleed in the future or even setting up false accounts. Divisions that are trending toward hitting 130 percent of their target may, on the other hand, take a very conservative view of accounting and set up large reserves they can draw from in future fallow years. In each of these outcomes, the division wins and the company loses.[8]

A total economic profit incentive plan has a floor but no ceiling. Overperforming is encouraged by being rewarded. In order to hinder exploitation, we recommend a bonus bank, in which bonuses are placed and paid out over several years, depending on the sustainability of the improvement over time. Management will be much less tempted to substitute its short-term gain for the company's long-term health. This is only the beginning, for a comprehensive incentive plan

8 For more detail see Ross L Watts and Jerold L Zimmerman, *Positive Accounting Theory* (Englewood Cliffs, NJ: Prentice Hall, 1986).

will not only have to address these issues but others too; for example, employee retention and minimizing the cost of compensation to shareholders.

Summary and Conclusion

Almost every publicly traded company will tell you that they manage for shareholder value. Yet the tools at their disposal often provide scant guidance because they are partial in focus, emphasizing today over tomorrow. Indeed, many management teams find themselves dedicating thousands, even tens of thousands, of workdays toiling over a political budgeting process only to find that the end product does not track toward the goal of shareholder value.

With the Accenture TRS Mapping methodology and our measurement of total economic profit, forward-looking executives can correct and extend their vision, getting their companies back on the high-performance business track, and keeping them there even in the face of a swiftly evolving competitive environment. Total economic profit brings today and tomorrow into a single view, and TRS Mapping connects the dots all the way back to the operational level. By aiming at total economic profit, management will aim their company directly for shareholder value.

(John J Ballow is a partner in the Accenture Finance & Performance Management service line and has more than 25 years of experience as a corporate finance officer, advisor and strategist in financial management. He specializes in economic value analysis, value management, finance operations and strategy, and corporate financial management. Mr. Ballow holds an MBA in finance. He can be reached at john.j.ballow@accenture.com

Brian F McCarthy joined Accenture in 1993 and has more than 10 years of experience in value and performance management and financial reengineering engagements. His primary focus is in helping client organizations increase shareholder value, where he also has led recognized primary research projects in this area. Mr. McCarthy holds an MS in mathematics and statistics. He can be reached at brian.f.mccarthy@accenture.com

Michael J Molnar is a visiting research fellow at the Accenture Institute for High Performance Business. His work has focused on assisting executive teams with finance, strategy and general decision-making issues across a variety of industries. He has earned an MBA in finance and an MS in decision sciences. He is a CPA (certified public accountant), CMA (certified management accountant), and CFM (certified in financial management). He can be reached at michael.j.molnar@accenture.com).

About Accenture

Accenture is a global management consulting, technology services and outsourcing company. Committed to delivering innovation, Accenture collaborates with its clients to help them become high-performance businesses and governments. With deep industry and business process expertise, broad global resources and a proven track record, Accenture can mobilize the right people, skills and technologies to help clients improve their performance. With approximately 90,000 people in 48 countries, the company generated net revenues of US$11.8 billion for the fiscal year ended August 31, 2003. Its home page is www.accenture.com.

About Accenture Institute for High Performance Business

The Accenture Institute for High Performance Business creates strategic insights into key management issues through original research and analysis. Its management researchers combine world-class reputations with Accenture's extensive consulting, technology and outsourcing experience to conduct innovative research and analysis into how organizations become and remain high-performance businesses. Its home page is www.accenture.com/institute and may be contacted at institute@accenture.com.

6

Contemporary Value Based Management: Fallacies of Today's Value Based Management and its Impact on Corporate Investment Behavior

Achim Seisreiner and Sebastian Träger

In its current design, Value Based Management (VBM) faces serious restrictions when it comes to assessing the real value a firm creates. Furthermore and even more problematic, we show that the contemporary approaches to VBM can lead to dysfunctional management decisions which, in the end, may actually neutralize or even destroy a firm's present and future value positions. As a consequence, we argue that a multidimensional value framework will help VBM to return on the right track. Unfortunately, today's VBM is predominantly restricted to the logic of shareholder satisfaction. As a consequence, corporate decision-making is mainly influenced by the future prospects of adding value to invested capital. But we will show that there exist an immense variety of value sources that also need to be included to fully assess corporate value added. Only by broadening VBM's present perspective on value, it can again be seen as a helpful guideline to secure corporate sustainability.

Source: SAM/IFSAM VII World Congress Proceedings, Goteborg, 2004 (Revised on 29 August 2006). This article was originally titled as "Value Based Management and the Multidimensionality of Value: Attempting to Overcome the Restrictions of Today's Value Based Management".

Introduction

Where and how to compete are the key issues of strategic management. A global business world offers multiple and diverse opportunities and threats to a firm in such a way that it is hard for executives to design and evaluate an optimal action plan. In general, firms respond to the diversity and complexity of the relevant business world with a requisite variety of commitments to handle immanent corporate risk: e.g. they exercise diversification to establish options for corporate growth; they become engaged in strategic alliances to optimize their value chain etc. (e.g. Figure 1). Among other motives—such as (personal) reputation, social responsibility or environmental sustainability—business activities in general are recognized to be focusing on the maximization of future corporate value. Under this guideline every planned activity or investment of a firm in a specific industry, market or technology must be checked for its rate of return and its impact on corporate value respectively.

Figure 1: Structural Options for Doing Business in a Complex Environment

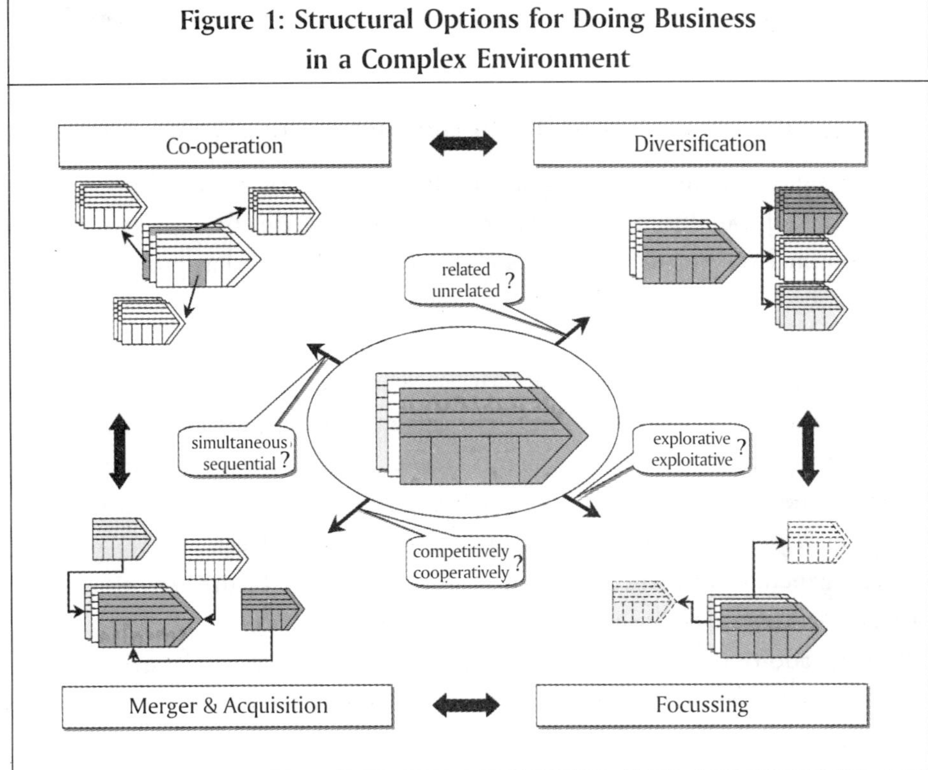

Accordingly, when planning a firm's competitive strategy one of the key questions to be answered by corporate decision-makers refers to the allocation of scarce resources in their most productive usage. Hereby, the decision-inherent restriction is to always deploy an existing and available resource in its most profitable application. A positive net value is eventually created when the monetary value of all resources used for the production of a product or service is lower than the resulting value of the final product or service. Additionally, this net value must also be higher than in every conceivable alternative investment. Even though this calculation seems to be an easy job at first sight, every valuation process gives expression to the underlying business strategy and this significantly complicates the determination of generally accepted "true" or "real" values. To calculate meaningful value figures and to support corporate decision-making, many valuation methods have been developed first and foremost by consulting firms. Therefore, a special market for valuation concepts has been established. This promising area of management science and its translation into action is labeled Value Based Management (VBM). It is obvious that VBM and the design of the corporate actions are closely related topics in strategic management.

Making Valuable Decisions in Multifarious Competitive Landscapes

If corporate environment is stable and decision-makers are fully informed about environmental conditions, a rational decision-making can be expected. In this world optimal value generation is reduced to a simple selection process. In case different value creating alternatives have been identified they will *ceteris paribus* be compared and the final choice will be based on the activity that will generate highest return. Further or additional activities will only occur if internal conditions such as resource endowment, technology, and managerial capabilities advance to a quality that match the requirements needed to successfully enter into, for example, a new line of business (Dundas/Richardson 1982; Prahalad/Bettis 1986). Unfortunately, reality provides quite a different picture. Decisions are—among others—generally influenced by uncertainty about the future, environmental fuzziness, corporate elites, and complexity (Dimitrov/Hodge 2002; Jensen/Zajac 2004). In addition, firms—as traditionally argued—are not only striving with competitors for consumers and market shares, but also for access to resources, technology, services, and favorable market conditions (e.g. patent protection) (Jayachandran et al. 1999). Moreover, firms often do not compete in the market place on their own but in alliances and networks that spontaneously emerge around a distinct issue. Depending on the situation, it is, for example, conceivable that strategic groups, industry clusters or even whole industry sectors compete with each other for raw materials, qualified personnel, and subsidies (Baum/ Korn 1999). Furthermore, the character of competitive actions is also very complex and ought not to be reduced to an entry-retaliation-relationship. There are many other ways to compete without simply trying to drive a competitor out of the competitive arena (Brandenburger/Nalebuff 1998). Different competitive scenarios such as collusion, peaceful coexistence or hypercompetition are also acknowledgeable (D'Aveni 1994). As a result, environmental complexity is characterized by multiple competitive modes of aggregation and interaction and therefore of different competitive targets (Rasche 2002). Accordingly, when firms think about an optimal mixture of business activities it would be a mistake to rest this decision and the underlying assumptions about the potential level of value improvements merely on anticipated sales and potential retaliation strategies. As shown, the competitive environment is too complex to be reduced to one-dimensional dependencies.

This means that exact causal relationships about the effects of certain activities cannot be easily derived at all. For every decision alternative there exists a variety of known and unknown outcomes where decision-makers are not sure about the probability of occurrence and the complexity-inherent factors that may positively or negatively affect them. Thus, whereas *ex post* measurement of value creation per business activity is relatively easy, because the necessary data is widely available or at least easily obtainable, companies face serious difficulties estimating the potential for value creation of a decision to be made in the future. To evaluate different investment alternatives in terms of value creation, the literature on VBM offers a variety of performance metrics that may support the managerial decision to enlarge or reduce the scope of activities (e.g. Bromwich/Walker 1998).

Today's Value Based Management as a Fallacious Guideline for Investment Decisions

VBM as a management and control system measures, encourages, and supports all those activities that contribute directly to a positive increase in a firm's value (Ameels et al. 2002). Therefore, the fundamental aspects of VBM are to analyze where and how value has been created, to identify new possible sources of wealth generation, and to avoid activities that destroy or neutralize value. Generally, it is an instrument for *ex post* as well as *ex ante* performance analysis. For this reason VBM seems to be a helpful guideline for a firm's decision-making. Furthermore, the emergence of VBM indicates that value creation has become a central issue for corporate management. Consequently, its main objective is to identify and facilitate actions that maximize return on investments and to make sure that these returns always exceed the capital costs of an investment. Additionally, VBM has to ensure that the returns on capital invested match at least the returns that could have been accomplished in its next best alternative use (opportunity costs). For this matter, academics and especially consulting companies have developed a great number of performance metrics, all of which claim to be a comprehensive foundation for sound decision-making and management accountability (Ameels et al. 2002).

We illustrate the logic of modern valuation practice by two systems of VBM that are the most frequently used concepts: The Cash Value Added (CVA) system, developed and promoted by the Boston Consulting Group (Olsen/Thomas 1987) and the Economic Value Added (EVA) system, developed and promoted by Stern Stewart (Stewart III. 1994) and McKinsey (Copeland et al. 1994). Both concepts have in common that they distinguish between an internal and an external performance measurement perspective (Schaefer 2002 and Figure 2).

Figure 2: Traditional Approaches to Determine Corporate Value Creation

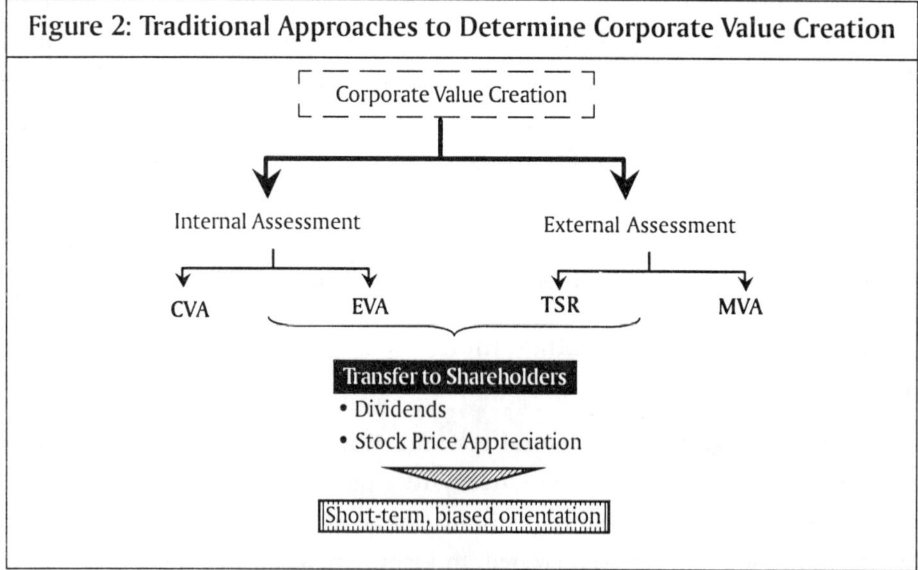

This reflects the managerial logic that value creation is internally controlled (foremost *ex ante*) but is evaluated externally (foremost *ex post*) by capital markets. For this reason the CVA as an internal measure is accompanied by the Total Shareholder Return (TSR) as the corresponding external figure, and the internal oriented EVA corresponds to the external figure of the Market Value Added (MVA). Before considering the calculations of the internal metrics CVA and EVA, it is important to realize that the credibility of the external metrics—*ex ante* as expected figures or *ex post* as realized performance measures—determine the investment options of a firm by playing the role of a financial gatekeeper. For that, in the long run, the internal calculations of expected value creations should correlate positively with these external metrics. Otherwise firms are systematically overrated or underrated according to the value creation and investment options are becoming volatile and hard to plan. The TSR is an internal rate of return calculation for a stockholding period considering the stock price development over time and the dividends paid in these periods. The second external measurement, the MVA, is the difference between the net capital value and the market value of a company. Unfortunately, the MVA is only relevant for investors who invested in a firm by the time it was founded and under the constraint that they invested at book value (Schaefer 2002). At the stock exchange this does not seem to be the standard case.

The internal measures of VBM, CVA and EVA differ very much according to the calculation mode: CVA is based on cash flow considerations while EVA is based on accounting information. One essential problem with the latter is that many adjustments are needed to correct for accounting rules that do not reflect economic reality. The CVA can be calculated directly—as Gross Cash Flow (GCF) less Economic Depreciation (ED) less Capital Charge (GK*c)—or indirectly—as the difference between Cash Flow Return on Investment (CFROI) and cost of capital (c) multiplied with Gross Capital (GK). To calculate EVA Stern Stewart and McKinsey use identical approaches only differing by the naming of the variables. For example, McKinsey does not refer to the EVA but to Economic Profit (EP). Nevertheless, the concepts are identical: EVA is calculated as the difference between Net Operating Profit After Tax (NOPAT) and capital charge (capital*WACC), that is the capital multiplied with Weighted Average Cost of Capital (WACC). EP is calculated in the same way.

It is Net Operating Profit Less Adjusted Taxes (NOPLAT) less invested capital that is multiplied with WACC.

Even without looking more closely at details of the calculation methods, it becomes obvious that today's view on VBM and its measures is primarily based on the maximization of cash flows or more generally of returns on capital invested and thus of Shareholder Value Added (SVA) (Bannister/Jesuthasan 1997). Within this perspective, whether or not a firm is creating value will be simply indicated externally by the dividends that each shareholder receives and the stock price increase at the end of a period. Hence, it is the sum of share price appreciation and paid dividends divided by the share price at the time of investment (Rappaport 1986).

As mentioned before, *ex post* calculations of the SVA are rather easy, since necessary data can be obtained from the accounting department and stock markets. Contradictory, *ex ante* projections of the potential of a new business to add to shareholder value is more difficult, because performance projections must rely on information about the future. To calculate the expected SVA resulting from a new business activity internally, projections are required about future cash flows or profits and an interest rate that discounts them to their present value. SVA is thus a value metric that is predominantly based on *projections* about the activity-induced performance and the discount rate with an unknown probability of occurrence. If we assume a situation where at the end of the planning period the free cash flow or the profit stemming from a business project will eventually be lower than the projected one, the SVA perspective suggests the investment to be critical, because in comparison to the underlying *projections* value has been destroyed. The managerial consequence could range between deeper investigations and rigorous divestments. In the end, such a controlling and management system may result in what we call a lemmings-game: Just like lemmings follow an intuitive signal to jump off a cliff, investors will withdraw their capital from the investment. But resting such a decision merely on *projected value added* is fallacious, because it does not say anything about the actual level of value the business activity created. SVA in this situation is only a performance metric that states a negative value compared to the projected one, but it fails to account for actual or real value creation respectively.

Another result of such a lemmings-like action is myopic investment behavior. This can easily be demonstrated by the case of investments with delayed payments (cash flows or profits). These are investments resulting in payments that do not affect the corporate performance until, let's say, 10 years after the investment started. Predicting the future payments to infinity is impossible. So introducing a so called Termination Value (TV) of an investment is helping to cope with this valuation problem. The TV represents the expected payments beyond the forecasting horizon (Schaefer 2002). The usual length of forecasting horizons is about 5 to 10 years (Böltzel/Schwilling 1998). Therefore, in practice, predictions of future payments are divided into two periods. One period (5 to 10 years) is characterized by an explicit forecast of annual performances whereas a subsequent period (>10 years) represents the hardly predictable payments of the distant future. In the case of investments with delayed payments the TV has logically a proportionally big share in the total present value of an investment. Unfortunately, investments of that kind are suspect with regard to the "hockey stick"-effect, which outlines the fact that poor forecasts are becoming good ones in an unrealistic manner the longer the planned horizon (Böltzel/Schwilling 1998). It is evident that investments without such a suspicious attitude are preferred, because the flow of payments simply takes place earlier. Unfortunately, the temporality of payments by itself does not say anything about the "real" value creation by an investment.

As a conclusion, since VBM is currently predominantly concerned with SVA, corporate decision-makers are required to focus primarily on the *early* fulfillment of the *projected* development of their capital costs, profits or free cash flows respectively. As a result of this one-dimensionality in focus, today's VBM is nothing but mere shareholder value management and the analyzed firm is treated merely as a "black box", because other valuable and thus potentially wealth-improving sources are simply left out of consideration. But in a complex world with multiple arenas of competition, the measurement of corporate success relying on only one performance metric such as the SVA is by no means sufficient. With regard to the real value generation of a business project, VBM in its present form has not much to add. Accordingly, to evaluate diverse business activities in a complex market environment, a closer look at additional sources of wealth creation and a more comprehensive system of performance metrics is required.

A Multidimensional Value Framework for Proper Value Based Management

As mentioned earlier, following the present view of VBM the process of corporate value creation is thus far simply set equal to the maximization of shareholder value. We already pointed out that we judge this view as being rather inadequate and refer to Lippman and Rumelt (2003) who argue that wealth creation results in payments (i.e. revenues) to *all* resources involved in the production process. Though the main recognized payments in VBM are those to shareholders, which take the forms of dividend payments and/or stock price increases. This problematic logic suggests that apparently no other resources but capital have been invested into the production process. Naturally, this is not the case. Capital is just one (scarce) resource in the resource portfolio of a firm and thus only a partial indictor of corporate wealth or value creation. As a result, "[the] language of cost obscures the simple facts that value is lodged in scarce factors, not 'economic profit'" (Lippman/Rumelt 2003: 904). Therefore, by relying on free cash flow or profit as the major measure of a firm's value added, it is very likely that the real or actual corporate value added is not reflected because other significant sources of corporate wealth are simply ignored. As a consequence, we firstly propose an extended conception of value *creation* which will give the opportunity to incorporate *all* sources of value as also illustrated in Figure 3.

Figure 3: An Extended Conception of Corporate Value

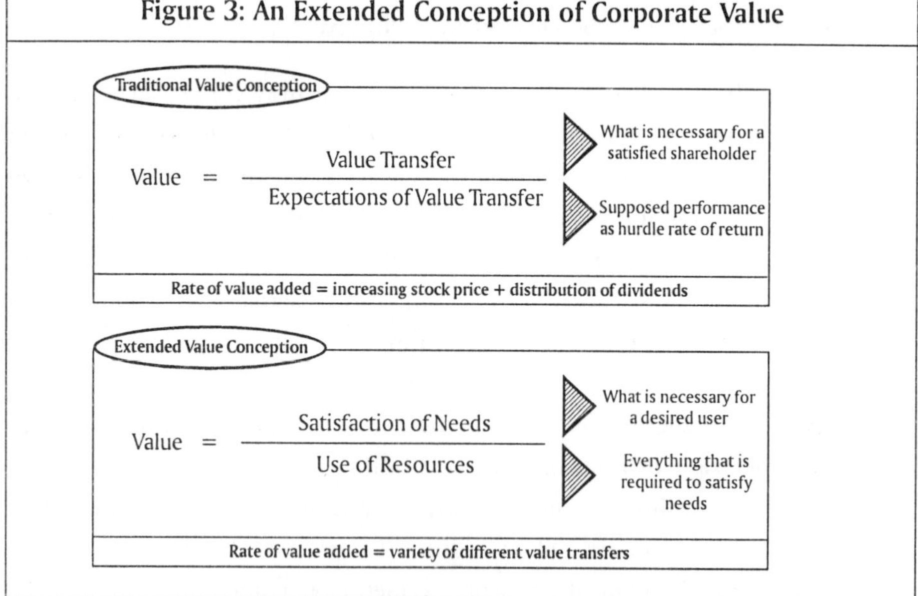

To evade the central shortcomings of VBM addressed above, we secondly present a three-dimensional model to explain how value should be *managed.* This model incorporates the Lippman/Rummelt-logic and introduces different performance metrics that measure the value added of all resources involved in the production process. This implies that it is necessary for a firm to assess, for example, how much value added was created for all its input factors (elementary factors). Furthermore, we argue that the complex process of managing corporate value consists of three interdependent dimensions: 1. *Value Investment,* 2. *Value Creation,* and 3. *Value Transfer.* Dividing the process of managing value according to these dimensions allows us to focus attention on several (resource and thus value) interactions that are simply neglected in present VBM. The model incorporates the three dimensions into an integrated framework, as shown in Figure 4.

Figure 4: A Multidimensional Value Framework

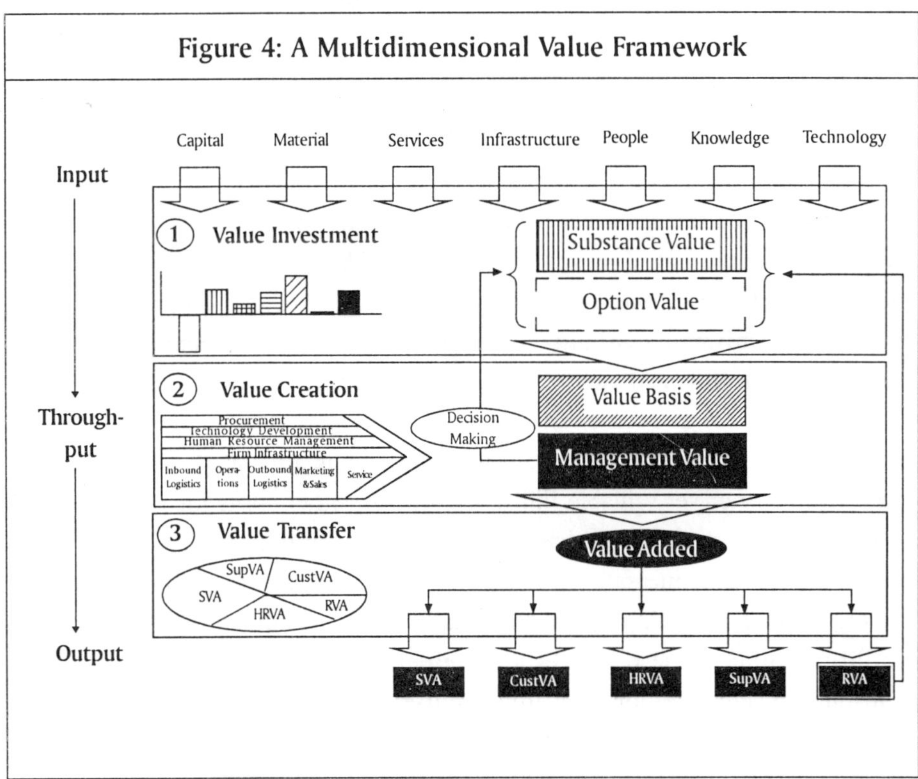

Value Investments

Firstly, the process of managing value can be seen as some kind of *investment activity* whereby input factors are tied to the firm. In the view of VBM, all these input factors (e.g. capital, material, services, infrastructure, people, knowledge, technology) contain a factor-specific Substance Value, which reflects the present necessity of a disposable resource for a firm and determines whether or not this factor contributes positively to the actual corporate performance and thus to value generation. This argumentation is similar to the resource-based view of the firm (e.g. Wernerfelt 1984; Barney 1991; Peteraf 1993) that corporate actions will only lead to competitive advantages and to increasing value generation if and only if individual or combined resources deployed are valuable, scarce or non-obtainable, non-substitutable and non-imitable. Accordingly, the quality of available resources and the superiority of the knowledge or technology that combine them into productive use particularly influence the performance of the firm over time. To a firm it is therefore of particular importance to ensure that value is added to the resources in use through permanent investments to ensure long-term growth.

In addition to the resources deployed, it is also imaginable that some of the firm's resources are not always in use (i.e. organizational slack) (Sharfman et al. 1988; Nohria/Gulati 1996). For example, as the literature on real options suggests, resource commitments should not be made before they become absolutely necessary or a deployment alternative has been identified that will result in highest possible returns for a specific resource or its combination with others (Trigeorgis 1996; Copeland/Antikarov 2001). Additionally, it is also imaginable that firms often invest in not yet valuable skills, resources or other assets for reasons of risk diversification or with no particular deployment in mind. Miller (2003) defines latter resource investments as investments in asymmetries that might serve as a starting point for developing valuable, rare, and non-substitutable resources in the future. Since these resources are presently not deployed and thus cannot contribute to value creation they are of course neglected in current value analysis. But due to the fact that they are likely to contribute to value generation in the future and that the resulting non-commitment induced flexibility is valuable itself, VBM ought to incorporate investments in corporate (real) options when assessing the value in present times. For this reason each input-factor also has a specific Option Value which is relevant for its future use. Accordingly, the basis of the value creation process is either resource-determined (Substance Value) or potentially resource-determined (Option Value). Whereas information about the former can generally be derived from the corporate accounting system the latter is largely a function of environmental developments and specifically a question of effective execution and abandonment or termination management (Adner/Levinthal 2004). Hence, *both* are the fundamental building blocks for the assessment of how much value a firm is able to generate in its relevant environment.

Value Creation

The process of managing value can further be seen as a *transformation process*. Following this view, the so called "value basis"—as the present stock and quality of the firm's value investments—is only a necessary but not a sufficient condition for value creation. It is the quality of management that makes the difference (disposition factor) (e.g. Jensen/Zajac 2004). This means that the elements of importance for value creation are managerial activities and the resulting outcomes (Penrose 1995). By explicitly considering the importance of managerial action, one gains insight into the influence of management actors on value creation. Therefore, this managerial quality is called Management Value. As a collective term, Management Value reflects the aggregated quality of diverse managerial areas of a firm like the actual corporate grade of leadership, organization, marketing, planning, controlling and strategic management. While Management Value is an important factor for value creation, it is also an essential element for value investment because it influences the quality of decision making directly. As mentioned above, a firm always has to manage the balancing act between present and future orientation in VBM. To succeed, management must permanently coordinate normative, strategic and operative issues (Seisreiner 1999). Because of this sophisticated task, Management Value seems to be a relevant "cognitive bottleneck" for corporate investment activities, too.

Value Transfer

Thirdly, managing value can finally be seen as a process of *value distribution* to a firm's respective stakeholders. Even if value investment and value creation are the very basis for considerations of value distribution, the value transfer theme is presently established as the core of VBM. The final dimension of our proposed perception of sound VBM is hence to evaluate whether or not the process of value creation, i.e. the management's ability to enlarge the (monetary) worth of the aggregated corporate value basis (SubV + OV) has been successful in a given period. At this point, we are able to close the "value cycle" by providing an overview to comprehensively understand how productively the resources (inputs) at corporate disposal have been used by decision-makers. Therefore, the crucial issue is how all relevant stakeholders benefit from corporate activities. Obviously, the different stakeholders of a firm have different expectations of value transfers they potentially gain from. Because of that it seems to be helpful to distinguish between four simplistic added value concepts: value added to shareholders, customers, the firm's human resources, and suppliers. All these value concepts represent a special kind of value transfer to distinct stakeholders even if they are not directly accompanied by payments like dividends to shareholders or increasing benefits to the staff. In our view, every corporate activity can therefore be seen as a value transfer, because it "consumes" resources (e.g., time, personnel, money). Consequently, financial payments are only a special kind of value transfer. Additionally, we further distinguish from the remaining value added that is not distributed among the respective stakeholders. Such a residual is usually reserved for reinvestments and thus becomes a residual-induced inside-transfer or payment. The following classification will help to identify the different payments.

Shareholder Value Added (SVA). Since shareholder value and its operating figures have thus far already been a major part of analysis in this paper, we would like to avoid a repeating discussion and simply refer to it as being the additional value to stock owners stemming from stock price appreciations and dividends paid in a certain period of time. This will be the case if the return on capital is higher than the price paid by the firm for its capital. Accordingly, it is an indicator that the value of equity increased compared to the value of market priced outside capital (e.g. Rappaport 1994). As a result, these circumstances lead to an increasing Shareholder Value Added (SVA).

Human Resource Value Added (HRVA). As already pointed out, a firm's human resources are of crucial importance with regard to the overall corporate performance, because they are acknowledged as being the main source of actual and potential competitive advantages (Prahalad/Hamel 1990). The design of corporate incentive systems is of significant importance for the performance of a firm, because such systems will eventually lead to a better-motivated workforce and thus to effectiveness gains. To invest value in an incentive system can help to satisfy a variety of motives ranging from fair compensation, extensive health and safety regulations to the safeguarding of jobs or peaceful labor relations. Furthermore, if a firm provides a comprehensive incentive system that covers most of the employee's needs the fluctuation rate will decrease and the firm as an employer will become more attractive. Finally, this in turn results in a higher retention rate. Therefore, since a firm's employees gain directly from incentive systems, a Human Resource Value Added (HRVA) is of particular importance and must be included in the discussion of how much value a firm created, because the quality or performance-induced payments to the stock of human capital are an essential parameter for assessing the value a firm was able to generate (Abowd et al. 1990). This means that if a corporate incentive system is by and large accepted by the workforce target groups the Human Resource Value Added (HRVA) increases as a result.

By referring to the material and immaterial "payments" to human resources as an indicator for incentive acceptance and thus value added, we are able to circumvent the difficulties that come along with the assessment of the actual value of the human resources at corporate disposal. Many scholars (e.g. Lev/Schwartz 1971; Flamholtz 1972; Jaggi/Lau 1974) have developed models that try to more or less successfully incorporate the value determining factors (i.e. the costs and/or benefits of education) of employees. It is needless to further elaborate the deficiencies of these approaches that have often been referred to by many critics. Instead, by suggesting a periodic comparison of HR-payments adjusted for current inflation rate, we are easily able to assess how much value was added to a firm's human resources.

Customer Value Added (CustVA). Moreover, not only the value of (internal) resources *per se* indicate the level of wealth creation. Another important determinant for the assessment of overall corporate value added is the perceived customer satisfaction. If the products or services offered by a firm significantly contribute to the satisfaction of customer needs—for example via a high degree of perceived quality (Reeves/Bednar 1994; Zeithaml 1988), extensive service coverage or rock bottom prices—an increase in Customer Value Added (CustVA) will be the consequence. This line of thought is congruent to Porter's (1985) argument that value is determined by the level of the consumer's willingness to pay for what a firm offers. Thus, if the distinct characteristics of a product or service significantly improve the satisfaction of consumer needs, their willingness to pay for this particular product or service will rise as well. Accordingly, in situations of constant prices the level of service and quality improvements will result in a value transfer to the consumer. Equally, if quality and service remain stable a price decrease will lead to the same result. In both cases producer surplus has been transferred to the respective customer. This means that the value added for customers is directly linked to corporate value added (Gupta/Lehmann 2003). Consequently, it is very fruitful for VBM to take a closer look at the possibilities of value creation for its respective customer groups, because it will payoff in value added for the firm (Nayyar 1995). Therefore, the chance of success for a business activity to contribute to corporate value creation crucially depends on the level of CustVA.

Methodologically, the calculation of the CustVA is relatively easy in terms of price decreases adjusted for current inflation rate. With regard to the CustVA contributions of service, quality and willingness to pay (if prices are kept unchanged for the latter) permanent surveys of the relevant customer groups are required to estimate the respective value contribution.

Supplier Value Added (SupVA). Another managerial topic that is a significant indicator of corporate value added stems from the relationships between a firm and its suppliers. Up-to-date supply chain management focuses on these relationships considering suppliers as important partners in the value chain (Rice Jr./Caniato 2003). To identify the value added to suppliers we propose to refer to the Supplier Value Added (SupVA). The generated SupVA is of distinct importance to a firm, because it ensures that the resources provided by suppliers are of good quality, relatively cheap, and that they arrive on time. For this matter, firms invest in contractual relationships with their suppliers to ensure that the supplied resources are of the same high quality and to enable the supply chain to run frictionless. This also includes investments in technology and infrastructure to be used by the supplier, which in turn adds value to the latter (Bowersox et al. 2003; Moberg et al. 2003). Suppliers, for instance, achieve an advantage by fair price fixing and long-term contracts with the purchasing firm. Therefore the suppliers also have an interest in products or services offered to the purchaser being produced with state of the art technology. This allows them to concentrate on specialization without permanently having to revise the plans of production. As a consequence, the Supplier Value Added (SupVA) reflects the quality of supply chain management from a supplier's point of view. But such a relationship is by no means unilateral, because the purchasing firms adding value to their suppliers are rewarded with a well functioning relationship and resources of superior quality. Consequently, it can be expected that SupVA-induced access to superior resources that are traded on a relationship stabilized by bilateral investments will result in an increasing corporate value added.

An assessment of how much value has been added per period to the respective suppliers is a topic yet unexplored by today's management literature. Nonetheless, relevant aspects of SupVA such as price decreases of (raw) materials, quality improvements, the value of long-term contracts and (bilateral) technology or infrastructure investments appear to be calculable through internal surveys and by analyzing the corporate accounting records.

Residual Value Added (RVA). In addition to these four stakeholder-specific value added conceptions, there is a remaining amount of value which in general is not meant to be distributed to stakeholders. This value added is called Residual Value Added (RVA) and reflects the part of the corporate value added which is designated to be reinvested or ploughed back to enhance the corporate value basis for future activities. Accordingly, these residual resources can be redirected to either enlarge the firm's input endowment (substance) or to extend a company's (real) options to expand and create future business opportunities. The calculation of the RVA is rather easy, because (re)investments usually are recorded in the accounting system.

The Possibility of Managing Corporate Sustainability

Preserving and enhancing the quality of the resources at disposal is the fundamental requirement for corporate sustainability. Due to the possibility of splitting corporate value generation into five different categories of value transfers, a firm is now able to analyze inter-temporally whether or not VBM lead to successful value appropriation by the different stakeholders (i.e. resource owners). However, it has to be recognized that Value Added (VA)—as the sum of SVA, HRVA, CustVA, SupVA, and RVA—only mirrors the *satisfaction* of relevant stakeholder groups, but it does not state anything about the actual value of a firm's substance. Accordingly, serious problems arise when intuitively drawing conclusions about overall value creation by referring to the VA magnitude in an unreflected manner. Hereby, three main problems appear to be the most challenging issues: Firstly, there is some kind of *causal ambiguity* about the origins of added value. Secondly, the VA does not say anything about the actual size of the value basis but only about its *changes*. And thirdly, corporate VA has to be compared with meaningful *benchmarks* to serve as a guideline for managerial action.

With regard to the first two problems it has to be pointed out that no inferences can be drawn from the actual level of value added to the origins of its creation. Consequently, a positive and increasing VA over time is not to be set equal to the supposition that each resource "produced" a similar contribution to the corporate value return. The VA is—as shown—an aggregated performance metric that measures the combined value return of *all* resources in actual use. While the transformation of some resources may contribute substantially to corporate VA, the transformation of others may actually "destroy" or "neutralize" value. Simultaneously, this also means that even a negative or decreasing VA is—in the short run—by no means a signal for inefficiencies. The opposite may be the case. It is obvious that every investment in future opportunities "consumes" value transfers in the present. As a consequence, the preparation of future value creation is often hardly distinguishable from the present destruction or neutralization of value, because it will eventually pay off in VA in future periods. So to simply look at the figures of value added gives an inadequate picture of the real corporate value basis. For example, if a firm decides to expand its business portfolio into new industries it is very likely that the firm's disposition of resources will be redirected and focused. As a result, value is transferred to resource investments that are particularly involved in this venture at the expense of others (e.g. R&D infrastructure vs. diminishing equity basis). It is hereby imaginable that the value basis increases while no added value can be realized for the stakeholders in this particular period. This aspect can easily be misinterpreted as a temporary inefficiency of specific resources, although they may create value in the long run.

For this reason, controlling the value cycle just with the five VA components is fallacious and has to be supplemented by a precise evaluation of the value basis development (i.e. Substance Value + Options Value).

The analysis for this may lead to the conclusion that a firm can be considered as doing business in a sustainable manner if it invests in its value basis and distributes value to its stakeholders in a durable way. However, for a company to be labeled as successful in the long run the condition of durable value additions to stakeholders is necessary, but by no means sufficient. It is of distinct importance to evaluate the quality of corporate VBM with adequate external references that will be considered as *target values*. This leads to the third problem of *benchmarking* the value cycle. Taking relevant benchmarks into account while evaluating the VBM of a firm leads to a relativization of corporate performance. Useful corporate references could be the achievable value additions per *industry*, *technology*, *product or service*, and *region*. By referring to specific benchmarks, any VBM-activity (value investment, value creation, and value transfer) can be evaluated according to the expected average performance that is possible with regard to a specific reference. So if a firm's performance data (e.g. about the value basis or value added) is eventually lower than the average, the firm may have operated more successfully than in earlier periods, but underperformed its benchmark or target value respectively. Though in this case a firm's overall VA is positive it does not contribute to corporate sustainability. While an internal analysis may result in a sustainable development an outside reference focus may lead to—as shown—completely contradictory results. That is why an assessment of VA without considering the relevant benchmarks is meaningless.

As a result, controlling the corporate value cycle is a complex phenomenon. To be able to manage the sustainability of VBM, three essential and interdependent conditions have to be met by corporate decision-makers: 1) The *value basis* has to be analyzed permanently with regard to its composition, development, and scale, 2) the relevant stakeholders need to be satisfied with adequate *value transfers*, and 3) the performance data of VBM have to be *benchmarked* constantly to avoid misjudgments and to prevent misfits with the environment. Consequently, by successfully following these guidelines Management Value will increase and corporate sustainability will be guaranteed. Therefore, we believe that in managing corporate sustainability a modern concept of VBM like the one proposed here, which takes a variety of value generating sources and value transfers into account, is superior to the one-dimensional concept of the presently used approaches to VBM. Even if our concept can only be seen as a first and certainly juvenile outline, we hope that this may be a promising starting point to revise the henpecking lemmings-logic of shareholder orientation in VBM.

As far as future research is concerned it is of crucial importance to operationalize the proposed performance metrics to methodologically support the improvement of the currently rather restricted practice of valuation to a more comprehensive measurement system. For this purpose the commonly used techniques to calculate the SVA and the introduction of a what we call "Value Balance Sheet" (Seisreiner 2006 and Figure 5) could serve as a starting point for the development of a comprehensive performance measurement system taking into account the multidimensionality of value. Moreover, it could then also be used as a tool to determine the *actual* contribution of a firm's management to value creation (i.e. Management Value) and derive precise payment systems, which currently still is a rather controversially debated topic (e.g. adequacy of stock option plans).

Figure 5: A Simple Value Balance Sheet

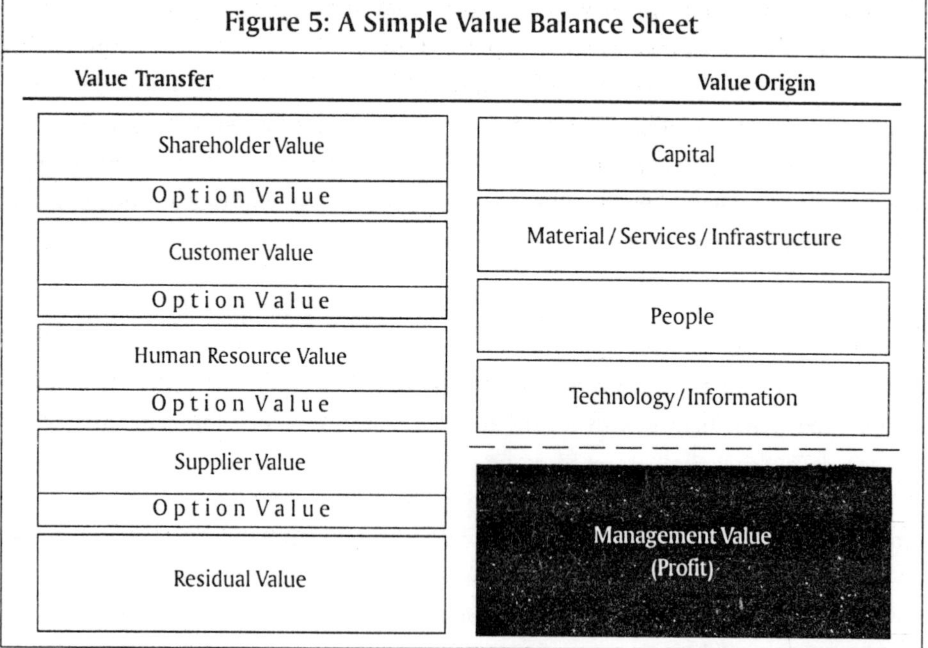

In order to make HRVA, CustVA, SupVA, and as a consequence RVA precisely measurable, we are required to open new doors and develop new methods to fully assess the value transfers stemming from corporate activities. Only if we are able to accomplish this arduous venture, a departure from the SVA as the dominant logic of VBM is likely to occur and will shed light on the "real" value of a firm.

(Achim Seisreiner, Chair of Business Administration, Organization and Human Resource Management/Scientific Advisor and Projects, Universität Potsdam, Deutsche Bahn AG/DB Akademie GmbH, Potsdam, Germany. He can be reached at achim.seisreiner@bahn.de

Sebastian Träger, Chair of Business Administration, Organization and Human Resource Management, University of Potsdam, Germany. He can be reached at traeger@rz.uni-potsdam.de).

References

1. Abowd, J. M. et al. 1990. "The Effects of Human Resource Management Decisions on Shareholder Value". *Industrial and Labor Relations Review*, 43: 203–236.
2. Adner, R. & Levinthal, D. A. 2004. "What is not a Real Option: Considering Boundaries for the Application of Real Options to Business Strategy". *Academy of Management Review*, 29: 74–85.
3. Ameels, A. et al. 2002. "Value-Based Management: An Integrated Approach to Value Creation. A Literature Review". Vlerick Leuven Gent Management School Working Paper.
4. Bannister, R. J. & Jesuthasan, R. 1997. "Is your Company Ready for Value Based Management?" *Journal of Business Strategy*, 18: 12–15.
5. Barney, J 1991. "Firm Resources and Sustainable Competitive Advantages". *Journal of Management*, 17: 99–120.
6. Baum, J. A. C. & Korn, H. J. 1999. "Dynamics of Dyadic Competitive Interaction". *Strategic Management Journal*, 20: 251–278.
7. Böltzel, S. & Schwilling, A. 1998. "Erfolgsfaktor Wertmanagement: Unternehmenswert- und Wachstumsorientiert Steuern". München/Wien: Carl Hauser.
8. Bowersox, D. J. & Closs, D. J. & Stank, T. P. 2003. "How to Master Cross-Enterprise Collaboration". *Supply Chain Management Review*, 7: 18–27.
9. Brandenburger, A. M. & Nalebuff, B. J. 1998. *Coopetition*. New York et al.: HarperCollins.

10. Bromwich, M. & Walker, M. 1998. "Residual Income Past and Future". *Management Accounting Research*, 9: 391–419.

11. Copeland, T. et al. 1994. *Valuation: Measuring and Managing the Value of Companies*. New York et al.: Wiley.

12. Copeland, T. & Antikarov, V. 2001. *Real Options: A Practitioner's Guide*. New York/ London: Texere.

13. D'Aveni, R. A. 1994. *Hypercompetition – Managing the Dynamics of Strategic Maneuvering*. New York et al.: The Free Press.

14. Dimitrov, V. & Hodge, B. 2002. *Social Fuzziology. Study of Fuzziness of Social Complexity*. Heidelberg: Physica.

15. Dundas, K. N. M. & Richardson, P. R. 1982. "Implementing the Unrelated Product Strategy". *Strategic Management Journal*, 3: 287–301.

16. Flamholtz, E. 1972. "Toward a Theory of Human Resource Value in Formal Organizations". *The Accounting Review*, 47: 666–678.

17. Gupta, S. & Lehmann, D. R. 2003. "Customers as Assets". *Journal of Interactive Marketing*, 17: 9–24.

18. Jaggi, B. & Lau, H.-S. 1974. "Toward a Modell for Human Resource Valuation". *The Accounting Review*, 49: 321–329.

19. Jayachandran, S. et al. 1999. "The Theory of Multimarket Competition: A Synthesis and Implications for Marketing Strategy". *Journal of Marketing*, 63: 49–66.

20. Jensen, M. & Zaja, E. J. 2004. "Corporate Elites and Corporate Strategy: How Demographic Preferences and Structural Position Shape the Scope of the Firm". *Strategic Management Journal*, 25: 507–524.

21. Lev, B. & Schwartz, A. 1971. "On the Use of the Economic Concept of Human Capital in Financial Statements". *The Accounting Review*, 46: 103 –112.

22. Lippman, S. A. & Rumelt, R. P. 2003. "The Payments Perspective: Micro-Foundations of Resource Analysis". *Strategic Management Journal*, Special Issue: Why is there a resource-based view? Toward a theory of competitive heterogeneity, 24: 903–927.

23. Miller, D. 2003. "An Asymmetry-Based View on Advantage: Towards an Attainable Sustainability". *Strategic Management Journal*, Special Issue: Why is there a resource-based view? Toward a theory of competitive heterogeneity. 24: 961–976.

24. Moberg, C. R. & Speh, T. W. & Freese, T. L. 2003. SCM: "Making the Vision a Reality". *Supply Chain Management Review*, 7: 34–39.

25. Nayyar, P. R. 1995. "Stock Market Reactions to Customer Service Changes". *Strategic Management Journal*, 16: 39–53.

26. Nohria, N. & Gulati, R. 1996. "Is Slack Good or Bad for Innovation"? *The Academy of Management Journal*, 39: 1245–1264.
27. Olsen, E. & Thomas, R. 1987. "Stock Price Performance: Corporate Agenda for the 1980's". *Journal of Corporate Finance*, 2: 3–15.
28. Penrose, E. 1995. *The Theory of the Growth of the Firm*. (3rd ed.). Oxford/New York.
29. Peteraf, M. 1993. "The Cornerstones of Competitive Advantage: A Resource Based View". *Strategic Management Journal*, 14: 179–191.
30. Porter, M. E. 1985. *Competitive Advantage*. New York: The Free Press.
31. Prahalad, C. K. & Bettis, R. A. 1986. "The Dominant Logic: A New Linkage Between Diversity and Performance". *Strategic Management Journal*, 7: 485–501.
32. Prahalad, C. K. & Hamel, G. 1990. "The core competence of the corporation". *Harvard Business Review*, May/June: 79–91.
33. Rappaport, A. 1986. *Creating Shareholder Value: The New Standard for Business Performance*. New York: The Free Press.
34. Rasche, C. 2002. *Multifokales Management. Strategien und Unternehmenskonzepte für den pluralistischen Wettbewerb*. Wiesbaden: Gabler.
35. Reeves, C. A. & Bednar, D. A. 1994. "Defining Quality: Alternatives and Implications". *The Academy of Management Review*, 19: 419–445.
36. Rice Jr., J. B. & Caniato, F. 2003. "Building a Secure and Resilient Supply Network". *Supply Chain Management Review*, 7: 22–30.
37. Schaefer, O. M. 2002. *Performance Measures in Value Management: A Model based Approach to explain the CVA and EVA Measures*. Bielefeld: Erich Schmidt.
38. Seisreiner, A. 1999. *Management Unternehmerischer Handlungspotentiale*. Wiesbaden: Gabler.
39. Seisreiner, A. 2006. *Rationalität wertorientierter Managementkonzepte: Einordnung und kritische Wirkungsanalyse*. Wiesbaden: Gabler, forthcoming.
40. Sharfman, M. P. et al. 1988. "Antecedents of Organizational Slack". *The Academy of Management Review*, 13: 601–614.
41. Stewart III, G. B. 1994. "EVA: Fact and Fantasy". *Journal of Applied Corporate Finance*, 7: 71-84.
42. Trigeorgis, L. 1996. *Real Options. Managerial Flexibility and Strategy in Resource Allocation*. Cambridge, MA: The MIT Press.
43. Wernerfelt, B. 1984. "A Resource-based View of the Firm". *Strategic Management Journal*, 5: 171–180.
44. Zeithaml, V. A. 1988. "Consumer Perceptions of Price, Quality, and Value: A Means-End Model and Synthesis of Evidence". *Journal of Marketing*, 52: 2–22.

Section II

Experiences

7

Implementing Value Based Management

Samuel C Weaver and J Fred Weston

We identify four alternative performance metrics used in value based management (VBM). (1) Basic is an intrinsic value analysis (IVA), the discounted cash flow (DCF) methodology. (2) We show that this framework will be consistent with returns to shareholder (RTS, capital gains plus dividends) measured over appropriate time horizons. (3) Economic profit (EP) [also called economic value added (EVA®)] takes from the DCF free cash flow valuation, net operating profits after taxes (NOPAT), divided by invested capital to obtain the return on operating invested capital (ROIC) less a cost of capital estimate (k); the difference multiplied times operating capital. (4) The relationship between the market value of the firm's financial instruments and the book value of the firm's operating assets can be expressed equivalently as market value added (MVA), the q ratio, and the market-to-book ratio.

We test the relationships of alternative financial accounting performance metrics versus market metrics on a historical basis as well as on a prospective basis. We find that the

---

Source: http://www.anderson.ucla.edu/faculty/john.weston/papers, 2003.

alternative financial performance metrics—discounted cash flow valuation, returns to shareholders, economic profit, the market to book ratio [equivalently, the q ratio and market value added (MVA)] are highly correlated. We also find that standard financial ratio analysis as expressed in the DuPont formulation are also significantly related to market performance metrics and in the implementation of VBM.

In implementation, each approach to value based management (VBM) starts with strategic planning processes, ties performance to incentive compensation, requires top management involvement, as well as information and training programs for employees. The four approaches to VBM also take into account other stakeholders (employees, consumers, community). VBM must also evaluate changing economic, cultural, and political environments. The strategic planning process analyzes long-term trends, cyclical economic changes, competitive forces, and effective development of managerial capabilities and other resources. Our clinical analysis centers on Hershey Foods Corporation.

The literature on value based management contains many unsettled issues, particularly alternative performance measurement theories (Martin and Petty, 2000; Rappaport, 1998; Stewart, 1991; Young and O'Byrne, 2001; Copeland et al, 2000). Divergent views are also reflected in the extensive bibliography developed by Korajczyk (2001).

This paper seeks to illuminate the nature of Value Based Management (VBM) by describing its implementation at the level of the firm. Its central elements are portrayed in Figure 1. The overview of relationships presented demonstrates that VBM is a continuous process. It begins with strategic planning to achieve competitive advantages which produce superior growth in economic profits and returns to shareholders. Strategic planning guides the firm's choice of a product-market scope and its resource requirements. The economic nature of the industry or industries in which the firm operates determines the patterns of its financial statements reflected in traditional financial ratio analysis. Based on a business economic analysis of the industry and the firm's competitive position, projections of financial relationships provide a basis for valuation estimates. Since these are subject to error and change, further analysis based on identification of the key drivers of value are made. This facilitates study of the impact of operating performance on the value driver levels and the resulting valuations. Periodic reviews lead to strategy revisions as well as to changes in policies and operations. Repeated iterations of the process shown in Figure 1 are made.

Four performance measurements are widely used in the literature. They are: (1) discounted cash flow (DCF) valuation using fundamental value analysis (FVA); (2) returns to shareholders (RTS); (3) economic profit (EP); (4) the relationship between the market value of the firm's financial instruments and the book value of the firm's operating assets. This relationship has been variously called market value added (MVA), the *q* ratio, and the market-to-book ratio.

This paper will compare the strengths and limitations of each performance measure. We use data for Hershey Foods to quantify the comparisons and relationships. In the third edition of Copeland et al (2000), data for Hershey was also used; we extend their study. Martin and Petty (2000) also made illustrative calculations for different companies for different measures; by using one company we can more directly compare alternative performance measures. Ittner and Larcker (1998, 2001) provide useful reviews of the current state of the literature. Our aim is to lay a foundation for additional company samples or generalized research. We discuss each of the four measures, in turn, followed by comparisons between them as a basis for our conclusions.

Valuation Measurements

To overcome the sluggish growth of its chocolate business, Hershey embarked on a program of diversification. In 1966 Hershey entered the *pasta* business by purchasing the San Giorgio Macaroni Company. It purchased other pasta companies over the years, culminating with the acquisition in 1990 of Ronzoni which made Hershey the number one pasta company in the United States. During this time period Hershey also acquired some restaurant chains and an ice cream chain. Neither of these two major diversification efforts utilized Hershey's manufacturing or distribution core competencies.

As a consequence of its unsound diversification efforts, Hershey's stock price closed at the end of 1990 at $18.75. Its growth record was unimpressive. The poor performance resulted in management changes and major restructuring activities. The pasta and restaurant business were unrelated to Hershey's core chocolate business and so were divested. Hershey also divested some foreign operations that it had not been managing effectively. It formulated some strategic objectives: (1) Broaden the scope of its chocolate products. (2) Further develop its lines of non-chocolate candy, chewing gum, and other confectionery products. (3) Make entries into high growth segments of other related snack products.

Divestitures of its restaurant and pasta businesses improved Hershey's gross margin. Hershey also sold off its chocolate operations in Germany and Italy to an affiliate of Huhtamäki Oy (based in Finland). Concurrently, it acquired Huhtamäki's Leaf North America (Leaf) confectionery operations. In addition, the parties entered into a trademark and technology license agreement under which Hershey will manufacture and/or market and distribute in North, Central and South America Huhtamäki's strong confectionery brands including *Good & Plenty, Heath, Jolly Rancher, Milk Duds, Payday* and *Whoppers.* In December 2000, Hershey completed the purchase of the breath freshener mints and gum businesses of Nabisco, Inc.

As a result of this restructuring, Hershey transformed itself into solely a chocolate and confectionery company while enhancing its domestic market share to 26.8% compared to Mars at 17.0% domestic market share. These strategy changes took Hershey out of two unrelated businesses (pasta and restaurants). Hershey moved from chocolate into broader candy markets. This major strategy shift improved profit margins. It also initiated some penetration into the broader snack market which grows at a 6% rate per annum compared to a 2% growth rate for the food industry as a whole.

Fundamental Value Analysis

These strategy changes are reflected in the valuation calculations presented in Table 1. The methodology employed is the widely used discounted cash flow (DCF) analysis which could be expressed in spreadsheets or in equivalent formulas (see Copeland et al, 2000; Cornell, 2001; Rappaport, 1998). Table 1 presents a

DCF spreadsheet valuation of Hershey Foods as of the end of 2002. The key determinants of value reflected the strategic and operating improvements that began to take effect by 1994. The resulting intrinsic share value was close to its closing price per share for 2002 of $67.44.

In Table 2 we perform a fundamental value analysis for Hershey over the years 1994 through 2002. In Lines 10 and 11 of Table 2, we compare our estimates of intrinsic value with the actual closing price per share for Hershey over the 1994-2002 period. Our estimates were based on steady improvements of the value drivers over the restructuring activity of Hershey during the 1990s. The actual market prices anticipated future improvements in value drivers more fully than our projections. The market reacted much more severely to the failures of the new inventory and shipping system installed by Hershey in 1999. Because of the glitches, Hershey was unable to ship products during the critical August to October sales opportunities associated with Back-to-School and Halloween. The market appeared to overact to some temporary bad news.

The calculations reflect both the historical data and projections. Since the number of years of competitive advantage shown in the base year 2002 column is 10 years, the calculations reflect yearly projections for 2003 to 2012 and for the terminal stage. To make the projections for the 17 value drivers, we drew on company presentations, analysts' reports, and our own studies of the economics of the industry and firm.

The behavior of the value drivers in Table 2 reflects the results of the operating and financial restructuring by Hershey during the 1990s. Hershey concentrated its business on its core competency of producing, marketing, and distributing chocolate and confectionery products. Management was able to improve growth, margins, and the period of competitive advantage while reducing investment needs (both working and fixed capital) and the cost of capital. These effects achieved a rising intrinsic value per share.

A major strength of the DCF models is that they seek to identify the underlying determinants of value. Since the expectations or projections inherently are subject to errors, the framework can be used as a valuable management planning and control system. An ongoing monitoring of expectations compared with changing estimates of the value drivers can be used in an information flow system. Policies and decisions can be revised in a feedback process to improve performance, as illustrated in Figure 1. The DCF estimates of intrinsic value can be used as a part of strategic planning processes to estimate the valuation consequences of alternative strategic plans.

Returns to Shareholders

Returns to shareholders (RTS) are measured by annual capital gains plus dividend yields. The logic of this performance metric is that it calculates the economic income to investors for specified time periods. In Table 3 we make these calculations for Hershey based on the yearend closing prices, shares outstanding, and dividend yield for the years 1980-2000. Because of Hershey's unsound diversification efforts, the results behave erratically. Two methods are employed to deal with this instability.

One is to calculate averages over longer time periods. In Table 4 we calculate the unweighted arithmetic average annual returns for 5- and 10-year time segments. We also calculate the compounded annual returns to shareholders using the endpoints of each time segment. We obtained similar results. For the entire period 1982-2002, the compound annual return was 16.8% per annum.

The most meaningful use of returns to shareholders involves comparisons with benchmarks. Table 5 compares the RTS measures for Hershey against the S&P500 and the Value Line food processing index for the years 1994-2002. For the entire time period, the RTS for Hershey shareholders averaged 6.41% above the S&P500. Benchmarked against the food processing index, the RTS for Hershey shareholders was 1.73% lower. (The beta risk measures of the food processing industry are similar to those of the chocolate and confectionary product industry).

The use of the RTS measure permits a reasonably firm conclusion. Hershey's performance was comparable to the broader industry segment of which it is a part. It was superior to the broader S&P 500 index. It would be useful to make a similar comparison with four or five firms with products more closely comparable to Hershey's. However, there are no other major public chocolate companies in the US Mars is privately held. The RTS measure is a useful indicator of performance. It can readily be applied by using appropriate benchmarks, groups of firms, or indexes.

As a performance metric, it compares the economic returns to investors in a firm relative to alternative benchmark investments. Hershey competes for the consumer's dollar; it also competes for the investor's dollar.

Economic Profit Measures

Economic profit has been distinguished from accounting measures of net income by deducting a charge for the use of capital invested. For example, suppose the accounting net income is \$120. If the firm has a book total investment of \$1000 and a cost of capital of 10%, the deduction would be \$100. The net \$20 would represent economic profit or residual income. This concept was applied by Donaldson Brown, the senior officer of General Motors, in the 1920s as a guide to allocating resources among the multiple divisions. It also began to be applied by General Electric in the 1950s. The consulting firm, Stern Stewart, has employed the concept in a measure called economic value added whose abbreviation EVA® has been copyrighted. In applying the concept, Stern Stewart makes adjustments to NOPAT and to the measurement of the invested capital base. Adjustments to NOPAT seek to capitalize expenses such as R&D and advertising over the estimated lives during which they contribute to revenues. A recent survey of 29 EVA® users revealed that all 29 calculated NOPAT and Invested Capital in different ways (Weaver 2001). We have chosen a standard approach that excludes non-US GAAP adjustments such as capitalizing advertising and R&D.

In Table 6, the measure of economic profit is calculated for Hershey for the years 1983-2002. First, NOPAT (Line 3) is calculated as in the FVA procedures. Next the Invested Capital (IC, Line 7) is calculated as the sum of Operating working capital, Net property plant and equipment, and Other assets net. Invested capital could also be measured as total assets less non-interest bearing liabilities or the book value of equity plus all interest bearing debt. The average of the beginning and ending invested capital figures are used in subsequent calculations. The return on average invested capital (ROIC, Line 9) is defined as the ratio of NOPAT to average invested capital. We use an average in the denominator since NOPAT is received throughout the year.

The WACC is specified in Line 10 and estimated to have declined over this twenty year period. The difference between ROIC and WACC is multiplied times the Average Invested Capital in Line 8 to obtain the Average Economic Profit numbers in Line 12. The measures demonstrate that Hershey's economic profits were small until after the restructuring activities during the 1990s. For sensitivity analysis, alternative costs estimates can be employed.

The Properties of Economic Profits (EP)

In his book on EVA® or EP, Stewart (1991) states that "MVA marches in lockstep with EVA, thus confirming the usefulness of EVA as a measure of corporate performance" (p. 209). He defines market value added (MVA) as the excess of the market value of the firm (V) over its book capital.

The nature of the relationship between EP and MVA is facilitated by a simple example in which:

r	= return on invested capital (ROIC)	=	12%
k	= cost of capital (WACC)	=	10%
C_o	= capital investment	=	$1,000

This firm was created by a capital investment of $1000, so for this example the investment also represents the total capital of the firm. The net present value (NPV) is calculated by subtracting the investment from the gross present value (GPV):

$NPV = GPV -$ Investment Outlay or Capital

$$= \frac{rC_o}{k} - C_o = \frac{0.12(1,000)}{0.10} - 1,000 = 1,200 - 1,000 = \$200$$

EP or EVA® is defined as before and calculated as:

$EP = (r - k)C_o = (0.12 - 0.10)\ 1,000 = \$20$

NPV is the discounted value of EP($20/0.10) which equals $200. Grinblatt and Titman (2002) prove the same result for the finite period case (pp. 341-342). In both the finite and infinite period examples, certainty is implicit. The value of the firm (V) is the book capital of $1000 plus the NPV of $200 which total $1200. Recall that MVA is $(V - C_o)$ which is the NPV of $200 ($1200 – $1000). Thus, in application, market value added (MVA) reflects expectations of future cash flows and discount rates.

Since economic profit (regardless of how it is named) is equivalent to an NPV measure, it is a sound guide to investment decisions as is traditional discounted cash flow analysis. Both economic profit and traditional intrinsic value (or fundamental value analysis) can be used to measure the effectiveness of investment decisions at the level of the firm or to segments such as divisions or plants.

Tests of EP Measures

Economic profit or economic value added has been widely evaluated and tested. Rappaport (1998) argues that even after adjustments for multi-year effects of R&D, as well as advertising and reversing cumulative goodwill amortization, the "shortcomings of EVA" remain those of "a historical, sunk-cost measure" (p. 226). Young and O'Byrne (YO) (2001) argue that with appropriate accounting adjustments such as sinking-fund depreciation which makes ROIC equal to the economic return, the criticisms of EVA® no longer hold. They also question the empirical study of Biddle, Bowen, and Wallace (1997) which found that earnings data have more explanatory power for changes in stock prices than EVA®(YO, pp. 263-267). Wallace (1997) studied the internal incentive effects of adopting performance measures based on residual income. He found that firms do get what they measure and reward. Managers make decisions consistent with the performance measures adopted. Hogan and Lewis (2000) studied 51 firms adopting economic profit plans. They have a control group of firms based on industry, size, and pre-event performance. They found significant performance improvements for firms which adopt economic profit plans. They also found similar performance improvements for control firms. They conclude that alternative performance measurement plans perform equally well in improving shareholders' wealth.

Market Valuation Ratios

Other studies of performance, particularly academic research studies, have a measure of market value in the numerator. The q (or Tobin's q) ratio has been widely used to analyze the sources of differential firm efficiency related to variables such as diversification, percentage of equity ownership by top management, etc. In theory, the q ratio is defined as the market values of equity and debt divided by the current replacement value of assets. In practice, the denominator is difficult to calculate. In their early use of the q ratio at the firm level, Lindenberg and

Ross (LR) (1981), arbitrarily select a beginning date on which the replacement costs of fixed assets and inventories are assumed to be their book values. For each subsequent year, the previous year estimate is adjusted for general price level changes and for technological changes plus the increase in investments less deductions for depreciation. Subsequent refinements in the LR estimates were made by Chung and Pruitt (1994), Howe and Vogt (1996), Lewellen and Badrinath (1997), Lee and Tompkins (1999), and Howe, Vogt, and He (2003).

Whited (2001) measures Tobin's q as the ratio of the market value of assets divided by the book value of assets, "following the literature on corporate diversification." (p. 1670) The market value of assets is obtained "by adding to the book value of assets the market value of common equity and subtracting the book value of common equity and balance-sheet deferred taxes" (p.1671). This is equivalent to adding to the book value of assets the difference between the market and book value of equity. The denominator would be equivalent to the book values of equity plus debt. Whited observes that constructing q using the algorithms of Lewellen and Badrinath in estimating the replacement costs of assets would have reduced the number of observations without significant change in the qualitative results (p. 1670, fn 2).

We use the Whited definition of the q ratio in Table 7 since it is highly correlated with the other measures of q and does not require the complex estimates of the current replacement costs of investments. Accordingly, in Table 7, the q ratio as measured by Whited and the M/B ratio are calculated. The data were obtained from the Hershey financial statements for 1983-2002. Starting from almost equal levels of about 1.6 in 1983, the q ratio rises to 4.58 by 2002 while the M/B ratio rises to 6.52. When the numerator is the market value of equity plus book debt and the denominator is the book value of both equity and debt, the q ratio rises less rapidly because a constant is added to each term of the M/B ratio. Also both measures are inflated by share repurchase accounting practices. When shares are repurchased, the book based equity account is reduced by the market value of the shares repurchased. Since 1993, when Hershey first began share repurchases, book equity was artificially reduced by the extent that its M/B ratio was greater than 1. Hence, share repurchase programs in practice inflate both the q ratio and the M/B ratio.

Further Implementation Considerations

In implementation, operational performance and all the performance measures can usefully be buttressed by financial ratio analysis. Table 8 presents a compact financial ratio analysis in the form of the traditional DuPont system. It analyzes to a more detailed level than the condensed published financial statements. The elements of cost of goods sold are identified. Targets for R&D, marketing, and administration are set. Taxes are managed. Working capital elements are tightly managed. Fixed assets are acquired based on net present value principles. These elements are structured into the relationship between NOPAT and invested capital. NOPAT is a key value driver in Fundamental Valuation Analysis (FVA). Invested capital is key in the measurement of economic profit since it is multiplied times (ROIC – WACC). The return on invested capital (ROIC) in application emphasizes costs controls in the income statement and effective use of economic resources from the asset side of the balance sheet. ROIC is depicted as a relationship between the NOPAT margin and the effective utilization of operating total assets measured by the turnover ratio. Note that the data in Table 8 and in the Table 6 measures for 2002 are consistent.

Table 8 provides a basis for a control system to monitor and assure that the value drivers inherent in the valuation are established, communicated, and targeted. An effort is made to continuously improve ROIC by the use of multiple performance metrics with targets for both the long- and short-term. Responsibility is assigned both on a primary and secondary basis. These planning and control efforts contribute to improved strategy formulation.

Financial Planning and Control to Improve Strategies

The use of performance measures to improve strategies has a long history. When General Motors was desperately seeking to survive the postwar recession of 1921, it sought to float a bond issue of $50 million. Investment bankers were unable to underwrite the issue because of the bleak financial outlook for GM. Ultimately, the DuPont Corporation supplied the financing required by the purchase of a 23% equity interest in GM. DuPont installed Donaldson Brown, its top financial executive, as the CFO of GM to help protect its investment. GM acquired a small company to obtain Alfred Sloan as its new president.

Sloan recounts in his *My Years with General Motors* (1963) that the financial controls installed by Brown made it possible to revamp the fundamental automobile strategy of GM.

We have already described Hershey's ill advised diversification efforts. Financial analysis revealed the errors of investments in the low margin pasta business in which the chocolate maker had no managerial capabilities or experience. It returned to its core competencies and improved its performance by all four measures.

Similarly in the late 1980s Briggs & Stratton overspent on attempts at automation and began to produce high end air cooled gasoline engines at a loss. By focusing on cost leadership in its traditional core businesses, Briggs & Stratton returned to improvements in its financial performance.

At Herman Miller (office furniture) losses resulted from undisciplined multiple product proliferation. The problems involved strategy, structure, and financial control (Stern et al, 2001). Similar stories for seven companies are told of how adopters of multiple performance metrics including nonfinancial criteria improved their strategic decisions and operating efficiency (Kaplan and Norton, 1996; Eccles et al, 2000).

Conclusions

The implementation of value based management (VBM) identifies multiple approaches. Four have been widely used in practice. One is fundamental value analysis (FVA). Two is returns to shareholder (RTS). Three is economic profit. Four is the relationship between the market value of the firm's financial instruments and the book value of the firm's operating assets (MVA, the *q* ratio, and the market-to-book ratio). Planning and control analyses of the structure of income, costs, and investments are employed in implementing the previous four approaches.

In implementation, the four approaches to VBM have a high degree of similarity. Each embraces and utilizes the framework we present in Figure 1. The key elements include strategic review and organizational structure related to strategy, performance measurements, implementation, involvement and support of top executives and training throughout the organization, and continuous review and renewal.

Despite the similarities in methodology, each of the proponents of a particular emphasis of VBM argues for its distinctive superiority and for defects or limitations in the approaches of its competitors. Fundamental value analysis (FVA) performs a DCF valuation of cash flows over long time horizons. Changes in value can also be measured yearly by reference to returns to shareholders (RTS) or by market value added (MVA), the market-to-book ratio, and the q ratio.

On conceptual and analytical criteria most writers emphasize the preeminence of fundamental value using DCF spreadsheets or formulas. Intrinsic value measures should relate to returns to shareholders as well as to market value changes. However, market expectations sometimes run ahead of or behind intrinsic value measurements. As a consequence there are no perfect correlations between intrinsic value, returns to shareholders, and changes in market value.

Economic profit or economic value added programs have been effectively promoted. Since they involve a return on invested capital and a discount factor, ROIC and WACC also need to be measured. The intrinsic value measures are most sensitive to estimates of sales growth and the NOI margin. In turn, the NOI margin depends on the control of costs. The return metrics require effective management of working capital and fixed investments which are analyzed in the DuPont chart shown in Table 8.

In theory the four alternative approaches to VBM are somewhat different. In practice, the implementations have similarities in methodology and coverage. They all center on strategic financial planning and appear to make valuable contributions to performance improvement and to value creation. Intrinsic value DCF analysis, returns to shareholders, economic value added, and the market-to-book analysis have all contributed to value improvements. Each of the performance measures has something to contribute. Each also has limitations. Clearly, the use of one measure alone when multiple measures can be readily calculated is unnecessarily self limiting. A combination of performance measures can provide useful information for planning and control systems.

The downturn beginning in 2000 emphasizes that external economic indicators are an important part of value based management. Also indicators of performance in relation to stakeholders such as employees and consumers are useful. If a firm does not score well in these areas, it is not likely to score well in the effort to add to shareholder value. With the aid of computers, multiple performance measures can be employed. This also permits communication of financial goals and performance widely throughout the organization. Continuous information exchange stimulates managers and informs top executives. Value based management requires multiple performance measures with support from top executives who interact over a wide range of managers on an informed basis.

Thus a complete value based management system includes financial measures, indicators of external economic and financial developments, as well as active top management and board involvement on a continuing basis.

Acknowledgement: We benefited from the comments of James S Wallace at the Meetings of the Financial Management Association, October 2002. Our thanks to Juan A. Siu for his assistance.

(Samuel C Weaver, College of Business and Economics, Lehigh University. He can be reached at scw0@lehigh.edu

J Fred Weston, The Anderson School at UCLA, University of California, Los Angeles. He can be reached at jweston@anderson.ucla.edu).

References

1. Biddle, Gary C., Robert M. Bowen, and James S. Wallace, 1997, "Does EVA Beat Earnings? Evidence on Associations with Stock Returns and Firm Values," *Journal of Accounting and Economics*, 24 (No. 3, December), 301-336.
2. Chung, Kee H. and Stephen W. Pruitt, 1994, "A Simple Approximation of Tobin's q," *Financial Management*, 23 (3, Autumn), 70-74.
3. Copeland, Tom, Tim Koller, and Jack Murrin, 2000, *Valuation: Measuring and Managing the Values of Companies, 3rd ed.*, New York: John Wiley & Sons.
4. Cornell, Bradford, 2001, "Is the Response of Analysts to Information Consistent with Fundamental Valuation? The Case of Intel," *Financial Management*, 30 (No. 1, Spring), 113-136.
5. Eccles, Robert G., Robert H. Herz, E. Mary Keegan, and David M. H. Phillips, 2001, *The Value Reporting Revolution: Moving Beyond the Earnings Game*, New York: John Wiley & Sons.
6. Grinblatt, Mark, and Sheridan Titman, 2002, *Financial Markets and Corporate Strategy, 2nd edition*, Boston: Irwin/McGraw-Hill.

7. Hogan, Chris, and Craig Lewis, 2000, "The Long-Run Performance of Firms Adopting Compensation Plans Based on Economic Profits," Owens Graduate School of Management Working Paper, (May).

8. Howe, Keith M. and Stephen Vogt, 1996, "On 'q'," *Financial Review*, 31 (2, May), 265-286.

9. Howe, Keith M., Steve Vogt, and Jia He, 2003, "The Effect of Managerial Ownership on the Short- and Long-run Response to Cash Distributions," *Financial Review*, 38 (2, May), 179-196.

10. Ittner, Christopher D. and David F. Larcker, 1998, "Innovations in Performance Measurement: Trends and Research Implications," *Journal of Management Accounting Research*, 10, 205-238.

11. Ittner, Christopher D. and David F. Larcker, 2001, "Assessing Empirical Research in Managerial Accounting: A Value-Based Management Perspective," *Journal of Accounting and Economics.*

12. Kaplan, Robert S., and David P. Norton, 1996, *The Balanced Scorecard*, Boston: Harvard Business School Press.

13. Korajczyk, Robert A., 2001, "Papers on Value-Based Management," October 12, <www.kellogg.nwu.edu/faculty/korajczy/htm/vbm.htm>.

14. Lee, Darrell E. and James G. Tompkins, 1999, "A Modified Version of the Lewellen and Badrinath Measure of Tobin's Q," *Financial Management*, 28 (1, Spring), 20-31.

15. Lewellen, Wilbur G. and S. G. Badrinath, 1997, "On the Measurement of Tobin's q," *Journal of Financial Economics*, 44 (1, April), 77-122.

16. Lindenberg, Eric B. and Stephen A. Ross, 1981, "Tobin's q Ratio and Industrial Organization," *Journal of Business*, 54 (1, January), 1-32.

17. Martin, John D., and J. William Petty, 2000, *Valued Based Management: The Corporate Response to the Shareholder Revolution*, Boston: Harvard Business School Press.

18. Rappaport, Alfred, 1998, *Creating Shareholder Value: A Guide for Managers and Investors*, New York: The Free Press.

19. Sloan, Alfred P., 1963, *My Years with General Motors*, Garden City, NY: Doubleday.

20. Stern, Joel M., and John S. Shiely, with Irwin Ross, 2001, *The EVA Challenge: Implementing Value-Added Change in an Organization*, New York: John Wiley & Sons.

21. Stewart, G. Bennett, III, 1991, *The Quest for Value*, New York: HarperBusiness.

22. Wallace, James S., 1997, "Adopting Residual Income-Based Compensating Plans: Do You Get What You Pay For?" *Journal of Accounting and Economics*, 24 (No. 3, December), 275-300.

23. Weaver, Samuel C., 2001, "Measuring Economic Value Added?: A Survey of the Practices of EVA? Proponents," *Journal of Applied Finance*, 11 (No. 1, Fall/Winter), 50-60.

24. Whited, Toni M., 2001, "Is It Inefficient Investment that Causes the Diversification Discount?' *Journal of Finance*, 56 (No. 5, October), 1667-1691.

25. Young, S. David, and Stephen F. O'Byrne, 2001, *EVA and Value-Based Management: A Practical Guide to Implementation*, New York: McGraw-Hill.

Figure 1: Interaction between Strategy and Value Based Management (VBM)

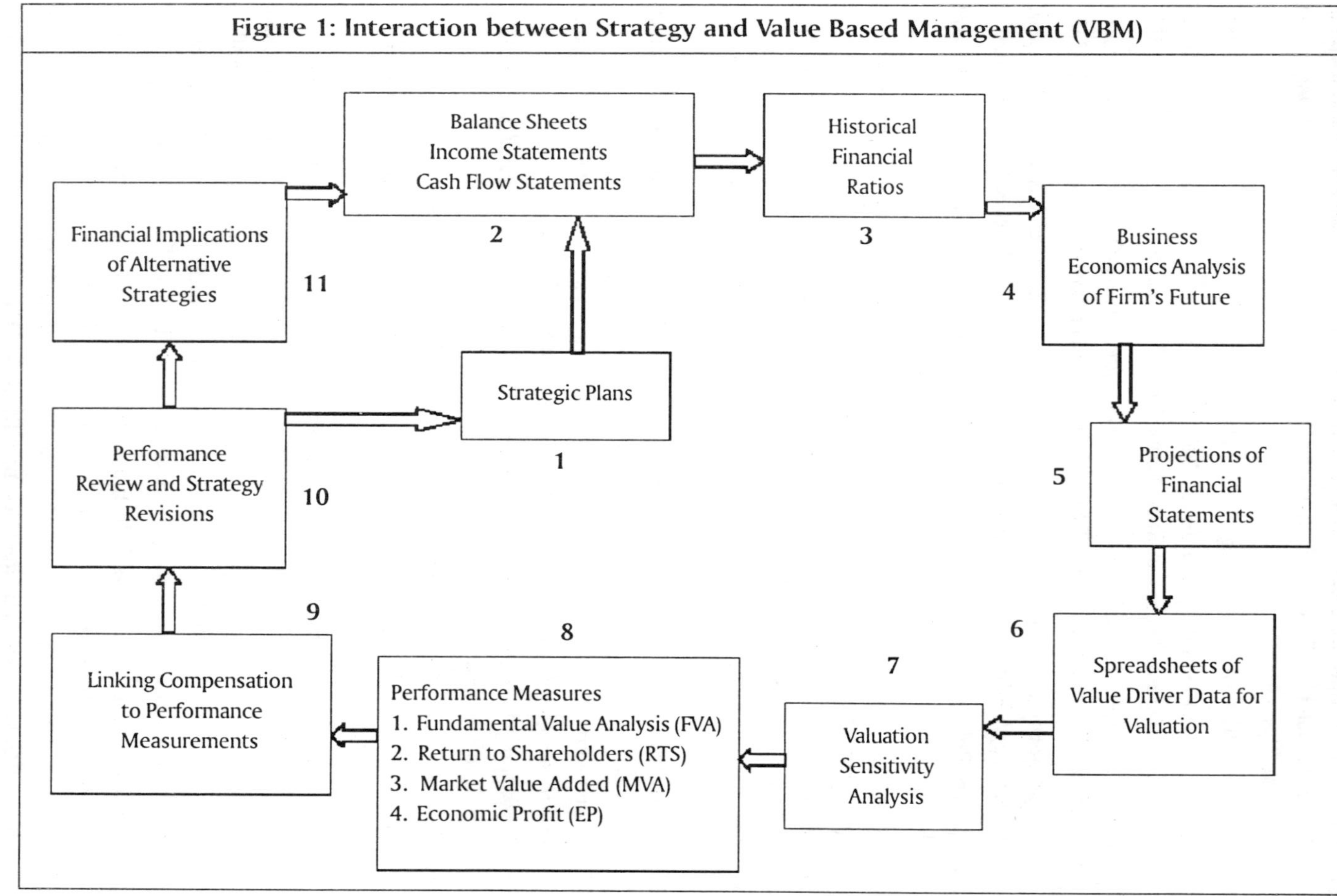

Table 1: DCF Spreadsheet Valuation of Hershey Foods (with Restructuring)

(Dollar Amounts in Millions Except per Share)

	2002	2003E	2004E	2005E	2006E	2007E	2008E	2009E	2010E	2011E	2012E	2013E
Panel A – Inputs for Present Value Calculations												
1. Net revenues	$4,582	$4,765	$4,955	$5,154	$5,360	$5,574	$5,797	$6,029	$6,270	$6,521	$6,782	$6,985
2. Revenue growth rate		4.0%	4.0%	4.0%	4.0%	4.0%	4.0%	4.0%	4.0%	4.0%	4.0%	3.0%
3. NOI		$ 715	$ 743	$ 773	$ 804	$ 836	$ 870	$ 904	$ 941	$ 978	$1,017	$1,020
4. Cash tax rate		38.0%	38.0%	38.0%	38.0%	38.0%	38.0%	38.0%	38.0%	38.0%	38.0%	38.0%
5. Income taxes		272	282	294	306	318	330	344	357	372	387	388
6. NOPAT		$ 443	$461	$ 479	$ 498	$ 518	$ 539	$ 561	$ 583	$ 606	$631	$ 632
7. + Depreciation		143	149	155	161	167	174	181	188	196	203	203
8. – Change in working capital		10	10	10	11	11	12	12	13	13	14	14
9. – Capital expenditures		133	139	144	150	156	162	169	176	183	190	196
10. – Change in other assets net		5	5	5	5	6	6	6	6	7	7	7
11. Free cash flows		$ 438	$ 456	$ 474	$ 493	$ 513	$ 533	$ 555	$ 577	$ 600	$ 624	$ 618
12. WACC		7.65%	7.65%	7.65%	7.65%	7.65%	7.65%	7.65%	7.65%	7.65%	7.65%	7.65%
13. Discount factor		0.92894	0.86292	0.80160	0.74464	0.69172	0.64256	0.59690	0.55448	0.51508	0.47848	
14. Present values		$ 407	$ 393	$ 380	$ 367	$ 355	$ 343	$ 331	$ 320	$ 309	$ 299	
Panel B – Operating Relationships (As a % of Revenues)												
NOI		15.0%	15.0%	15.0%	15.0%	15.0%	15.0%	15.0%	15.0%	15.0%	15.0%	14.6%
NOPAT		9.3%	9.3%	9.3%	9.3%	9.3%	9.3%	9.3%	9.3%	9.3%	9.3%	9.1%
Depreciation		3.0%	3.0%	3.0%	3.0%	3.0%	3.0%	3.0%	3.0%	3.0%	3.0%	2.9%
Change in working capital		0.2%	0.2%	0.2%	0.2%	0.2%	0.2%	0.2%	0.2%	0.2%	0.2%	0.2%
Capital expenditures		2.8%	2.8%	2.8%	2.8%	2.8%	2.8%	2.8%	2.8%	2.8%	2.8%	2.8%
Change in other assets net		0.10%	0.10%	0.10%	0.10%	0.10%	0.10%	0.10%	0.10%	0.10%	0.10%	0.10%
Free cash flow		9.2%	9.2%	9.2%	9.2%	9.2%	9.2%	9.2%	9.2%	9.2%	9.2%	8.9%

Contd...

Contd...

Panel C – Valuation Calculations

Part I – Cost of Capital Inputs			Part II – Terminal Value (TV)	Part III – Valuation Calculation		
(a)	Risk-free rate	5.60%	TV = Free Cash Flows$_{n+1}$ / (WACC–g)	(1)	PV of cash flows, Year 2003-2012	$ 3,504
(b)	Beta	0.60	= 618 / (0.0765 – 0.030)	(2)	PV of terminal value	$ 6,363
(c)	Equity risk premium	6.00%	= $13,298	(3)	Marketable securities	–
(d)	Tax rate	38.0%		(4)	Total value of the firm	$ 9,866
(e)	Cost of equity	9.20%		(5)	Value of debt	880
(f)	Cost of debt (before-tax)	6.50%		(6)	Value of equity	$ 8,986
(g)	Cost of debt (after-tax)	4.03%		(7)	Shares outstanding	133
(h)	Capital structure, % equity	70.00%		(8)	Intrinsic share price	$ 67.79
(i)	Base WACC	7.65%				

Table 2: Fundamental Value Analysis, Hershey, 1994-2002
(Dollar Amounts in Millions Except Per Share)

	1994	1995	1996	1997	1998	1999	2000	2001	2002
Panel A – Value Drivers									
R_0 =Base year revenues	\$3,606	\$3,691	\$3,989	\$4,302	\$4,436	\$3,971	\$4,221	\$4,557	\$4,582
Initial growth stage									
m_s = Net operating income margin	13.9%	14.3%	14.4%	15.0%	15.0%	15.0%	15.0%	15.0%	15.0
T_s = Tax rate	45.4%	33.8%	38.3%	36.2%	24.0%	37.9%	38.8%	38.8%	38.0%
g_s = Growth rate	5.1%	5.4%	6.0%	6.6%	6.8%	6.8%	7.0%	7.0%	4.0%
d_s = Depreciation	3.0%	3.0%	3.0%	3.0%	3.0%	3.0%	3.0%	3.0%	3.0%
I_{ws} = Working capital requirements	0.2%	0.2%	0.2%	0.2%	0.2%	0.2%	0.2%	0.2%	0.2%
I_{fs} = Capital expenditures	3.7%	3.5%	3.4%	3.1%	2.6%	2.6%	2.8%	2.8%	2.8%
I_{os} = Change in other assets net	0.1%	0.1%	0.1%	0.1%	0.1%	0.1%	0.1%	0.1%	0.1
k_s = Cost of capital	10.0%	9.9%	9.8%	9.5%	9.5%	9.5%	9.5%	9.5%	7.65%
n = Number of growth years	5	6	7	9	9	9	10	10	10
Terminal stage									
m_c = Net operating income margin	12.0%	12.2%	14.3%	14.6%	14.6%	14.6%	14.6%	14.6%	14.6%
T_c = Tax rate	38.8%	38.8%	38.8%	38.8%	38.8%	38.8%	38.8%	38.8%	38.0%
g_c = Growth rate	4.0%	4.1%	4.2%	4.3%	4.3%	4.4%	4.5%	4.5%	3.0%
d_c = Depreciation	2.9%	2.9%	2.9%	2.9%	2.9%	2.9%	2.9%	2.9%	2.9%
I_{wc} = Working capital requirements	0.10%	0.12%	0.14%	0.15%	0.16%	0.18%	0.20%	0.20%	0.20%
I_{fc} = Capital expenditures	2.4%	2.5%	2.6%	2.6%	2.7%	2.7%	2.9%	2.9%	2.8%
I_{oc} = Change in other assets net	0.1%	0.1%	0.1%	0.1%	0.1%	0.1%	0.1%	0.1%	0.1%
k_c = Cost of capital	10.0%	9.9%	9.8%	9.5%	9.5%	9.5%	9.5%	9.5%	7.65%
$1 + h = (1+g_s)/(1+k_s)$	0.9555	0.9591	0.9654	0.9735	0.9753	0.9753	0.9772	0.9772	0.9661

Contd...

Contd...

Panel B – Calculating Firm Value									
1. PV of initial growth stage cash flows	$ 1,038	$ 1,661	$ 1,991	$ 3,110	$ 4,059	$ 2,976	$ 3,383	$3,652	$3,504
2. PV of terminal value	3,805	3,941	5,112	6,090	6,307	5,750	6,047	6,529	6,363
3. Enterprise operating value	$ 4,843	$ 5,602	$ 7,102	$ 9,199	$ 10,366	$ 8,725	$ 9,430	$10,181	$9,866
4. Add: Marketable securities	-	-	-	-	-	-	-	-	-
5. Entity value	$ 4,843	$ 5,602	$ 7,102	$ 9,199	$ 10,366	$ 8,725	$ 9,430	$10,181	$9,866
6. Less: Total interest-bearing debt	505	796	996	1,317	1,282	1,118	1,136	885	880
7. Equity value	$ 4,338	$ 4,806	$ 6,106	$ 7,882	$ 9,084	$ 7,607	$ 8,294	$9,296	$8,986
8. Number of shares	173.5	154.5	152.9	142.9	143.1	138.5	136.3	135.6	132.6
9. Intrinsic value per share	$ 25.01	$ 31.10	$ 39.92	$ 55.15	$ 63.46	$ 54.94	$ 60.86	$68.53	$67.79
10. Actual closing price per share	$ 24.19	$ 32.50	$ 43.75	$ 61.94	$ 62.19	$ 47.44	$ 64.38	$67.70	$67.44
11. Percent difference from closing price	3.4%	-4.3%	-8.7%	-11.0%	2.0%	15.8%	-5.5%	1.2%	0.5%

Table 3: Hershey, Returns to Shareholders Relationships, 1982-2002
(Adjusted for stock-splits)

	1982	1983	1984	1985	1986	1987	1988	1989	1990	1991	1992
1. Closing Price	$4.70	$5.27	$6.44	$8.58	$12.31	$12.25	$13.00	$17.94	$18.75	$22.19	$23.50
2. Common Shares Outstanding (millions)	188.0	188.0	188.0	188.0	180.4	180.4	180.4	180.4	180.4	180.4	180.4
3. Dividend per share	$0.17	$0.18	$0.21	$0.24	$0.26	$0.29	$0.33	$0.37	$0.50	$0.47	$0.52
4. Dividend yield		3.9%	3.9%	3.7%	3.0%	2.4%	2.7%	2.8%	2.8%	2.5%	2.3%
5. Capital gain		12.2%	22.1%	33.3%	43.4%	-0.5%	6.1%	38.0%	4.5%	18.3%	5.9%
6. Total return to shareholders		16.1%	26.1%	37.0%	46.5%	1.8%	8.8%	40.8%	7.3%	20.8%	8.2%
		1993	**1994**	**1995**	**1996**	**1997**	**1998**	**1999**	**2000**	**2001**	**2002**
1. Closing Price		$24.50	$24.19	$32.50	$43.75	$61.94	$62.19	$47.44	$64.38	$67.70	$67.44
2. Common Shares Outstanding (millions)		175.2	173.5	154.5	152.9	142.9	143.1	138.5	136.3	135.6	132.6
3. Dividend per share		$0.57	$0.63	$0.69	$0.76	$0.84	$0.92	$1.00	$1.08	$1.17	$1.26
4. Dividend yield		2.4%	2.6%	2.8%	2.3%	1.9%	1.5%	1.6%	2.3%	1.8%	1.9%
5. Capital gain		4.3%	-1.3%	34.4%	34.6%	41.6%	0.4%	-23.7%	35.7%	5.2%	-0.4%
6. Total return to shareholders		6.7%	1.3%	37.2%	37.0%	43.5%	1.9%	-22.1%	38.0%	7.0%	1.5%

Data Source: Compustat

Table 4: Average Returns to Shareholders, Hershey (1982-2002)		
Period	Average Annual Return	Compound Annual Return
1982-1992	21.4%	20.5%
1993-1997	29.7%	28.5%
1998-2002	5.2%	3.5%
1982-2002	18.3%	16.8%

Table 5: Annual RTS Benchmark Comparisons		
Year	Hershey – S&P500	Hershey – Food Index
1994	–0.23%	–6.94%
1995	3.33%	11.51%
1996	13.83%	12.29%
1997	12.80%	–4.88%
1998	–24.92%	–9.16%
1999	–41.96%	–19.23%
2000	49.88%	9.74%
2001	20.16%	–0.54%
2002	24.80%	–8.34%
Average	6.41%	–1.73%

Table 6: Calculation of Average Invested Capital and Economic Profit, Hershey, 1983-2002

(Dollar Amounts in Millions)

	1983	1984	1985	1986	1987	1988	1989	1990	1991	1992
1. NOI	$ 205	$ 220	$ 245	$ 271	$ 294	$ 266	$ 310	$ 351	$ 390	$ 428
2. Cash Tax Rate	40.7%	37.4%	35.2%	38.9%	48.7%	36.7%	39.8%	42.6%	33.9%	34.2%
3. NOPAT	$ 122	$ 138	$ 159	$ 165	$ 151	$ 168	$ 187	$ 201	$ 258	$ 282
4. Operating Working Capital	$ 207	$ 210	$ 241	$ 203	$ 256	$ 358	$ 319	$ 385	$ 382	$ 409
5. NPPE	575	643	702	793	863	736	830	952	1,146	1,296
6. Other Assets Net	(36)	(39)	(81)	(26)	90	229	221	244	199	320
7. Invested Capital (IC)	$ 746	$ 814	$ 862	$ 971	$1,209	$1,323	$1,371	$1,582	$1,726	$2,025
8. Average Invested Capital (AIC)	$ 719	$ 780	$ 838	$ 916	$1,090	$1,266	$1,347	$1,476	$1,654	$1,876
9. AROIC = NOPAT/AIC	**16.9%**	**17.6%**	**18.9%**	**18.0%**	**13.8%**	**13.3%**	**13.9%**	**13.6%**	**15.6%**	**15.0%**
10. WACC	12.0%	12.0%	12.0%	12.0%	12.0%	12.0%	12.0%	12.0%	12.0%	11.0%
11. AROIC – WACC	4.9%	5.6%	6.9%	6.0%	1.8%	1.3%	1.9%	1.6%	3.6%	4.0%
12. AEP = AIC (AROIC – WACC)	**$ 35**	**$44**	**$ 58**	**$ 55**	**$ 20**	**$16**	**$ 25**	**$ 24**	**$ 59**	**$ 76**
	1993	**1994**	**1995**	**1996**	**1997**	**1998**	**1999**	**2000**	**2001**	**2002**
1. NOI	$ 457	$ 475	$ 511	$ 563	$ 630	$ 643	$ 558	$ 615	$ 672	$ 698
2. Cash Tax Rate	39.7%	45.4%	33.8%	38.3%	36.2%	24.0%	37.9%	41.8%	54.1%	15.1%
3. NOPAT	$ 276	$ 259	$ 338	$ 348	$ 402	$ 488	$ 347	$ 358	$ 309	$ 593
4. Operating Working Capital	$ 443	$ 500	$ 496	$ 509	$ 527	$ 722	$ 807	$ 787	$ 569	$ 745
5. NPPE	1,461	1,468	1,436	1,602	1,648	1,648	1,510	1,585	1,535	1,486
6. Other Assets Net	42	(23)	(54)	45	(5)	(46)	(101)	(61)	(72)	21
7. Invested Capital (IC)	$1,946	$1,946	$1,878	$2,156	$2,170	$2,324	$2,217	$2,311	$2,032	$2,252
8. Average Invested Capital (AIC)	$1,985	$1,946	$1,912	$2,017	$2,163	$2,247	$2,271	$2,264	$2,171	$2,142
9. AROIC = NOPAT/AIC	**13.9%**	**13.3%**	**17.7%**	**17.2%**	**18.6%**	**21.7%**	**15.3%**	**15.8%**	**14.2%**	**27.7%**
10. WACC	10.5%	10.0%	9.9%	9.8%	9.5%	9.5%	9.5%	9.5%	9.5%	7.65%
11. AROIC – WACC	3.4%	3.3%	7.8%	7.4%	9.1%	12.2%	5.8%	6.3%	4.7%	20.0%
12. AEP = AIC (AROIC – WACC)	**$67**	**$65**	**$ 149**	**$ 150**	**$ 196**	**$ 275**	**$ 131**	**$ 143**	**$ 102**	**$ 429**

Date Source: Compustat

Table 7: Valuation Ratios, Hershey, 1983-2002
(Dollar Amounts in Millions)

	1983	1984	1985	1986	1987	1988	1989	1990	1991	1992
1. Year-end Market Value of Equity	$991	$1,210	$1,614	$2,221	$2,210	$2,345	$3,235	$3,382	$4,002	$4,239
2. Book Value of Equity	$596	$661	$728	$728	$832	$1,006	$1,117	$1,244	$1,335	$1,465
3. Interest-Bearing Debt (IBD)	$150	$153	$134	$243	$377	$317	$254	$338	$391	$560
4. IBD + Market Value of Equity = (1) + (3)	$1,141	$1,363	$1,748	$2,464	$2,587	$2,662	$3,489	$3,720	$4,393	$4,798
5. Average Invested Capital = Avg[(2) + (3)]	$719	$780	$838	$916	$1,090	$1,266	$1,347	$1,476	$1,654	$1,876
6. Market Value Added (MVA) = (4) – (5)	$422	$584	$910	$1,547	$1,496	$1,396	$2,142	$2,244	$2,739	$2,923
7. q-ratio* = (4)/(5)	1.59	1.75	2.09	2.69	2.37	2.10	2.59	2.52	2.66	2.56
8. Market-to-Book Equity = (1)/(2)	1.66	1.83	2.22	3.05	2.65	2.33	2.90	2.72	3.00	2.89
	1993	**1994**	**1995**	**1996**	**1997**	**1998**	**1999**	**2000**	**2001**	**2002**
1. Year-end Market Value of Equity	$4,293	$4,196	$5,022	$6,691	$8,853	$8,902	$6,568	$8,773	$9,183	$8,940
2. Book Value of Equity	$1,412	$1,441	$1,083	$1,161	$853	$1,042	$1,099	$1,175	$1,147	$1,372
3. Interest-Bearing Debt (IBD)	$534	$505	$795	$995	$1,317	$1,282	$1,118	$1,136	$885	$880
4. IBD + Market Value of Equity = (1) + (3)	$4,827	$4,701	$5,818	$7,687	$10,170	$10,184	$7,686	$9,909	$10,068	$9,819
5. Average Invested Capital = Avg[(2) + (3)]	$1,985	$1,946	$1,912	$2,017	$2,163	$2,247	$2,271	$2,264	$2,171	$2,142
6. Market Value Added (MVA) = (4) – (5)	$2,841	$2,755	$3,906	$5,669	$8,007	$7,937	$5,416	$7,645	$7,896	$7,678
7. q-ratio* = (4)/(5)	2.43	2.42	3.04	3.81	4.70	4.53	3.39	4.38	4.64	4.58
8. Market-to-Book Equity = (1)/(2)	3.04	2.91	4.64	5.76	10.38	8.54	5.98	7.47	8.00	6.52

* Measured as in Whited (2001)

Date Source: Compustat

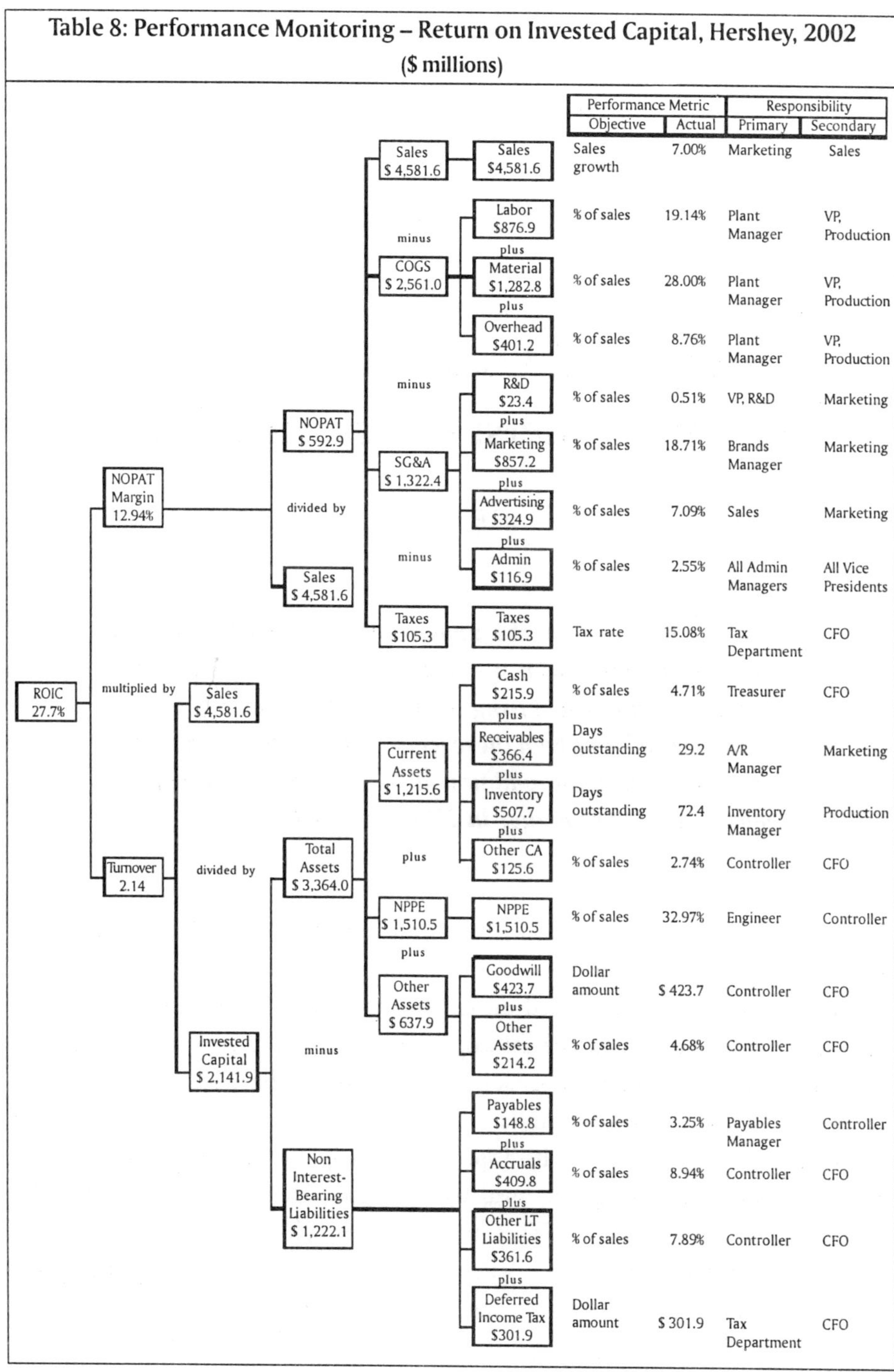

Table 8: Performance Monitoring – Return on Invested Capital, Hershey, 2002 ($ millions)

	Performance Metric		Responsibility	
	Objective	Actual	Primary	Secondary
Sales $4,581.6	Sales growth	7.00%	Marketing	Sales
Labor $876.9	% of sales	19.14%	Plant Manager	VP, Production
plus Material $1,282.8	% of sales	28.00%	Plant Manager	VP, Production
plus Overhead $401.2	% of sales	8.76%	Plant Manager	VP, Production
R&D $23.4	% of sales	0.51%	VP, R&D	Marketing
plus Marketing $857.2	% of sales	18.71%	Brands Manager	Marketing
plus Advertising $324.9	% of sales	7.09%	Sales	Marketing
plus Admin $116.9	% of sales	2.55%	All Admin Managers	All Vice Presidents
Taxes $105.3	Tax rate	15.08%	Tax Department	CFO
Cash $215.9	% of sales	4.71%	Treasurer	CFO
plus Receivables $366.4	Days outstanding	29.2	A/R Manager	Marketing
plus Inventory $507.7	Days outstanding	72.4	Inventory Manager	Production
plus Other CA $125.6	% of sales	2.74%	Controller	CFO
NPPE $1,510.5	% of sales	32.97%	Engineer	Controller
Goodwill $423.7	Dollar amount	$ 423.7	Controller	CFO
plus Other Assets $214.2	% of sales	4.68%	Controller	CFO
Payables $148.8	% of sales	3.25%	Payables Manager	Controller
plus Accruals $409.8	% of sales	8.94%	Controller	CFO
plus Other LT Liabilities $361.6	% of sales	7.89%	Controller	CFO
plus Deferred Income Tax $301.9	Dollar amount	$ 301.9	Tax Department	CFO

8

Concept and Usage of EVA by Two Indian Leaders: Infosys and HLL

T R Shastri

This article discusses the implementation of EVA by two Indian companies who are leaders in their own areas—service and manufacturing sectors. After comparing the economic profits of both these leaders, the author concludes that economic value addition as a percentage of capital deployed is always higher in HLL than in Infosys.

The words 'value added' look like the formation of an adjective but are used as a noun in financial accounting. Strange are the principles of accounting! Initially accounting discipline concentrated on tallying of numbers representing the assets, liabilities, revenue and expenditure. Its scope extended to interpretation of the numbers and working as tool to the managerial personnel. Now we have branches with exotic names like forensic accounting, inflation accounting, human resource accounting, creative accounting and so on. These specialized disciplines try to evolve accounting principles and guidelines to specific areas and principles. The corporates are responsible to the society in which they live. They are also responsible to the other stake holders and of course to the stock holders. Value added in financial accounting attempts to measure the social and performance aspect of the concept of value added.

Valued added can be defined as the measure of economic performance. It is not simply the net profit of the company but the increase in the wealth of the economic entity. The concept can be applied for the nation as a whole or for a corporate. The net profit is always measured as income minus expenses. But value added can be measured in two ways. In subtractive method, Value added is defined as equal to output less input. In other words, it is the value addition done at the entity by its own economic activities. It can also be calculated by additive method under which it is the sum of all distributed wealth. The entity normally distributes its wealth to employees (wages etc), to the government (tax etc), to the capital providers (dividend etc) and balance of course is retained. Thus under this method, Value added = Remuneration of employees + Remuneration of government + Remuneration of capital providers + Retained earnings.

While subtractive method reflects the performance aspect of the VA, the second method indicates the social aspect of the performance. Though, it can also be argued that one method subsumes the other since ultimately the remunerations paid represent the surplus created i.e. output less input. It may also be inferred that VA represents more than the income because it vividly describes how the wealth created is distributed. It therefore indirectly tries to enforce the concept that an economic entity does not just belong to the equity holders (though economically, it may be true) but to other stake holders, who appear in the additive model of VA.

The application of VA has been discussed quite extensively in financial accounting in Australia, France, Germany, The Netherlands, South Africa and UK. In Asian countries like Singapore and Japan, VA has been used in managerial accounting.

The concept of VA has been discussed in India in recent years in academic and business circles widely. However its actual application and disclosure in annual statements is limited to a few of the companies. Companies which are well known for their corporate governance are known to be in the forefront in discussing and arriving at VA in their annual statements.

The extent of VA discussed and disclosed in two of the leading companies viz.: Infosys and Hindustan Lever Ltd (HLL) are discussed below. It may be noted that each is a leader in its own area viz.: service and manufacturing sector and each is known for its professional approach to business situations.

Infosys

Infosys measures the EVA as the profitability after taking into account the cost of all capital. In other words it is the post-tax return on capital employed after adjusting for the tax benefit i.e. tax shield on the debt and as deducted by the cost of capital employed. The cost of equity is calculated as return on risk-free investment + expected risk premium on equity investment adjusted for beta variant in India. Till fiscal 2003, the average beta variant for software stocks in the US had been used in the above calculation, perhaps since a local equivalent was not available.

Infosys recognizes that for adding value i.e. for increasing EVA, the company has to earn higher returns than cost of capital. As a part of corporate governance, Infosys has disclosed several non-financial and intangible performance measures such as Brand valuation, Economic Value-Added (EVA) statement, Intangible asset scorecard, Human resource accounting and value-added statement in the annual statements. Infosys expects to bridge the gap between the information available to the management and the information available to the stakeholders through such disclosure.

Hindustan Lever Ltd

HLL defines VA or Economic value added (EVA) as net operating profit after tax less cost of capital employed. EVA is the residual income after providing for the cost of capital (due to lenders and shareholders). It represents the value added to the shareholders by generating operating profits in excess of the cost of capital employed in the business.

Here profit is after depreciation and after taxes but before deducting interest costs. Thus it represents the total funds available with the company for distribution among shareholders and lenders, though of course, it will not distribute all that is thus available! The cost of capital employed is arrived at multiplying the Weighted Average Cost of Capital (WACC) with Average Capital Employed. For this purpose, cost of debt is taken at the effective rate of interest applicable to an "AAA" rated company like HLL with an appropriate mix of short, medium and long term debt, net of taxes. This rate will vary from year to year. For the year 2005, HLL has taken a pre tax rate of 5.10% (8.2% for 2004). Cost of Equity is defined by HLL as "the return expected by the investors to compensate them for the variability in returns caused by fluctuating earnings and share prices".

Cost of Equity is arrived at by multiplying risk free return equivalent to yield on long-term Government Bonds (taken at 6.95% for 2005) and adding market risk premium (taken at 9%) multiplied by the beta variant for the company, taken at 0.95. Beta is the relative measure of risk associated with the Company's shares as against the market as a whole, as generally understood.

Thus HLL's cost of equity is arrived at as = 6.95% + 9% x 0.95 = 15.50%

HLL also recognizes that EVA will increase when there is increase in operating profit without adding to capital and where additional capital is deployed in projects, their returns should be more than the cost of new capital. In other words, EVA will increase under situations of greater efficiency and profitable growth. Similarly capital should be drawn out of activities that do not cover the cost of capital. HLL records that EVA has been computed under very conservative assumptions.

Conclusions

The two companies have their years ending on March 31st and December 31st and hence the figures for the years marked as 2006 & 2005 above are nearly comparable. The financial indicators of EVA of the two companies from the published accounts can be summarized as per chart below.

					Rs. in crores
Infosys					
Year ended March 31	**2002**	**2003**	**2004**	**2005**	**2006**
Economic Value-Added	510	454	689	1132	1540
EVA® as a percentage of average capital employed (%)	29.40	18.23	22.07	26.14	24.93
HLL					
Year ended December 31	**2001**	**2002**	**2003**	**2004**	**2005**
EVA	1080	1236	1429	887	1014
EVA as % of capital employed	38.4	36.4	37.8	23.9	39.6

The summary indicates that the economic value addition as a percentage of capital deployed is always higher at HLL compared to that at Infosys. The ratio at HLL has been consistently increasing in the recent years indicating the efficient use of capital and the value added thereon. As a percentage of average capital employed, EVA at Infosys has been erratic and hence there is inconsistency in the value additions and hence uncertainty to the shareholders in terms of value addition. The nature of business being different, the uncertainty may therefore be natural. The volume of operations, nature of activity, the business models and the geographical spread are completely different for the two companies. Hence the comparison of the absolute figures may not be correct. But on a cursory glance, it looks like Infosys is more consistent in growth of VA. The correct conclusion therefore could be that it is wiser to compare the VA of a company over the years rather than comparison with results of other companies.

(Prof. T R Shastri is a Faculty Member at Icfai Business School, Bangalore. He can be reached at trshastri@ibsindia.org).

Economic Value-added Analysis – Infosys

					Rs. crore
Fiscal	**2006**	**2005**	**2004**	**2003**	**2002**
Cost of Capital					
Risk-free debt cost (%)	7.50	6.80	5.20	6.00	7.30
Market premium	7.00	7.00	7.00	7.00	7.00
Beta variant	0.78	0.98	1.27	1.57	1.41
Cost of equity (%)	12.96	13.63	14.09	16.99	17.17
Average debt / Total capital (%)	–	–	–	–	–
Cost of debt – net of tax (%)	NA	NA	NA	NA	NA
Weighted Average Cost of Capital (WACC) (%)	12.96	13.63	14.09	16.99	17.17
Average capital employed	6,177	4,331	3,125	2,493	1,735
PAT as a percentage of average capital employed (%)	40.14	42.63	39.80	38.29	46.57
					Contd...

Contd...					
Economic Value-Added (EVA®)					
Operating profit (excluding extraordinary income)	2,654	2,048	1,357	1,079	943
Less: Tax	313	326	228	201	135
Cost of capital	801	590	440	424	298
Economic Value-Added	**1,540**	**1,132**	**689**	**454**	**510**
Enterprise Value					
Market value of equity	82,154	61,073	32,909	26,847	24,654
Add: Debt	-	-	-	-	-
Less: Cash and cash equivalents*	4,709	2,998	2,873	1,684	1,027
Enterprise value	77,445	58,075	30,036	25,163	23,627
Ratios					
EVA® as a percentage of average capital employed (%)	24.93	26.14	22.07	18.23	29.40
Enterprise value/average capital employed	12.53	13.41	9.61	10.09	13.62

Hindustan Lever Limited			
			Rs. Crores
Years	EVA	Average Capital Employed	EVA as % of Capital Employed
2001	1080	2816	38.4
2002	1236	3396	36.4
2003	1429	3780	37.8
2004	887	3704	23.9
2005	1014	2560	39.6

EVA Trends: 1996-2005 (Unaudited)

(Rs. crores)

	1996	1997	1998	1999	2000	2001	2002	2003	2004	2005
Cost of Capital Employed (COCE)										
1. Average Debt	156	160	165	162	93	50	45	881	1588	**360**
2. Average Equity	815	1127	1487	1908	2296	2766	3351	2899	2116	**2200**
3. Average Capital Employed : (1)+(2)	971	1287	1652	2070	2389	2816	3396	3780	3704	**2560**
4. Cost of Debt post-tax %	7.88	8.82	9.10	8.61	8.46	7.72	6.45	4.88	5.19	**3.38**
5. Cost of Equity %	19.70	19.70	19.70	19.70	19.70	16.70	14.40	12.95	14.77	**15.50**
6. WACC %	17.80	18.34	18.64	18.83	19.27	16.54	14.30	11.07	10.66	**13.80**
7. COCE : (3) x (6)	173	236	308	390	460	466	486	418	395	**353**
Economic Value Added (EVA)										
8. Profit after tax before exceptional items	413	580	837	1070	1310	1541	1716	1804	1199	**1355**
9. Add: Interest After taxes	32	21	19	14	8	5	6	43	82	**12**
10. Net Operating Profits after Taxes	445	601	856	1084	1318	1546	1722	1847	1281	**1367**
11. COCE (7) above	173	236	308	390	460	466	486	418	395	**353**
12. EVA (10) – (11)	272	365	548	694	858	1080	1236	1429	887	**1014**

(Data from the published annual accounts of the two companies)

Source: http://www.hll.com/mediacentre/annualreport2005.pdf#search=%22EVA%20Trends%3A%201996-2005%20(Unaudited)%20%2B%20 HLL%22

9

Empowerment and Growth: The EVA Story at TCS

S Mahalingam

Tata Consultancy Services is on its way to become a truly global organization. It is looking towards institutionalising leading edge practices in hiring, training, and people care, with an innovative EVA-based compensation model. The target model will be one that offers a high growth, high performance internal environment, to empowered, proactive, high-brand consultants operating in a dynamic external environment. This article outlines the evolution of EVA, the EVA model, strategic benefits and a comprehensive, EVA-based Incentive Compensation Plan in TCS.

Tata Consultancy Services (TCS) employs over 15000 professionals, has offices in 23 countries and projects in 50 countries across the world, and revenues around $700 million. Among its clientele are a number of Fortune 500 companies and it is in the league of 30 top IT consulting firms in the world.

TCS today is an Indian enterprise with a global reach. Its hiring and people care practices are in line with the industry practices and the compensation model has been traditional. The company has now set its sights on becoming a truly global organization. Its vision is to be among the top 10 IT consulting organisations in the world, a global employer of choice. It is looking towards institutionalising leading edge practices in hiring, training, and people care, with and innovative EVA-based compensation model. The target model will be one that offers a high growth, high performance internal environment to empowered, proactive, high-brand consultants operating in a dynamic external environment.

One important factor in understanding the context of TCS growth is that the company veritably set up the industry in India and metamorphosed in phases from an industry-builder to a lead-player in the industry it created. In the new marketplace it has defined for itself, it has to run alongside the new breed of competitors in the country on the one hand, and on the other, the established giants in the global league it is breaking into, as a logical culmination of its growth.

In the initial phase, the mission within TCS, right from 1968 when the organisation came into being, appeared to the creation of the industry and the setting standards. The expansion of the market took place in the 70s and 80s when the company grappled with issues of fixing rates in different countries and the cost structure of the company was being formed internally. It was also part of a group which had its own tradition to follow in terms of creation of infrastructure, communication, training the workforce, continuing education and many such issues. Creating an identity of purpose and shared vision for the employees was critical as also the building of a number of assets.

Given the expediencies of the trail-blazing phase in the 70s and the 80s, profit maximisation was not the only goal. The company, nevertheless, was profitable. In the 90s, with the globalisation of Indian software, there was a spurt of competitors with operational excellence as their capability. In this phase too, TCS continued to grow, but it had to grow higher than the competition, which was no longer small. It needed to go ahead and start looking at itself all over again.

Evolution of EVA

The current operating environment is characterised by players who are increasingly moving into globalisation and towards a more perfect marketplace. The industry is faced with stiff competition, consolidation, rapid technological advancement and obsolescence, high R&D costs and talent retention. As a strategy-focused organisation, TCS was looking at growth beyond competition, defining for themselves an expansion path that would sustain their leadership in a world shaped by continuously evolving market forces. They thus had to think above operational excellence into product innovation to evolve projections for multi-year growth framework. EVA seemed to provide the tool for this self-propelling growth model.

The search lights now beamed on a different set of focus paths: How to grow at a rate higher than just the increase in numbers? How to sell competency and value rather than skills? How to manage commitment without over-committing? How to reduce wastage and increase efficiency to avoid the trappings of a very high cost organisation? The answers translated into measures at all levels. The total pre-occupation with customer's satisfaction had to be returned to introduce an element of profit orientation. This needed a system of efficient resource management, better control of outstanding, performance evaluation that would link reward to revenue generation. The company had to make sure the operational and tactical levels were aligned with the strategic, so that customer satisfaction was reflected through higher revenues, and sales officers were responsive to selling the more valuable services of TCS rather than just meeting targets.

To take proactive steps to enhance value for themselves as well as their customers, in around 1996, the company organised its structure into a three dimensional model defined along industry practices (which are verticals like engineering, transportation, telecom), service practices (assignment themes such as e-Business, outsourcing, architecture and technology consulting), and geographies (which are regional groupings). The TCS business units now belong to one cell or span across multiple cells in this cubic grid. Each is a revenue generating unit outside the grid, which do not have a direct revenue earning capability. These include the corporate office support functions and R&D, which contribute in an indirect way towards the organisation's earnings.

The EVA Model

In giving shape to the EVA model, an organisation needs to keep its focus towards the ultimate goal of aligning its people to the corporate mission, creating an entrepreneurial culture through an empowered workforce, and building ownership with accountability. TCS worked out an EVA framework to align corporate value with the performance of the constituent business units and the individuals who comprised these. It translated to a compensation model, where the employee had a share in the corporate pie with add-ons from the profits of the Business Unit and the Individual Performance Factor. At the individual level, an employee needs to know the drivers to tweak to enhance the EVA of the company, of the business unit, and his own contribution towards all these. There are three basic drivers—revenue, cost, and capital charge. Revenue is driven by the rate or license price put into the product, sales, billable hours, response time, and domain skills. On time delivery obviously has an impact on revenue because better delivery cycles improve the turnaround to the customers. Cost is managed through productivity, is affected by sales and marketing costs, recruitment and others. Receivables and training are the bulk of the capital charge. These are a representative list, and there are many others.

The individual works towards the improvement of the benefit package, which essentially has three components—the Corporate EVA, the Business Unit EVA, and the Individual Performance Factor. Out of the total EVA payment a certain percentage goes to each employee on the basis of corporate EVA improvement. Secondly, if your business unit did better than another business unit, then automatically you got more than the other business unit. Again it is a team reward concept. The third one depends on the evaluation of individual performance.

Strategic Benefits

With the introduction of EVA, yet another plank has fallen into place in the systemic efforts towards optimisation. Activity Based Costing, implemented 1992 onwards, was a major factor facilitating the smooth transition to EVA. Balance Scorecard was another adaptation in the journey towards excellence. TCS also participated in the Tata Business Excellence Model, (TBEM), which is really an adaptation of the Malcolm Baldridge award, for the Tata companies.

Initiatives such as the process map, a metrics definition, a number of data collection points are other enablers in data driven management. With the introduction of EVA, the company has to take a fresh look at the integrated system in a holistic perspective, and evolve ways and means of optimising it.

Implementation of EVA requires the integration of the planning and the tracking process. TCS sought to achieve this through a home grown tool called e-pilot, which essentially drills down from strategy to day-to-day activity. This facilitates the integrated planning approach, in defining the corporate EVA, linking it to the business unit/cell, and further to various components down the line, all the way to the drivers connected to each activity. With the drill-down of targets, the tracking becomes automated.

Incentive Scheme

A comprehensive EVA-based Incentive Compensation Plan has been designed for the employees. Building the incentive scheme requires a detailed exercise in arriving at the target EVA. The TCS model was defined, backed by a market analysis and a study of 24 competitors, largely outside India. The framework had specifications for target EVA, with carefully defined EVA intervals and provision for the positioning of zero EVA. The gradation continued through incentives corresponding target attainment, the double incentive. Implementation now covers the whole consulting organisation.

TCS is also implementing the bonus bank at the individual level. This exercise begins with a target bonus being earmarked for allocation on corporate target realisation, with a built in multiplication factor for exceeding the targeted EVA. When the corporate target is exceeded, a 'potential bonus' is declared. This accrues to the bonus bank of the individual as two components: Component A, the result of the share in the corporate pie; Component B, a composite factor depending on the business unit and individual performance. The accruals are cumulated over the years and the pay out each year is decided as a portion of this cumulative balance, leaving a surplus in the bonus bank. This concept of bonus bank allows an unlimited multi-year decision horizon, replacing the traditional thresholds and caps. It demands sustainable performance improvements, and maintains the important cumulative relationship between pay and performance.

The firsthand experience was a revelation, as we could see how we actually get paid out from the increases, demonstrating the dictum that EVA pays for itself. The reward is that the size of the pie could become different as its gets enlarged and the individual and the corporation appear to benefit considerably. It ensures the channelisation of information across levels and each entity can see how it fares against targets. It enhances the sense of participation through the realisation of the share in the larger pie, and provides the motivation to contribute to enlarge the pie. EVA really forces the organisation to adopt a proper business planning approach, gets a focus on strategies, and helps to monitor the accountability of people. In a nutshell, it gives a barometer on how the organisation is being run and mandates critical stocktaking to evolve on a continuous improvement path.

(S Mahalingam is Chief Financial Officer, Tata Consultancy Services. He joined TCS in 1970 immediately after qualifying as a Chartered Accountant. His career in TCS has seen him participating in consulting assignments in many parts of the world. He managed the London and New York offices of TCS in the early days of TCS's internationalization. Mahalingam was Executive Vice President before being appointed as CFO in February 2003).

Tata Steel: Rolling Out EVA

– *S Mahalingam*

Tata Steel is not content with being India's only world-class steel maker. The urge to improve and to emerge as the most cost-efficient steel producer induced it to consider quality and performance-improvement initiatives. It adopted the value-engineering technique, ISO 9000, ISO 14000, QS 9000, Six Sigma, and the JRD Quality Value, among other things. So why did the company choose to go in for one more value-based management initiative?

The company had been lagging behind in shareholder returns. Traditional measures like operating profit and price earnings ratio placed the company at the top. But it still had a long way to go. As a performance-monitoring tool, EVA speaks about value creation for shareholders. "EVA is more relevant for us as we are in a capital-intensive business, and EVA lays stress on investment management," says B Muthuraman, Tata Steel's managing director.

Tata Steel had not expected major benefits in the short term. But it expected to identify the levers that would help plan future initiatives. In the medium to long term, it plans to create a mindset where initiatives across all levels can be linked to EVA growth. Cascading accountability and decision making downwards is challenging. "Stern Stewart and Co will be providing extensive training to 40 of our officers, who will customise the training programme and take it down to each employee," Mr. Muthuraman adds.

Luck of the Team

Tata Steel is lucky in many ways. Despite its size and historical baggage, the teams have a lot of enthusiasm and ability to undertake and improve upon the number of large initiatives concurrently. They have the best team to extract the best out of consultants, says Tej Pavan Gandhok of Stern Stewart.

Tata Steel adopted a five-stage process for implementing EVA:

- Sharing the vision: Creation of awareness among employees
- Value diagnostic: Identification of gaps and opportunities
- Value audit and goal setting
- Measurement and management
- Training and knowledge transfer from working groups to employees

So far the implementation has progressed along expected lines. Tata Steel's experience with 'total operating performance' and the Performance Ethic Programme (PEP) have helped. These initiatives have instituted a meritocracy-based management structure, which has improved decision-making processes even prior to the EVA rollout. Earlier initiatives, like the balanced scorecard, helped align employee goals with the company's objectives. Tata Steel did not have to spend time on identifying EVA centres and drivers as the PEP was already structured on those lines. The company was able to integrate all initiatives and make speedy progress on multiple initiatives.

"We have set ourselves the target of turning EVA-positive by 2007, which implies that we should be able to meet the expectations of our investors," says Mr. Muthuraman. If the recent capital expenditure plans are anything to go by, there is every reason to believe EVA is on a roll.

Source: http://www.tata.com/tata_steel/articles/20030326_rolling_out_eva.htm

10

Value Based Management Concepts: Suitable Tools for Airline Management?

Carsten Homburg, Andrea Theissen and Alexander Knigge

This article discusses the level of implementation of VBM concepts in major global airlines through a survey. The survey examines the importance of value based key performance indicators for both the perennial operative business plan and the strategic subordinated business plan which show that airlines consider VBM as an important strategic planning instrument. The survey reveals that the importance of these concepts for airline management is lower than it is in other industries.

Introduction

The deregulation process in the aviation industry in Europe during the seventies and eighties led to a long-term structural change. The aim of this liberalization was to facilitate market entry, to reduce aviation capacity limitations and to increase efficiency with an open price structure.

Due to growing competition from "low-cost" carriers and external shocks such as the increased oil price, the Iraq war, the terrorist attacks on 11th September and the SARS crisis, the price pressure on airlines has increased considerably.

Furthermore, the capital procurement options have changed. For state owned companies the risk of bankruptcy is regarded as very low, so that new investments can be financed by means of borrowed capital.

Today, as the proportion of privately owned airlines has surged constantly in the last two decades, the aviation industry is more dependant on the capital market as a source for new capital.

The generally low profitability of airlines and the increased number of bankruptcies, combined with the decline in passenger numbers following 11th September has led to a deterioration in the potential and conditions for borrowing capital for aircraft acquisition.

In the course of globalization and deregulation, the demands of the capital market have changed. International competition for capital and the growing importance of institutional investors have forced companies to view the maximization of shareholder value as the central strategic company goal.

The aim is to gain investors, through value-creating investments which increase the company value giving investors the prospect of a satisfactory rate of return.

Value Based Management: An Overview

The Idea

The idea of Value Based Management (VBM) is that the value of a company can only be increased if the yield of all new investments is higher than their cost of capital. VBM is based on the application of value-based performance indicators. They are used for the following three purposes:

- Strategic, Financial and Operational Planning
- Performance Measurement
- Performance Control.

The major objective of VBM is to achieve a sustainable raise in firm value over time.

Different Concepts

Value based performance indicators can be divided into two categories:

- On the one hand there are indicators that examine past performance data. These indicators facilitate the control of defined performance objectives.
- On the other hand there are future oriented indicators that rely on earnings or cash flow protection. They are mainly used for investment appraisals as well as planning processes, such as the allocation of internal resources.

Ideally, an indicator can be used for both, performance measurement and controlling as well as planning.

All VBM concepts require the preceding determination of the cost of capital.

Discounted Cash Flow Methods (DCFM)

DCF-methods are based on the idea that the value of a company is determined by the present value of the operating cash flows plus the value of the firms' non-operating assets. In order to use DCF-methods for company valuation, future operating cash flows have to be estimated. Therefore, implementing a DCF-method implies a relatively high planning effort. Furthermore, cash flow forecasting at airlines is difficult because of the high sensitivity of airlines to cyclical fluctuations.

To determine a value based performance indicator. The following three DCF-concepts are used:

- Free Cash Flow to Equity Approach
- Free Cash Flow to Firm Approach
- Adjusted Present Value Approach.

Value based performance indicators based on DCF-methods are best used for financial planning and evaluation purposes, particularly for investment appraisals. They are not very suitable for performance measurement and control due to their reliance on future cash flow projections which can be easily manipulated by the management to achieve the defined targets.

Cash Flow Return on Investment (CFROI) and Cash Value Added (CVA)

The CFROI-concept which treats a company in a similar way to an investment project produces an economic cash-based performance indicator. Value growth is measured by the comparison of the internal rate of return and the cost of capital.

Key input factors of the CFROI—concept are gross investment, gross cash flows, assets lifetime as well as the residual value of non-depreciating assets (e.g. intangibles such as rights to routes or slots) (see Figure 1). The gross investment consists of all assets and working capital before depreciation. The gross cash flow to the company's debt and equity holders is computed by adding depreciation and interest to the net income. One of the main assumptions for the CFROI determination is that the gross cash flow which is determined for the most recent year is kept constant over the assets' life. Thus, the CFROI does not constitute a cash flow projection but an examination of the present situation.

Accordingly, CFROI is a suitable tool for performance measurement and control rather than a planning instrument.

Figure 1: Calculation of CFROI

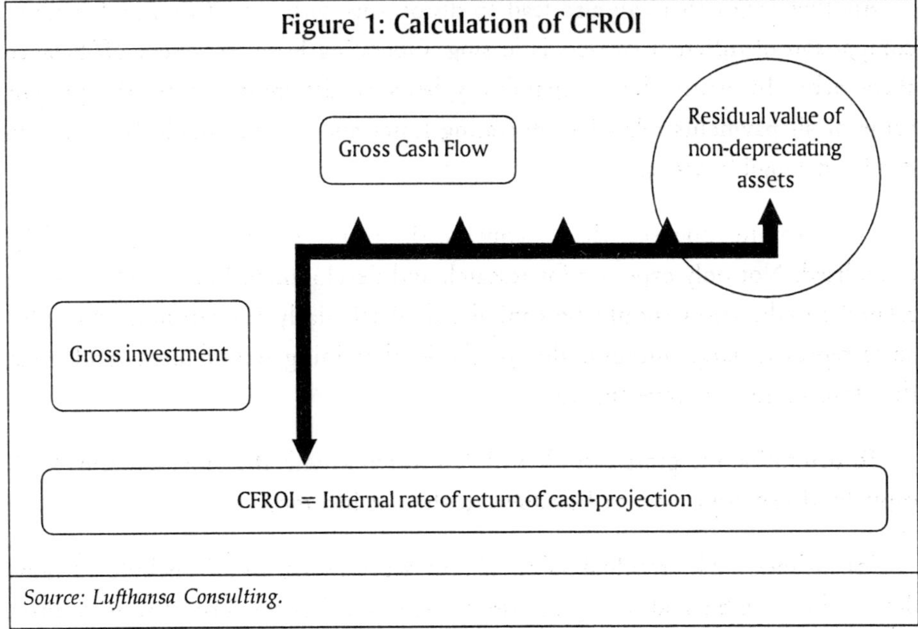

Source: Lufthansa Consulting.

In this context, the accounting treatment of assets is, particularly for airlines, very important. In the airline industry idle capacity is a common phenomenon.

The value of fully depreciated assets constitutes an important component of gross investment and therefore must be carefully estimated. Generally speaking, the usage of fair market values rather than residual values for fully depreciated assets facilitates a more realistic determination of gross investment.

However, the determination of fair market values for used aircraft is difficult because the used aircraft market is affected by cyclical fluctuations. When market prices decrease the gross investment also declines which causes a surge in the CFROI. Thus the performance indicator CFROI shows an increase in value although no value has been created. Consequently, the comparability of different time periods can be limited if the market prices have experienced volatility.

On the other hand, the usage of residual values will limit the comparability of the resulting performance indicator with other airlines since each carrier applies its own specific depreciation methods and policies.

Another factor that can also lead to distortions with regard to a performance comparison of different carriers is leasing. Operating leases represent off-balance sheet debt. To assure the comparability between different airlines the present value of all payments related to operating leases and rentals should be added to the fixed tangible assets.

Furthermore expenses, that encourage the future earning power, should be capitalized. Not only expenses for research and development but also all expenses related to education should be capitalized. Particularly for airlines, education costs represent large amounts due to the legal training requirements and must therefore be seen as investments.

To determine the gross cash flows in consistency with the gross investment all capitalized expenses have to be added to the net income.

For airlines, "The residual value of non-depreciating assets" include all non-depreciable tangible and intangible assets, such as real estate, airport slots, licenses and traffic rights.

Because of the complex calculation of the CFROI a simplified version, CFROI*, was developed. This simplified model also consists of the variables gross investment, gross cash flow and residual value of non-depreciating assets. The difference is that the gross cash flow is assumed to be a perpetuity. This assumption can only be justified if investments for replacement equal depreciations. Accordingly, in this concept an economic depreciation is established.

$$\text{CFROI}^* = \frac{\text{gross cash flow} - \text{economical depreciation}}{\text{gross investment}}$$

[1]Economical depreciation $= \dfrac{\text{WACC}}{(1+\text{WACC})^{T} - 1}$ x depreciating assets

The economic depreciation allocates the assets over their useful life and invests the corresponding depreciation charges in the WACC. Thus, it is assumed that investments undertaken in the past generate their costs of capital. This assumption is problematic because value based management claims to invest generated cash in investments that generate a return higher than the costs of capital. Where a profitable investment does not exist it is reasonable to use the generated cash for redemption of loans.

Profitability based indicators, such as the CFROI* are not suitable for performance controlling because an increasing profitability does not necessarily mean that value is created.

To extend the usage of this concept an absolute indicator, the Cash Value Added (CVA) can be determined. The CVA can be calculated in two ways:

$$\text{CVA} = (\text{CFROI}^* - \text{WACC}) \times \text{gross investment}$$

or

[2]CVA = gross cash flow – economical depreciation – capital charge

This concept can be used for all three purposes of Value Based Management: strategic, financial and operational planning; performance measurement; and performance controlling.

1 T = asset life and depreciating assets = gross investment – residual value of non-depreciating assets

2 Capital charge = WACC x Gross Cash Flow

To determine the company's value the future CVAs have to be estimated:

$$\text{Company's value} = \sum_{t=1}^{\infty} \frac{CVA_t}{(1+WACC)^t} + \text{invested capital}_{t=0}$$

Because of this future orientation the CVA-indicator is particularly suitable for investment appraisals. However, the same problems as discussed before with the CFROI-concept exist in this case.

Economic Value Added (EVA) and Market Value Added (MVA)

The [3]EVA® – concept was developed by the consulting firm Stern Steward & Co. The concept is based on the traditional residual income measure. It is calculated in the following way:

$$EVA = NOPAT_t - WACC \times NOA_{t-1}$$

In order to ensure that EVA more closely reflects the real economic situation of a company, [4]NOPAT and NOA which are derived from the accounting system can be adjusted. Although the academic literature presents a wide range of necessary adjustments, four major adjustment groups can be distinguished.

- The objective of **Operating Conversions** is to eliminate all non-operating assets, such as real estate and stocks at airlines' subsidies as well as loss or gains from exchange rate fluctuations. Accordingly depreciation for non-operating assets also should be excluded from NOPAT.
- **Funding Conversions** are used to adjust the NOA for the leverage effect. This includes the capitalization of operating leases as well as rentals. The net present value is added to NOA. To assure consistency the interest included in the payment has to be added to NOPAT.
- **Shareholder Conversions** involve adjustments to determine the economic value of equity. The sum of the shareholder conversions is added to the NOA. Expenses that encourage the future earning power such as cost for research and development, advertising as well as expenses for training and

3 EVA is proprietary. In the following the trade mark is omitted

4 NOPAT = Net operating profit after taxes and NOA = Net operating assets

further education are capitalised and depreciated over time. Consistently the change in capitalised expenses should be added to NOPAT. Since minority holdings are a common phenomenon in the airline industry and most of them are considered as strategic investments, they should be included in the NOA and NOPAT computation.

- **Tax Conversions** constitute the adjustment for tax expenses. For instance, if certain non-operating expenses are excluded, their tax cost also must be excluded.

The NOA comprises the tangible assets of a firm at its book value. Because of depreciation, the earning power of companies with younger assets can be underestimated.

Depreciations decrease the NOA and thereby increase the EVA although the NOPAT is still unchanged. Thus, it is difficult to compare companies on the basis of EVA if they differ in aging structure of assets or in depreciation policies.

Accordingly, a comparison of EVA over time is difficult because the EVA automatically increases over time due to the decreased book value of assets.

The EVA-concept is most suitable for performance measurement. It can also be used for valuation purposes. Similar to the DCF-methods, future EVA‘s can be estimated on an annual basis and discounted by the WACC. The present value of the future EVA's is called the Market Value Added (MVA).

The MVA can also be calculated by deducting the capital employed from the company's market value. Differences between the result of both concepts are most likely due to incorrect EVA estimations or an over or under valuation of the airline stock.

Empirical Study

Methodology

From May to July 2004 a survey was conducted with the objective to examine the level of implementation of VBM concepts at the major global airlines. The questionnaire that was sent to the Finance Department of selected airlines worldwide contained 43 questions.

The selection of the 80 airlines that were approached, was based on the number of transported passengers during 2003. However, airlines which are fully government-owned were excluded from the survey since they do not rely on capital markets and therefore an application of VBM concepts is highly unlikely.

22.5 percent of the approached airlines fully completed the questionnaire.

Results

The survey started with the evaluation of primary company objectives. Surprisingly the aim to "increase shareholder value" obtained the second lowest ranking. In contrast, "classic" objectives like "customer satisfaction" and "competitiveness" were given the highest importance.

This result is quite different from the results of comparable studies, that did not concentrate on one particular industry sector. In those studies the goal "increase

Figure 2: Primary Company Objectives*

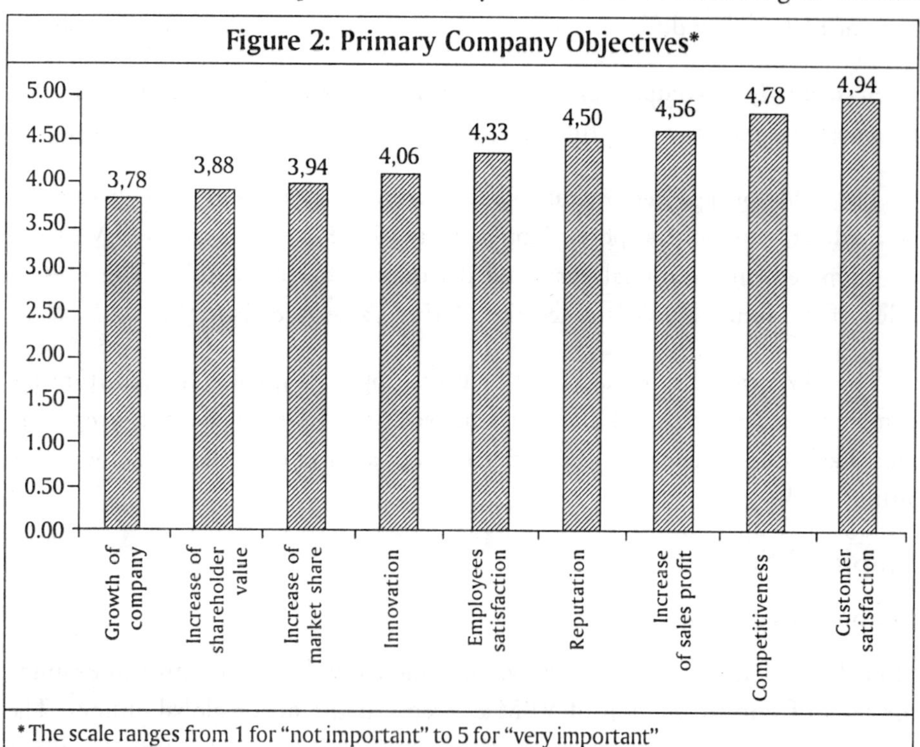

*The scale ranges from 1 for "not important" to 5 for "very important"

Source: Empirical Study, Lufthansa Consulting.

of shareholder value" was given the greatest importance. Despite the increased relevance of the capital market as provider of equity for airlines, the idea of value based management does not dominate the airline industry, as shown in Figures 2 and 3.

The most important target groups for airlines are still their customers and their employees.

It is not surprising that the government is still regarded as an important target group, as many governments still hold significant shares in their country's airlines.

Figure 3: Major Target Groups*

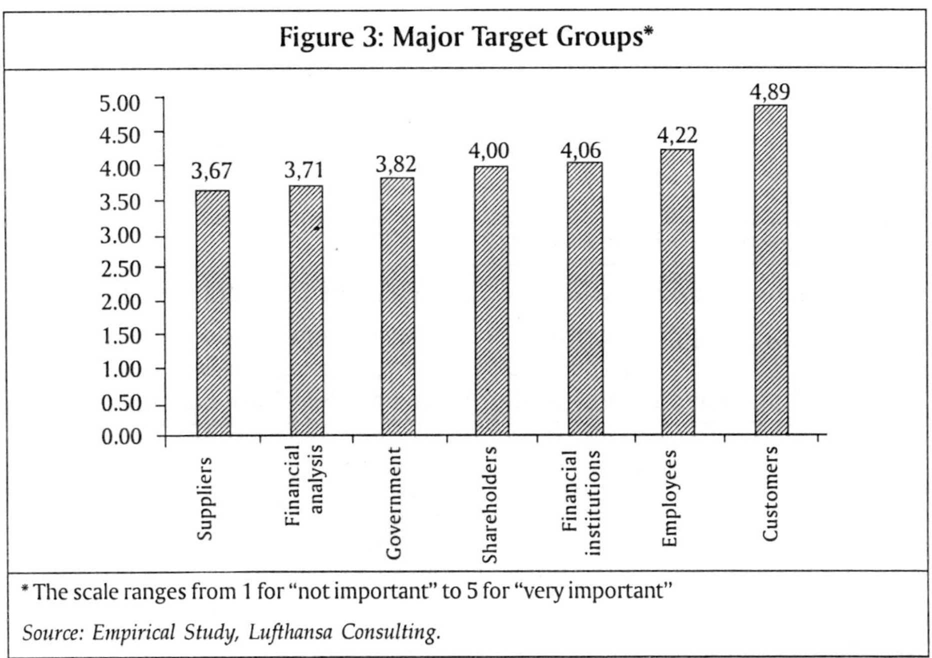

* The scale ranges from 1 for "not important" to 5 for "very important"

Source: Empirical Study, Lufthansa Consulting.

Most major airlines seem to have a basic understanding of the value based management concept. On a scale of 1 for "no knowledge" up to 5 for "very good knowledge", an average value of 3,53 was achieved. Only 41% of airlines evaluate their own knowledge as either good or very good.

Of the 18 airlines that completed the survey, only seven use a value based key performance indicator.

In contrast to comparable studies, profit-based key performance indicators do not dominate cash-flow-based key performance indicators (see Figure 4).

Figure 4: Used Value Based Key Performance Indicator

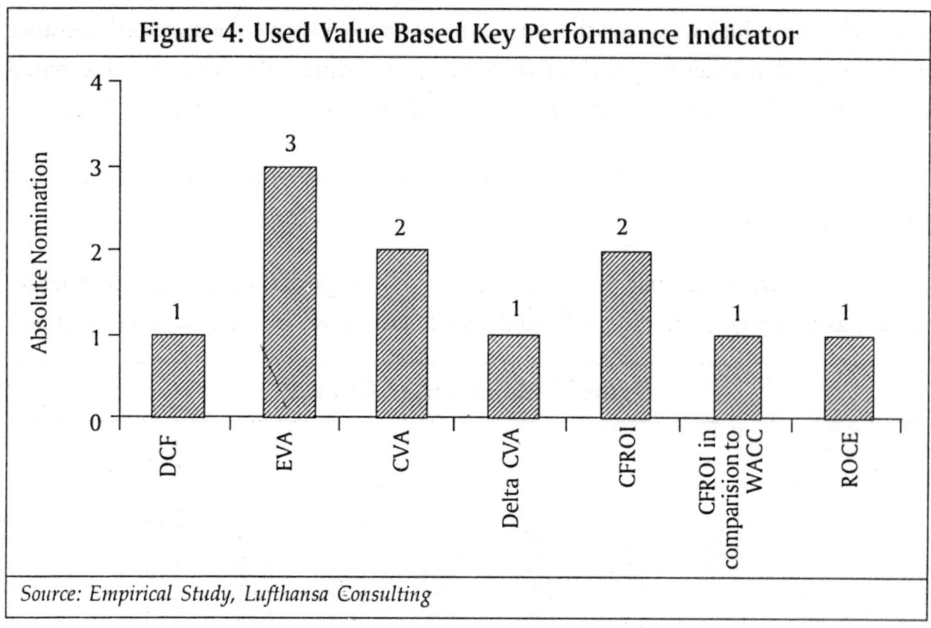

Source: Empirical Study, Lufthansa Consulting

This is most probably due to both the capital-intensive nature of the aviation industry and the high divergence in depreciation methods and policies.

Figure 5: Planned Introduction of Value Based Performance Indicator

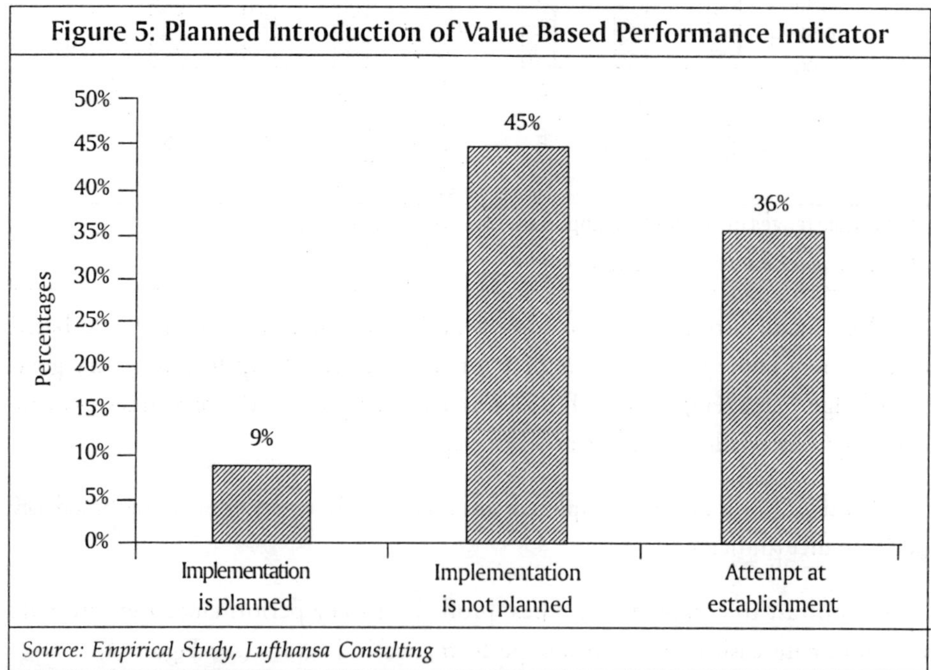

Source: Empirical Study, Lufthansa Consulting

Of the airlines, that do not use a value-based performance indicator, 45% are not planning to introduce one in the future and 36% attempted an implementation in the past (see Figure 5).

In order to obtain information about the implementation and realisation of value based management the following questions were only addressed to airlines that use such a concept.

43% of value conscious and controlling airlines introduced their key performance indicator in 2001.

In 83% of all cases, the implementation took approximately one year. Whereas 57% undertook the introduction with internal recourses, 43% also relied on external support.

The introduction was initiated in particular by Top Management and by the CEO, who both obtained the highest value for their efforts to introduce the concept (see Figure 6).

Figure 6: Level of Effort Towards the Introduction of the Value-Based Concept*

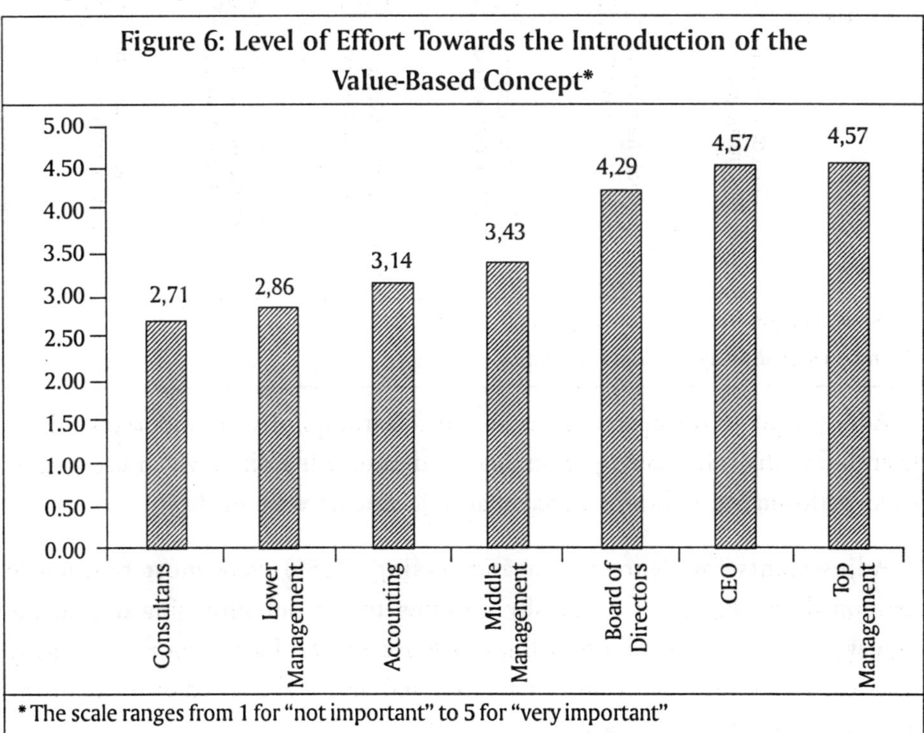

* The scale ranges from 1 for "not important" to 5 for "very important"

Source: Empirical Study, Lufthansa Consulting.

The measurement and planned increase of the enterprise value was the most frequently nominated reason for the introduction (see Figure 7). Thus the basic theoretical principle of value based management seems to coincide with it's primary objective in the practice.

Figure 7: Factors for the Decision to Introduce the Concept*

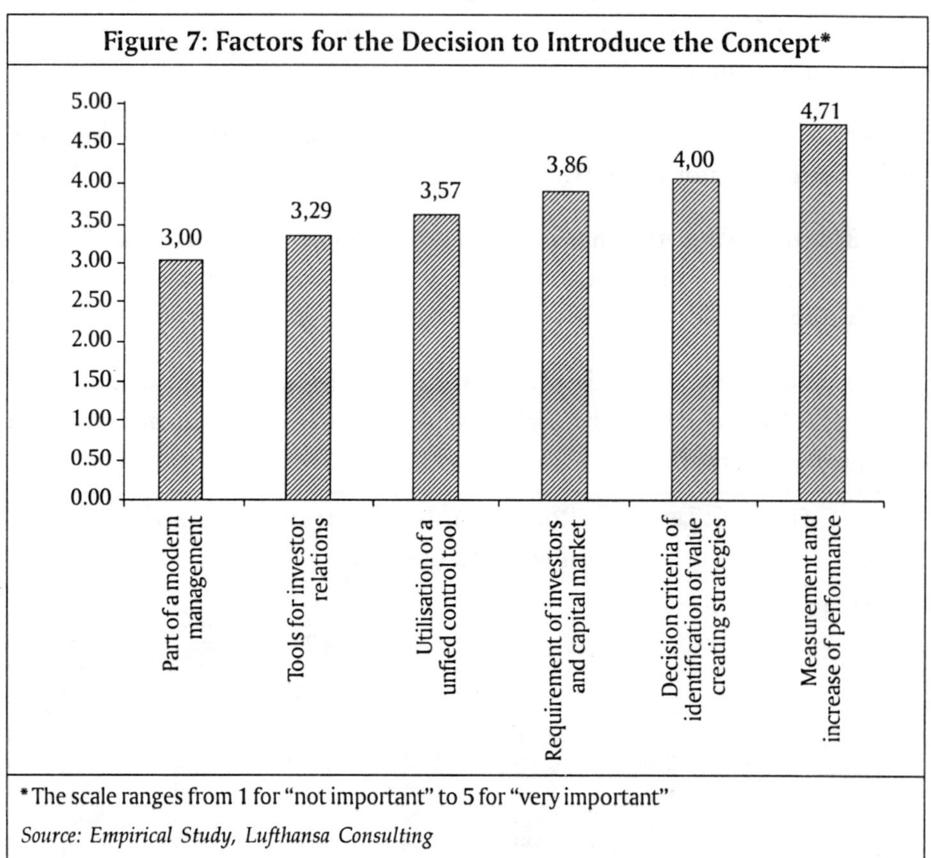

*The scale ranges from 1 for "not important" to 5 for "very important"

Source: Empirical Study, Lufthansa Consulting

Adjustments to the operating result and to earnings play an important role in determining the value based performance indicator. All airlines which use a value based performance indicator stated that adjustments were made.

Adjustments for depreciation and leasing (71%) were most frequently mentioned (see Figure 8). Generally speaking this is not surprising due to the high weighting of aircraft on airlines' balance sheets. Furthermore, operating leases constitute off-balance sheet liabilities and also make an adjustment to the raw accounting data necessary.

However, it is surprising that other important adjustments are neglected in many cases as shown in Figure 8.

Figure 8: Adjustments to the Determination of Earnings or Cash Flow and Fixed Income

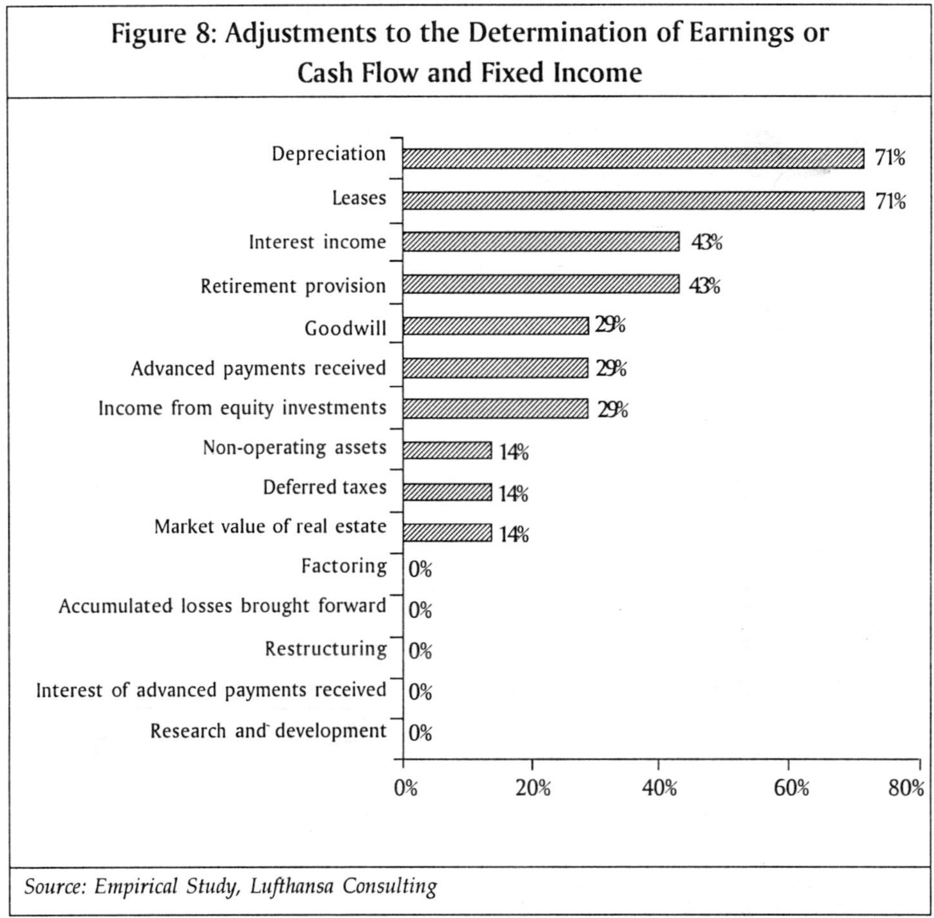

Source: Empirical Study, Lufthansa Consulting

Regarding the determination of the cost of capital the study shows homogenous results. 86% of all airlines use the WACC and 71% determine the costs of equity based on the Capital Asset Pricing Model (CAPM). 71% of the airlines determine the costs of debt by looking at the interest rates of their long-term bank loans.

To fully implement a value-based management concept, it is necessary to break down the key performance indicator to subordinate levels of the corporate hierarchy.

Figure 9 illustrates that only 43% of all airlines which use the key performance indicator on a company level also determine separate key performance indicators for their divisions. This result should be viewed critically because the heterogeneity of airline divisions can create great differences with regard to the underlying risk structure as well as the operating profitability. Consequently, an individual assessment as well as the break-down based on the overall corporate indicator is desirable.

Figure 9: Break-down Levels of the Value-based Key Performance Indicator

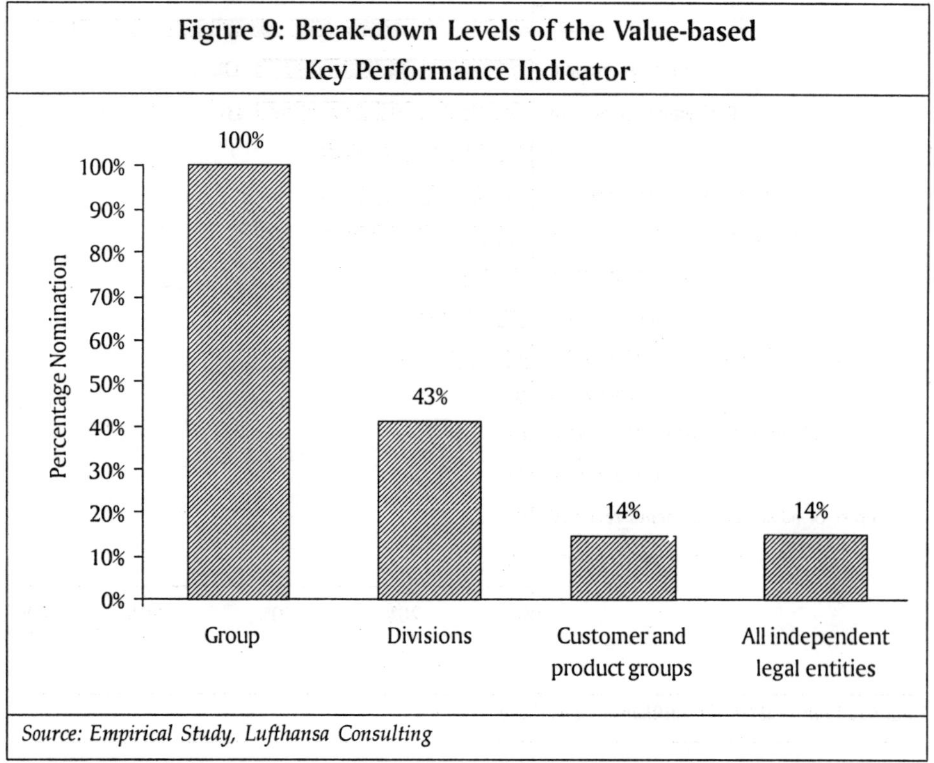

Source: Empirical Study, Lufthansa Consulting

While 86% indicate, that the value-based key performance indicators for subordinate levels can be reconciled with the shareholder value key performance indicator established for the company as a whole, 14% explain that this coordination is only partly possible.

In order to link the remuneration with the key performance indicator at subordinated levels it is reasonable to perform adjustments e.g. to isolate components, which cannot be influenced.

Although 50% apply these adjustments, 33% state that it is generally not desired. 17% comment that these adjustment are too complex are therefore disregarded (see Figure 10).

Figure 10: Necessity for Adjustments for Subordinated Levels

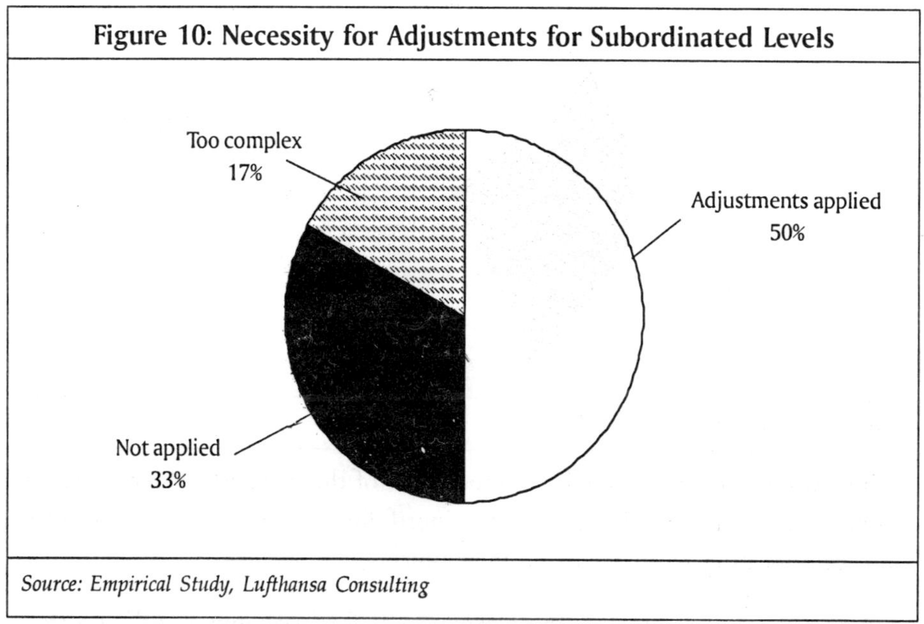

Source: Empirical Study, Lufthansa Consulting

To evaluate the implementation of the key performance indicator at different company levels the question was asked whether different costs of capital for different operational areas are determined. Since the heterogeneous divisions have different risk structures a separate examination of the departmental cost is recommended from an academic standpoint.

However, the vast majority of airlines do not calculate individual costs of capital for different operational areas. Only 29% compute individual capital costs on division level (see Figure 11).

Apart from the implementation on subordinated levels, value driver trees can help to identify the major performance drivers and thereby create the transparency necessary for cause analysis. Only 43% of the value based managing airlines break down the key performance indicator into operational indicators with the help of value driver trees.

Figure 11: Determination of Different Costs of Capital for Different Operational Areas within the Airline

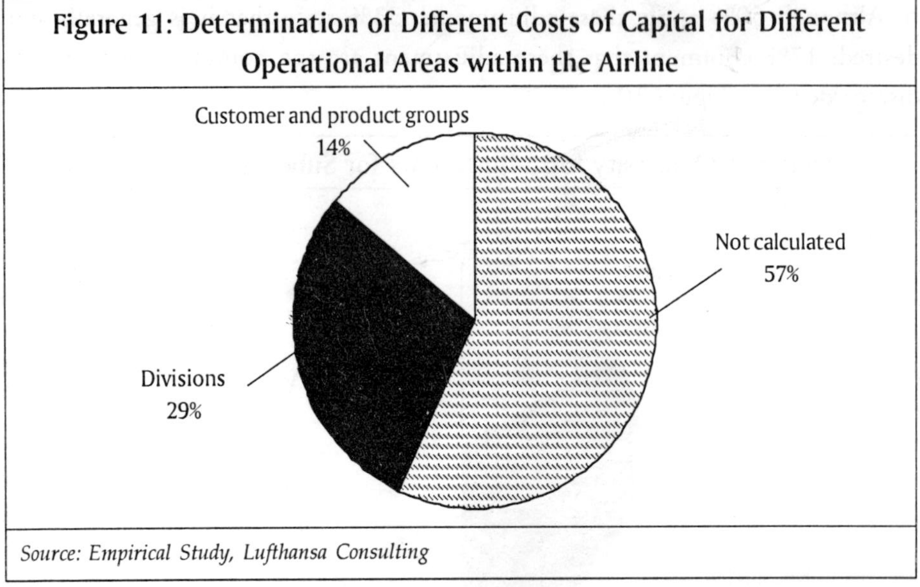

Source: Empirical Study, Lufthansa Consulting

Finally, the survey examined the importance of the key performance indicator on one hand for determining the business portfolio of an airline and on the other hand for allocating resources to business units.

On a scale from 1 (for "not important") to 5 (for "very important"), portfolio determination and resource allocation score 3,86 and 3,71 respectively.

These results suggest, that these decisions are not totally value based but that they are affected by other highly valued company objectives (see Figure 2).

To guarantee that management and employees act in line with shareholders interests many companies use compensation remuneration bonus systems based on performance indicators. 71% of the airlines indicated using such a compensation remuneration bonus system, while 21% indicated not using one.

In order to use value based management for planning it is necessary to formulate target returns (key performance indicator) for all major strategic and operational areas.

The survey examined the importance of value based key performance indicators for both the perennial operative business plan and the strategic subordinated business plan. Figure 12 shows that airlines consider VBM as an important strategic planning instrument.

Figure 12: Importance of Value Based Key Performance Indicators as Target Return

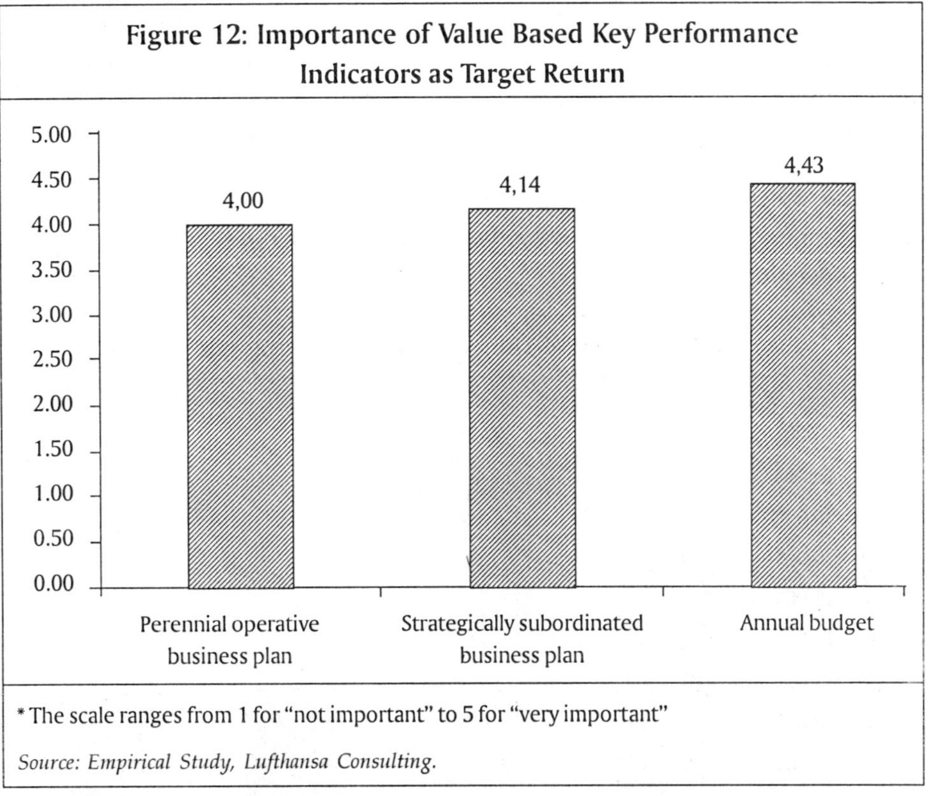

* The scale ranges from 1 for "not important" to 5 for "very important"

Source: Empirical Study, Lufthansa Consulting.

In contrast, the general importance of the key performance indicator for planning and control on an operational level is estimated lower, with an average value of 3,86.

However 71% of the airlines determine the substantial value drivers for their key performance indicator on the operational level.

Besides its role in planning, value based management is essential for performance measurement and performance control.

All airlines using value based management indicate defined target goals for subordinated levels to aid performance measurement and control. But it should be noted that (as you can see in Figure 10) only 50% of the airlines make adjustments when using the key performance indicator at subordinated levels. Performance measurement based on indicators that include components which cannot be influenced can cause a diminished acceptance by employees.

Furthermore 43% additionally use the balance scorecard as a control concept on an operational level in order to integrate non-financial indicators. But 57% do not use any other control concept that includes non-financial indicators in addition to the purely financial focus.

Figure 13 shows, that approximately 71% of airlines accomplish performance control quarterly or monthly. Furthermore 50% control project or process progress at the operational level.

Figure 13: Frequency of Undertaking a Performance Control

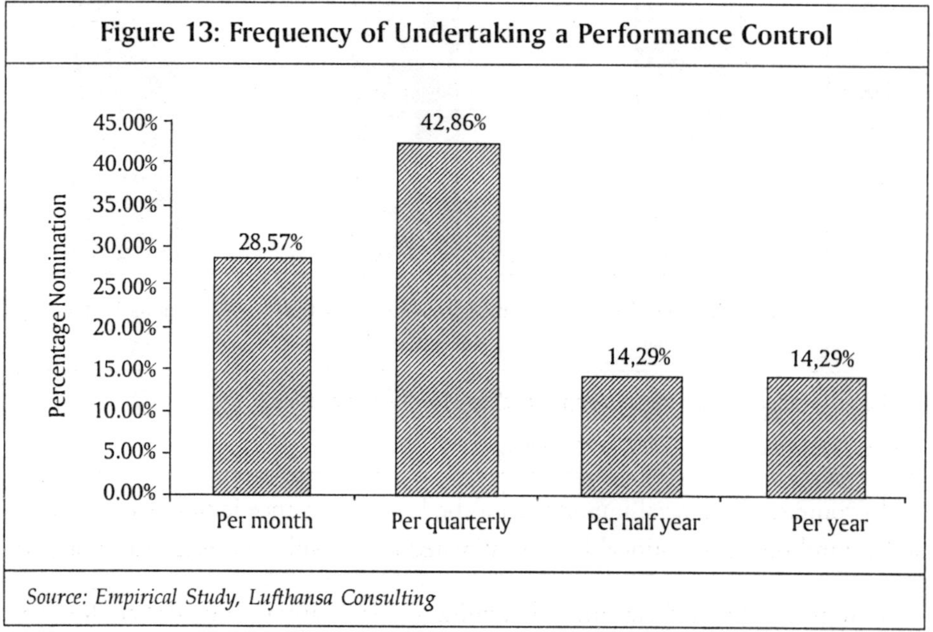

Source: Empirical Study, Lufthansa Consulting

The aim of VBM is to increase the fundamental enterprise value by value creation and to bind new investors with the potential of an appropriate yield.

Thus the capital market communication is very important. This communication should include the VBM-concept as well as the planned and realized value creation.

This study shows that large deficits still exist in the field of capital market communication. 57,14% of the airlines state that neither the achieved figure nor the annual development of the value based performance indicator is publicly reported.

Information about the calculation of the performance indicator as well as about the future planning are not revealed to the public at 71.43% of airlines (see Figure 14). Only 14.3% of airlines provide this information to analysts or institutional investors separately.

Compared with other industries the capital market communication in the airline industry is very underdeveloped.

Figure 14: Reporting on the Value Based Key Performance Indicator

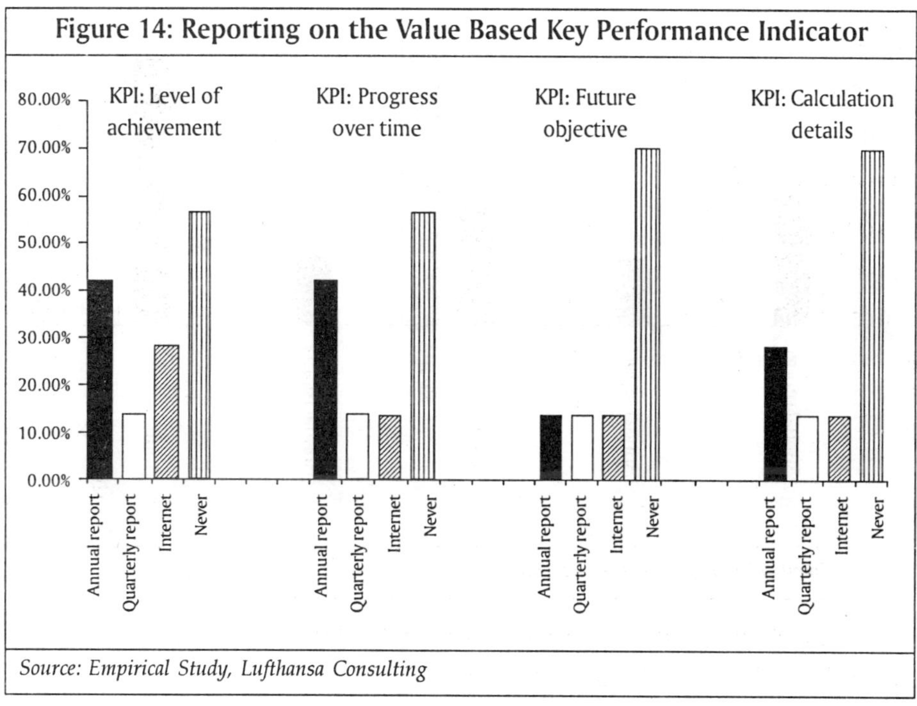

Source: Empirical Study, Lufthansa Consulting

Similar results were received for the reporting on the different components of the key performance indicator. 71.43% of the airlines do not give information about the cost of capital for the group or the planned cash flows. Only 14.29% report on the divisional costs of capital and on the planned EBIT or EBITDA (see Figure 15). Nevertheless it is positive that 57.14% of the airlines give information about the planned invested capital in the annual report. This result can be attributed to the capital intensity of airlines and the accordingly high value. It can be concluded, that airlines have not yet realized the importance of communication with the capital market.

Figure 15: Reporting on the Different Components of the Value-based Key Performance Indicator

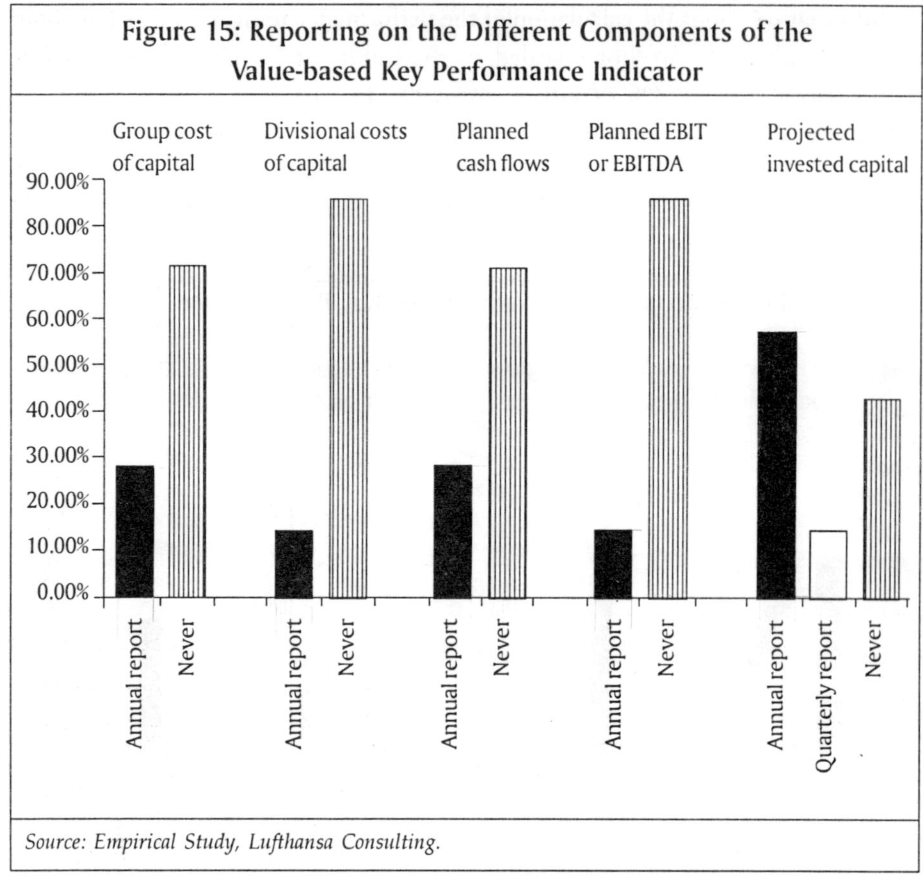

Source: Empirical Study, Lufthansa Consulting.

The concluding analysis of the implementation of the shareholder value concept shows that substantial deficits still exist here.

Although 71% of the airlines indicate having provided training about value based management the attitude or acceptance of the employees towards VBM is valued with an average of 3,5 (possible answers from 1 for "no acceptance" up to 5 for "high acceptance").

It should be noted that the implementation of the shareholder value concept is only graded with an average value of 3,86. 43% of value based managing airlines rate the implementation as only satisfactory (see Figure 16).

Figure 16: Level of Implementation of Shareholder Value Concept

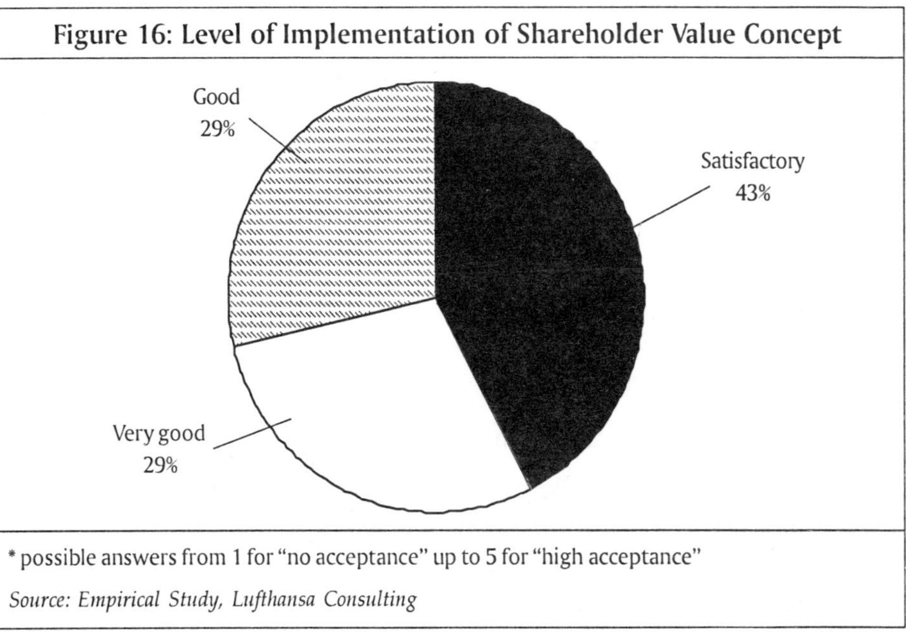

* possible answers from 1 for "no acceptance" up to 5 for "high acceptance"

Source: Empirical Study, Lufthansa Consulting

It seems that VBM at airlines could not yet be satisfactorily integrated in the company philosophy. According to recent results the success of value based management is estimated with an average value of 3,29. 71% of the airlines classified the success of VBM as satisfactory or less (see Figure 17).

Figure 17: Grading of the Success of VBM

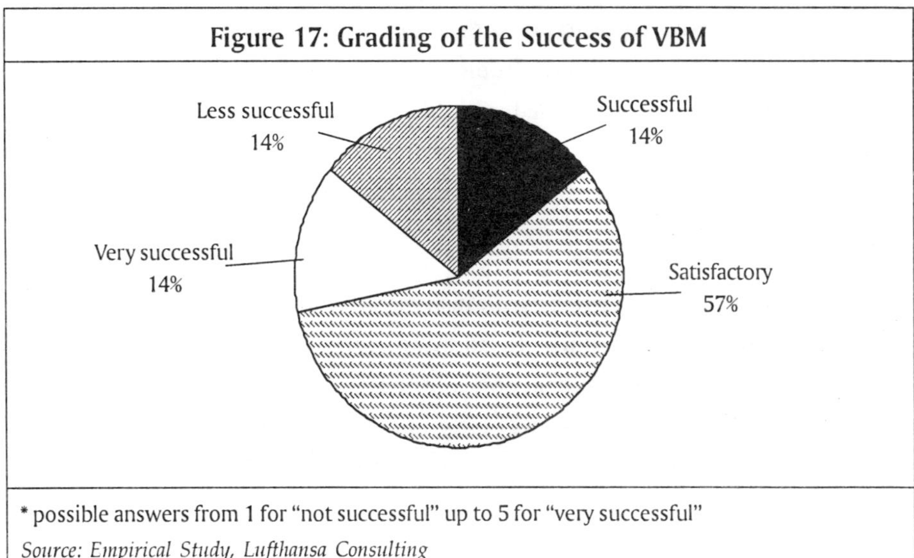

* possible answers from 1 for "not successful" up to 5 for "very successful"

Source: Empirical Study, Lufthansa Consulting

This result, however, could be attributed to the generally poor economic situation of the airline industry.

However, the continuing global deregulation process as well as the high level of competition for both capital and passengers will most likely enhance the distribution and depth of Value Based Management concepts applied in airline management in the future.

Lufthansa Consulting

Aviation is our business

Since 1988 Lufthansa Consulting, an independent subsidiary of Lufthansa German Airlines, has provided services and solutions to the air transportation industry worldwide. Our portfolio and our consulting experts are dedicated to assist aviation specific client groups: airlines, airports and aviation authorities as well as related industries such as ground handling companies, cargo terminal operators, aircraft manufacturers and financial institutions.

Our industry focus originates from our parent organization, one of the world's leading airlines and founding member of the StarAlliance, the international airline network. Thus we ensure that clients benefit from customized business solutions designed by consultants with a global understanding of the industry and in-depth knowledge of those topics that are critical for success. We know the aviation business! This knowledge enables us to quickly identify improvement potentials and offer customized consulting solutions including know-how transfer and implementation, applying the diversified experience of the entire Lufthansa Group.

Our consultants possess extensive industry experience and a profound command of pertinent methods and skills. In addition, they have access to sophisticated databases containing valuable data and information about markets, processes and technologies. These resources are being continuously developed to meet the dynamically changing requirements of our aviation clients.

Lufthansa Consulting maintains contact with leading German universities and other academic institutions to enrich practical experience with current results from research and development. Supporting our endeavor to extend the range and to improve the quality of our products and services we thereby develop innovative approaches towards improving our consulting services and methods, especially in the organizational and technical aspects of the airline and airport sector.

(*Professor Dr. Carsten Homburg is the Director of the Controlling Faculty at the University of Cologne.*

Andrea Theissen recently graduated in Business Administration from the University of Cologne.

Alexander Knigge is a consultant in the Finance Team at Lufthansa Consulting.)

11

PKN ORLEN: Polish Energy Giant's Growth Strategies

Shalini and Sumit Kumar Chaudhuri

Poland's largest oil refining and fuel retailing company, PKN (Polski Koncern Naftowy) ORLEN, has grown rapidly since its establishment in 1999. With the aim of becoming a major oil company in Europe, the company has forayed into foreign markets through acquisitions of companies. The case offers scope to discuss the growth strategies of PKN ORLEN in western and central Europe's energy markets through a 'value based management project' that would consolidate its various business operations.

"We want to build a powerful company with a strong identity."[1]

"With our well-thought-out concepts and plans, as well as Poland's improving economic conditions, we are ready to face new challenges on the way to increasing PKN ORLEN's value with growing optimism."[2]

– Zbigniew Wrobel, CEO of PKN ORLEN

1 Turek, Bogdan, and Fairlamb, David, "Poland's PKN Orlen Is Buying As Fast As It Can", www.businessweek.com, May 31, 2004.

2 "Annual Report 2003", www.orlen.pl

PKN ORLEN, Central Europe's largest oil refining and fuel retailing company,[3] has grown tremendously since its establishment in 1999 and contributes to 10% of Poland's state budget revenues.[4] Despite the Iraq war, PKN ORLEN experienced favourable market conditions in 2003 with 6% growth in fuel consumption. Also, a 16% rise in car sales in Poland added to PKN ORLEN's sales growth and enabled the company to clock revenues of 24,412 PLN million[5] in 2003 [Exhibit 1]. The market capitalisation of PKN exceeds PLN[6] 11 billion. While foreign shareholders constitute 10% of the total stake, nearly 28% is held by Nafta Polska[7] and Polish State Treasury[8] [Exhibit 2]. The company aimed to grow through acquisitions and forayed into the international markets by entering into agreements with Basell Europe Holdings[9] in 2002, Europe's leading oil company, 'BP Plc' in 2003 and Czech-based petrol company, 'Unipetrol' in 2004. It was also looking forward to the consolidation with a Hungarian oil company, 'MOL' in 2004. In an endeavour to strengthen itself as a major regional player by expanding internationally, the CEO of PKN ORLEN, Zbigniew Wrobel, devised a long-term plan called the 'Value based management project' that underlined the strategies required 'to build a strong corporate presence in central Europe, fully prepared to take a proactive role in the regional consolidation process.'[10]

A Brief Overview

'Polski Koncern Naftowy Orlen' (PKN ORLEN) was formed in 1999 following the merger between two large conglomerates of Poland, 'Petrochemia Plock SA' (Petrochemia) and 'Centrala Produktów Naftowych SA' (CPN). The establishment of CPN dates back to 1944 with the establishment of Polski Monopol Naftowych,

---

3 "PKN Orlen", www.orlen.pl

4 "World Economic Forum – PKN Orlen", www.weforum.org

5 op cit, "Annual Report 2003".

6 Poland Zlotych (PLN) is the Poland currency (1 USD = 3.794721 PLN as on June 18th 2004).

7 Poland's privatisation agency established in 1996.

8 A state-owned entity established in 1996 which is responsible for the privatisation of the oil and gas sectors in Poland.

9 Basell is a Dutch-based joint venture established by Royal Dutch Shell and BASF and is active in the development, manufacture and sale of polyethylene, polypropylene and special-purpose polyolefin materials. The company also prepares and sells licenses to produce polyolefins.

10 www.orlen.pl

which was later renamed as Centrala Produktów Naftowych in 1945. CPN was given the exclusive rights to manage the distribution of oil products in Poland. Headquartered in Warsaw, CPN underwent a reorganisation that resulted in the establishment of 17 branches. The regional branches had operational independence but the product pricing and purchasing was governed centrally from the headquarters. In 1995, CPN was transformed into a joint stock company that was wholly owned by the Polish State.

Petrochemia was formed in 1959 as a government enterprise to manufacture and manage an oil refinery that started its production in 1964. In 1968, Petrochemia expanded its operations from refining to processing of crude oil into fuels, lubricants and bitumen. It also started processing refinery gases, gasoline and hydrocarbons to yield a variety of semi-finished products, detergents and plastics. In 1970, it started producing petrochemicals and in June 1993, Petrochemia became a joint stock company wholly owned by the Polish State Treasury.

In 1996, a holding company named Nafta Polska was established which was 100% owned by the Polish State Treasury. The company was formed to carry out the privatisation process in the Polish oil sector and chemical industry. Its functions included monitoring the developments in the oil market, preparation of legislations related to the oil sector and forming strategies for the oil sector along with the Polish government.

By 1998, the Petrochemia group consisted of 51 companies with 28 subsidiaries. It had 520 gas stations in Poland and processed 11.2 million tonnes[11] of crude oil. In May 1998, the merger of Poland's largest oil refinery, Petrochemia and the largest motor fuel retailer and distributor, CPN, was approved. The result was the formation of PKN ORLEN (ORLEN) in 1999. By May 1999, CPN was providing 40% of the fuel supply in the Polish market with 2000 service stations,[12] and Petrochemia constituted 75% share in the domestic market producing 66% liquid fuel[13] domestically. PKN ORLEN was to be privatised by offering public

---

11 "Polski Koncern Naftowy", www.warsawvoice.pl, May 16th 1999.

12 "Energy Market Actors", www.eva.ac.at

13 op. cit. "Polski Koncern Naftowy".

shares on the local and foreign stock exchanges with the government retaining more than 25% stake in the company and selling 25% stake to a strategic investor.[14] The privatisation started in November 1999 with the listing of PKN ORLEN's shares on the Warsaw stock exchange.

After the merger, PKN ORLEN continued to be the largest fuel refinery and distributor of oil products in Poland. The privatisation of PKN ORLEN continued in June 2000 when 109.25 million shares of the company were passed to investors in the private sector through public offerings, with Nafta Polska and the State Treasury together constituting 28.44% stake [Annexure 1]. The company's shares were listed on Warsaw Stock Exchange and also as depository receipts on the London Stock Exchange.

The Post-Merger Developments

In June 2000, PKN ORLEN invested PLN 1.6 billion in the state-of-the-art technology and equipments for its Orlen Capital Group.[15] For instance, in its Plock factory the company installed C5–C6 isomerisation units[16] for the production of engine fuel components. This was the first plan to be implemented after the merger with maximum expenditure at the Plock refinery. The projects under the investment plan included the building of a modern fuel complex that would enhance the company's capability to produce high volume and top quality oil products. According to the then President and CEO of PKN ORLEN, Andrzej Modrzejewski (Modrzejewski), apart from increasing the operational efficiency, such investments were believed to make PKN ORLEN one of the most attractive listed companies in Poland. PKN ORLEN in partnership with KBC[17] in 2000 implemented the 'Profit Improvement Program' (PIP) that resulted in the savings of $13 million due to improvements in production and managing energy. PKN ORLEN was also able to save 25% of its estimated savings of PLN 300 million

---

14 "Poland Powers Up For The Twenty-First Century", www.dieselpub.com

15 The ORLEN Capital Group consists of 90 subsidiaries and associated companies of PKN with total headcount of 14,534, of which 5,871 were employed in PKN ORLEN. In 1Q 2004, companies from the ORLEN Capital Group generated net profit of PLN 37 million.

16 The C5/C6 isomerization unit converts normal pentane and normal hexane streams commonly found in straight run gasoline to isopentane and isohexane, thereby increasing their octane numbers. The isopentane and isohexane streams are then used for blending in the gasoline pool.

17 UK-based KBC is the leading independent process engineering consultancy and provides technical consulting services to the hydrocarbon processing industry.

between 2000 and 2002 due to a widespread reorganisation. This included the opening of twelve Regional Organisational Units consisting of Regional Wholesale and Logistics Offices, Regional Retail Trade Offices, Regional Financial Offices and Regional Investment and Overhaul Offices, all connected through an IT network. PKN ORLEN also reduced its storage and distribution facilities to 42 and sold, leased and liquidated the remaining 110. PIP also aimed at saving $0.40 per barrel in processing crude oil by the end of 2001.

The company strategically launched its 'ORLEN' brand along with its public offering of shares in June 2000 and that helped it to save the additional cost of promoting the brand among all the stakeholders. The company established 57 service stations and modernised 117 retail stations to maintain its 40% market share in fuel retail trade in Poland. By 2000, PKN ORLEN's fuel network consisted of 2,077 stations. Leveraging on its retail network, PKN ORLEN introduced 'FLOTA POLSKA' for fleet operators operating at the national level. The program allowed the operating fleets to purchase fuel, other products and services through the FLOTA card.[18] In spite of difficult market conditions as a result of increased fuel prices and economic slowdown that reduced the fuel consumption, PKN was able to increase its profits through the sales of 4.6 billion litres of fuel in 2000. The company also developed wholesale and logistics facilities by establishing a store with capacity of 55,000 meter cube at Ostrów Wielkopolski. PKN ORLEN also initiated the construction of a 212 km product pipeline to connect the store with the Plock refinery.

By 2001, FLOTA was being accepted at 1100 service stations of the company and its success prompted the company to introduce the 'VITAY' loyalty card scheme in 2001 for the individual customers. The VITAY card scheme was aimed at increasing customer loyalty by rewarding those customers who made regular purchases at the company's service stations. The rewards were in the form of points given to the customers, which they could redeem for fuel or gifts. The cards could be used at any of the company's service stations across Poland and had a built-in microchip that helped the cards to store and process more data apart from ensuring more security to the cashless transactions.

---

18 FLOTA POLSKA fuel card programme is aimed at business customers operating fleet of vehicles. The programme allows for the noncash purchase of fuel and certain other selected products, as well as services offered at its stations, by means of cards issued for a specific vehicle registration number or in a customer's name.

Commenting on PKN ORLEN's initiatives to transform itself as the largest energy company in Poland, Modrzejewski said, "In the next few years PKN ORLEN SA will seek to build on its status as the largest Company in Poland, and one of the largest enterprises of its kind in Central Europe, to expand its operations both in Poland and abroad. Mindful of the intensified consolidation sweeping through fuel and petrochemical companies in Central Europe, we are determined not to be left behind by our competitors. Indeed, the current situation presents a unique opportunity for a large Polish Company to participate in international consolidation. As well as benefiting PKN ORLEN SA, this would also reinforce Poland's position within the European Union."[19]

The company signed a three-year agreement with Poland's major fuel storage firm, 'Naftobazy Sp.' for storage and reloading of PKN ORLEN's oil products in order to gain benefits from the economies of scale in logistics. It also started building its international network by entering into an agreement with 'BMP Trading' to diversify its supply sources. Under this agreement, 2,000,000 tonnes of crude oil was to be supplied to BMP Trading. To guarantee the stable supply of crude oil, PKN ORLEN entered into a transaction with a leading Russian oil company, 'Yukos', for $300 million per year,[20] which would serve as a major supply source of crude oil. It also entered into a contract with Shell, BP and Statoil to supply them fuel for one year by the end of 2001. In 2001, PKN spent PLN 125 million to open 35 new stations and update 140 service stations excluding 86 that were unprofitable and failed to meet the quality standards. By 2001 end, VITAY cards were being used by 2 million customers in Poland and constituted 50% of its retail sales. FLOTA garnered 1000 companies constituting 30% of the retail fuel sales.[21]

With these initiatives, the company was able to increase its retail margins and sales of LPG, unleaded gasoline and diesel. However, the September 11 attacks in New York aggravated the economic recession across the world. The market conditions worsened in Poland and the fluctuation in oil prices decreased fuel demand, and declining margins in refining led to lowering of sales and net profit

---

19 "Annual Report 2000", www.orlen.pl

20 "PKN ORLEN Renews Contract for Crude Oil Supplies", www.orlen.pl, July 17th 2001.

21 "Annual Report 2001", www.orlen.pl

of PKN ORLEN in the fiscal year ending December 31, 2001 [Refer Exhibit 1]. The new challenges prompted the Chairman of PKN ORLEN's supervisory board, Prof. Andrzej Herman, to appoint a new and competent management team in 2001 that would successfully implement the strategic initiatives.

The new management team saw the appointment of Zbigniew Wrobel as the new CEO and the President of the Management Board. He said, "I assumed the position of the President of PKN ORLEN's Management Board in February 2002, and at the very beginning I adopted a management strategy oriented towards transforming the company into one of the largest and best companies in the fuels and petrochemicals industry, both in Poland and Europe." He further added, "We operate the largest wholesale and retail network in Poland, through which we are distributing our own refining products and petrochemicals—all of the highest quality. We also plan to invest in expanding our petrochemical units to enhance our capabilities and achieve compatibility with international markets and standards."[22]

With these developments, the company further planned to maintain its competitive advantage through the adoption of high standards in the company's operations and its strategy stated, "Through alliances and mergers, we intend to become a major player within Central Europe's international oil consortium in the future. PKN ORLEN's market position and potential allows us to assume the leading position in consolidation processes in the fuel and energy sector in Central Europe."[23]

Strategic Initiatives

PKN ORLEN's strategies in 2002 included further privatisation of PKN ORLEN and participation in consolidation of the oil sector, strategic alliances to access oil reserves, increasing the retail margin, cost cutting programs in all activities, promoting the ORLEN brand at company's service stations by 2003, increase in the production capacity of the petrochemical plant and reducing the storage costs by 50%.

---

22 ibid.

23 op cit "Annual Report 2001".

In 2002, PKN's network increased to 1954 service stations of which 631 were franchise outlets. The year 2002 also ended with a 50:50 joint venture agreement between PKN ORLEN and Basell Europe Holdings BV. Wrobel said, "Increased polyolefins production from world-scale plants integrated with an adjacent cracker, both of which are tailored to market conditions, and the opportunity to integrate with the world's leading polyolefins player, are the driving forces of the project."[24] The company invested 300 million, in the project, which by 2004 end, was expected to increase the capacity of PKN ORLEN's polyolefin units to 320,000 tonnes of polyethylene and 400,000 tonnes of polypropylene per year. Wrobel said, "It is vital that under the agreement, we not only acquire a world-class and state-of-the-art technology, with an 80%-guaranteed utilisation ratio for our installations, but also access to the international sales network operated by Basell Europe Holdings BV."[25]

The company also shifted its focus from production to marketing. It was evident from the introduction of branding elements like information pylons to help the consumers in easily locating the oil stations and the thrust on the FLOTA and VITAY card programs. Trained employees, friendly and professional in their behaviour, aided the company's marketing efforts. To ensure further profitability, the company reduced the number of directors in its management board from 60 to 22 and low-tier executives from 160 to 100. Although the volatility in oil prices, low GDP growth of Poland [Annexure 2], an unemployment rate of 20% and decreased sales of new cars led to reduced fuel consumption in 2002, the cost cutting program helped PKN ORLEN to increase its operating profit (EBIT) by 18% and net profit by 12% in 2002 [Refer Exhibit 1]. Retailing was chosen as a strategic growth area as it provided the company high margin and trade volume. PKN also concentrated on expanding its product range by concentrating more on the nonfuel products as their sales and retail margins had increased considerably in 2002.

The most significant event marking the company's growth and development in the international market included the agreement signed in December 2002 with BP to purchase its 494 service stations in Northern Germany for €140 million. The acquisition was completed on February 28, 2003. The service stations sold 2.98 million litres per year and the company believed that selling of PKN's

---

24 "Basell and PKN Orlen Sign Agreement to Form Polish Polyolefins Joint Venture", www.basellorlen.pl, September 30th 2002.

25 "Annual Report 2002", www.orlen.pl

products through these service stations would enhance its retail as well as refining margins and enable the company to achieve 7% market share in Northern Germany and 3% market share[26] in the entire German market. Commenting on this acquisition, the Vice President of the Management Board and Chief Marketing Officer of PKN ORLEN, Slawomir Golonka, said, "This is an extremely significant step in our strategy of expanding our marketing operations both in and outside Poland. This acquisition is an important first stage in building a strong and lasting presence in western Europe's largest energy market."[27] In line with the expansion strategy, the company also invested €35 million to update the German stations in order to make them profitable by early 2004.

To reap the maximum benefit from these international manoeuvres, the company devised and implemented a 'Value Based Management' project that primarily included five strategic key elements—employment rightsizing, cost cutting, reorganisation, modernisation and expansion in the retail segment, optimum utilisation of the capacities at refinery (including the development of petrochemical segment), and reorganisation and sale of the non-core assets. A comprehensive cost cutting program was initiated in July 2003 that helped in cost savings to the tune of PLN 144 million in 2003. The aim was to increase the annual cost savings to PLN 800 million by 2005. The company also succeeded in rightsizing its employee strength through Voluntary Retirement Scheme and disposal of 25 non-core companies. This reduced the employees' count by 2700. The intensive cost cutting, rightsizing and restructuring programs aimed at strengthening the company's finances through cost savings to enable PKN to carry out domestic and international expansion.

In November 2003, PKN ORLEN signed an agreement with the Hungarian fuel giant, MOL with the intention of making joint investments in business projects. In addition, the cooperation was believed to have paved the way for the merger of two entities, which would provide benefits from the economic opportunities occurring in the near future. On this agreement, former Prime Minister of Poland, Leszek Miller, said, "The agreement initiates work on a Central European fuel corporation; the process of establishing this corporation is an

---

26 "Annual Report 2003", www.orlen.pl

27 "BP Sells German Service Stations to Polish Oil Major PKN ORLEN", www.pressi.com, December 11th 2002.

important part of the strategy for the preparation of the Polish and Hungarian fuel sectors for competition in the European market."[28] Wrobel further said, "The companies share the view that cooperation will enable MOL and ORLEN to benefit from the synergy effect and pave the way for more effective competition with leading companies in the oil sector"[29].

The year 2003 reported a remarkable growth in revenues and net profit despite the eruption of war in Iraq. Poland recorded a GDP growth of 3.7% that enabled 6% increase in fuel consumption and 16% growth in the sales of new cars. The same year, the 500 service stations in Germany became profitable adding 400,000 tonnes of fuel sales to the company with non-fuel sales exceeding €81 million. Besides, Basell ORLEN became the largest producer and distributor of polyolefin with production capacity of 295 kilotonnes.[30]

The first quarter of 2004 marked PKN's largest acquisition, of Czech-based 'Unipetrol'. The sale of Unipetrol to PKN was completed with the approval of the Czech government on April 28, 2004 and PKN acquired 63% stake for CZK[31] 13.05 billion [Exhibit 3]. PKN was the only bidder for Unipetrol after MOL and Shell moved out of the tender. Pavel Kuta, the Deputy Chairman of National Property Fund, said, "Even though it isn't ideal that there was only one bidder left in the tender, the price (PKN ORLEN) offered is an acceptable one."[32] Although PKN was the only bidder, it was working in consortium with two other companies, Agrofert[33] and ConocoPhillips.[34] PKN and ConocoPhillips were interested in the refinery and fuel distribution business of Unipetrol while Agrofert was likely to take over the chemical subsidiaries of Unipetrol. It was believed that ConocoPhillips would help PKN in making Unipetrol's subsidiaries, Benzina and Ceska Rafinerska profitable. The cooperation with Agrofert was believed to

---

28 "Love at First Sight", www.warsawvoice.pl, November 26th 2003.

29 ibid

30 "PKN Orlen – Company Overview", www.orlen.pl

31 Czech Republic Koruny (1 USD (USA Dollar) = 26.2048 CZK as on July 2nd 2004).

32 "PKN Orlen only bidder for Unipetrol", www.gasandoil.com, May 18th 2004.

33 Agrofert is the second-largest chemical group in the Czech Republic. In addition to producing chemical products, the company's main business, its other activities include agriculture and food. In 2002, chemical business accounted for 62% of total sales.

34 It is the third-largest integrated energy company in the United States, and the largest refiner in that country. This group, which was created recently by the merger of Conoco and Phillips Petroleum, has many subsidiaries around the world. The focus is on exploration, refining and fuel distribution businesses.

allow PKN to restrict itself to only those assets, which were core to its business. Further, the deal was expected to strengthen PKN's position in relation to other competitors in Central and Eastern Europe [Annexure 3] apart from offering synergistic advantages of raw material procurement, utilisation of logistics infrastructure and chemical production.

In the first quarter of 2004, the company achieved the highest net profit of PLN 397 million [Exhibit 4]. Apart from factors like increase in car sales, domestic industrial production, GDP growth and domestic fuel consumption, the company benefited from the implementation of its strategic measures.

An Energetic Future

PKN ORLEN aimed to expand its network in future through acquisitions and increase its sales volume by 1.2% in 2004. It also aims to achieve consolidation with MOL and restructuring of Unipetrol in 2004. Poland joined the European Union on May 1, 2004 and the company expects an overall positive outcome with benefits exceeding the number of threats [Annexure 4]. PKN ORLEN plans to increase its retail network by increasing the total number of services stations in Poland to 1100 by the end of 2005. PKN ORLEN is also planning to merge its core companies and divest 40 non-core companies by 2006. The strategies are expected to yield sales of 3 million litres of fuel per service station and increase the non-fuel margin to 30% by 2006. By 2006, the company intends to modernise its total retail network with an investment of PLN 1 billion that will offer highest quality fuel and services.

Also, with the implementation of VBM, PKN ORLEN expects to double its economic value by 2006 [Annexure 5] and become a strong regional player [Annexure 6]. The German operations are expected to provide a net profit of €10-15 million by 2005 with an increase in the German market share to 10% by 2007. Wrobel said, "My vision is that in five years the Central European fuel and energy market will be dominated by a Regional Oil Concern, whose one of the core elements will be PKN ORLEN."[35]

(Shalini was a Research Associate, Icfai Business School Case Development Center, Hyderabad.

Sumit Kumar Chaudhuri is a Faculty Member at Icfai Business School Case Development Center).

[35] op cit, "Annual Report 2003".

Exhibit 1: Financial Highlights 2000-03

	2000 PLN m	2001 PLN m	2002 PLN m	2003 PLN m
Revenues	18,602	1 7,038	16,902	24,412
EBITDA	2,335	1,706	1,861	2,474
EBIT	1,425	617	731	1,267
Net profit	902	376	421	987
Total Assets	14,087	14,383	15,073	17,149
Shareholder' equity	7,596	7,958	8,329	9,510
Net Debt[1]	2,542	2,549	2,341	2,402
Net cash provided by operating activities	1,073	2,112	1,292	1,707
CAPEX[2]	1,459	1,533	967	1,337
	2000 PLN	**2001 PLN**	**2002 PLN**	**2003 PLN**
EPS	2.15	0.89	1.00	2.35
CF per share	2.55	5.03	3.07	4.06
Total assets per share	33.53	34.23	35.87	40.10
Book value per share	18.08	18.98	19.82	22.23
	2000 In %	**2001 In %**	**2002 In %**	**2003 In %**
Gearing[3]	33.5	32.0	28.1	25.3
ROACE[4]	10.7	4.3	5.0	8.2
	2000	**2001**	**2002**	**2003**
Number of employees in PKN ORLEN Group	1 3,342	17,582[5]	1 7,81 8	15.133

[1] Net debt = short and long-term interest-bearing debt – (cash and cash equivalents)

[2] Purchase of tangible and intagible assets

[3] Gearing = net debt/shareholders' equity

[4] ROACE = EBIT after actual tax rate/average (shareholder's equity + net debt)

[5] Full consolidation of Anwil started in 2001

Source: "Annual Report 2003", www.orlen.pl

Financial Data by Business Segments

2003	Refining PLN m	Petrochemical PLN m	Other PLN m
Revenues	24,476	4,545	1,653
Profit of the segment	1,251	418	6
Non-attributed revenues and costs	–407		
Operating Profit	1,267		
Assets	11,571	2,268	1,968
Capex	756	534	128

Source: "Annual Report 2003", www.orlen.pl

Exhibit 2: Shareholder Structure of PKN ORLEN

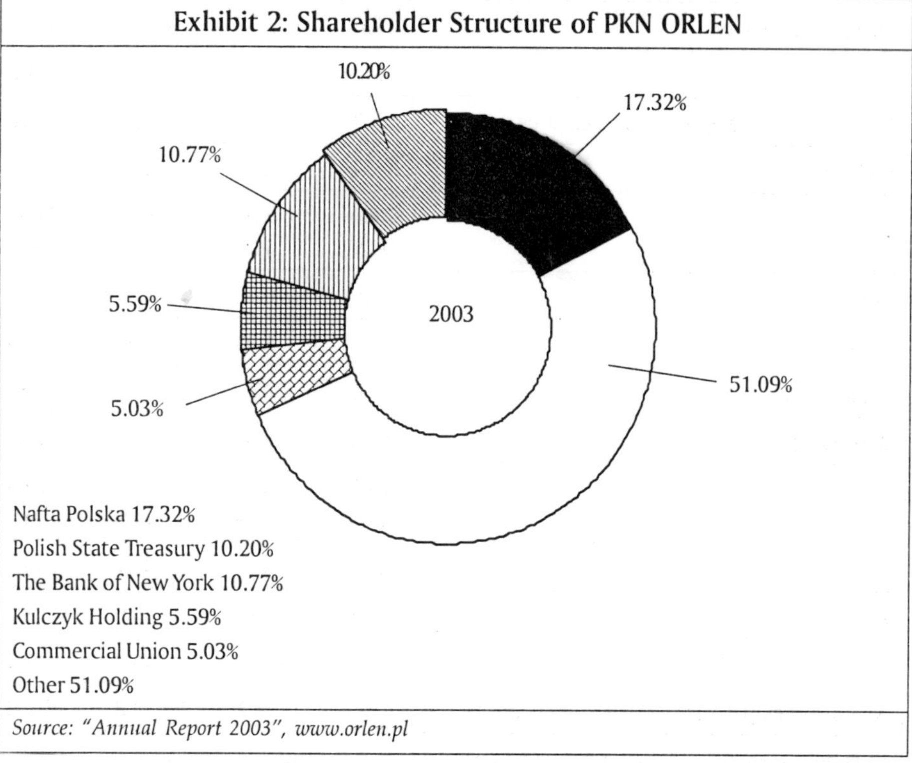

Source: "Annual Report 2003", www.orlen.pl

Exhibit 3: PKN ORLEN's Offer

The NPF's 62.99% Stake in Unipetrol	CCA's 9.76% Stake in Spolana	CCA's Receivables	PKN's Total Offer
11.30 bn CZK	1 mn CZK	1.75 bn CZK	13.05 bn CZK

Source: "Unipetrol", www.atlantik.cz, May 14, 2004

Exhibit 4: Financial Highlights of PKN ORLEN in the First Quarter of 2004

IFRS Basis PLN m	Q1 04	Q1 03	Change
Revenues	6.325	4.962	27.5%
Cost of sales	–5112	–3793	34.8%
Distribution costs	–542	–455	19.1%
Administrative expenses	–184	–209	–12.0%
Other	18	85	–78.8%
Profit from operations	505	590	–14.4%
Profit before income tax and minority interests	517	513	0.8%
Net profit	397	355	11.8%
Net profit – LIFO	305	205	48.8%
PLN	**Q1 04**	**Q1 03**	**Change**
EPS	0.93	0.84	10.7%

Source: "1Q 2004 – results", www.orlen.pl

Annexure 1: Privatisation of PKN ORLEN

Shareholder Structure of PKN ORLEN SA before Initial Public Offering [%]

State treasury – 10.38%
Nafta Polska – 74.06%
Petrochemia Plock SA Employees – 12%
CPN SA Employees – 3.56

Shareholder Structure of PKN ORLEN SA after Initial Public Offering [%]

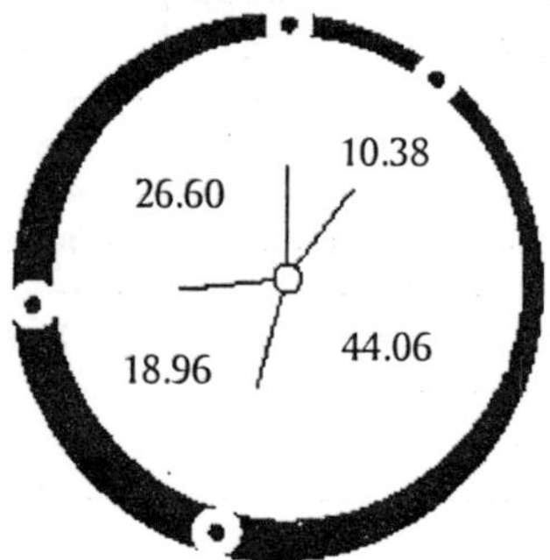

State treasury – 10.38%
Nafta Polska – 44.06%
The Bank of New York –18.96%
Other Stock Market Investors – 26.60%

Shareholder Structure of PKN ORLEN SA after Secondary Public Offering [%]

State treasury – 10.38%
Nafta Polska – 18.06%
The Bank of New York – 27.07%
Other Stock Market Investors – 44.49%

Source: "Annual Report 2000", www.orlen.pl

Annexure 2: Real GDP Growth in Poland

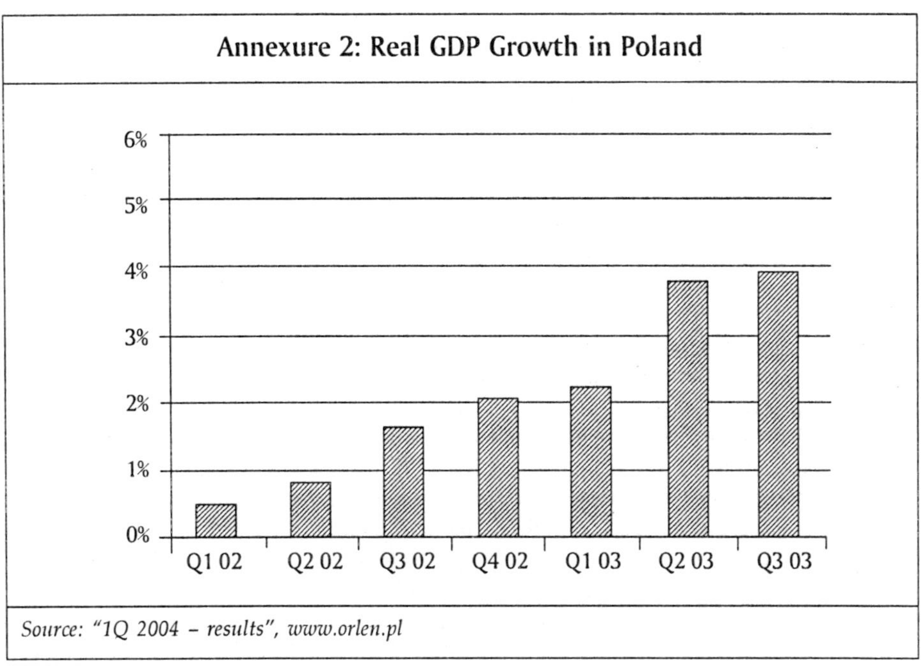

Source: "1Q 2004 – results", www.orlen.pl

Annexure 3: List of Competitors

Hungary

OMV Aktiengesellschaft

MOL (Magyar Olaj Gazi)

The Netherlands

Royal Dutch/Shell Group of companies

The UK

BP

France

TotalElfFina

Russia

OAO LUKOIL

Compiled by Icfai Business School Case Development Center.

Annexure 4: Benefits and Threats to Poland for Joining EU

Benefits

Opportunity to leverage expenditure incurred on:

1. PKN ORLEN's technological adjustment to the requirements set forth in the EU directives:
   - Investments in the construction of modern crude oil processing facilities (over USD 2 bn)
   - Extensive preparation of the refining installations and the distribution network for the reduction of harmful emissions, i.e. implementation of the provisions of the IPPC (Integrated Pollution Prevention Control) system and the European Parliament and Council Directive 94/63 (on the control of volatile organic compound (VOC) emissions resulting from the storage of petrol and its distribution from terminals to service stations);
   - Active development of the system of mandatory stocks and the infrastructure for their storage (e.g. at IKS Solino SA);
2. Acquiring the skills required to operate on a free and open market—the upgraded and restructured distribution network is a modern and efficient system, which ensures best-of-breed customer service, the source of our success on the Polish market where:
   - There are no logistics or formal barriers to fuel imports;
   - The financial regulations are compatible with EU requirements—the import duty rate on fuels is 0% and excise tax rates exceed the minimum set by EU;
   - We compete with the distribution networks of the world's largest oil companies.
3. More effective enforcement of provisions governing fuel quality controls and fair competition:
   - Use of unfair competitive practices by other market participants will become more difficult given the continuous monitoring and control of engine fuel quality;
   - Limited ability of the state to provide aid to inefficient companies.
4. The prospect of faster economic growth, translating into the development of the fuel market and better financial results for PKN ORLEN.
5. Possibility to use EU funds for restructuring the company by joining in the implementation of the National Development Plan, particularly in the field of activities promoting the innovativeness and competitive edge of companies operating in the single European market.

Threats

1. More stringent quality requirements for engine fuels: from 2009 the maximum admissible content of sulphur will be 10 ppm, and fuels with such sulphur content will have to be available in the market by 2005; another requirement will be the introduction of a separate kind of diesel oil for off-road engines and farming equipment and the reduction of the admissible sulphur content in marine oils.
2. Increase in costs related to the more stringent environmental protection regulations concerning such issues as pollution liability, prevention of excessive contamination, or reduction of greenhouse gas emissions.
3. Wider scope of the mandatory analyses of chemical substances introduced to the market.
4. Weaker position of crude-oil derivative fuels as a result of energy saving regulations to be enacted by the EU (providing for a reduction in energy consumption by 1% annually in each country, reduction of engine fuel consumption to 5.8 litres per 100 km, more common use of alternative fuels, such as hydrogen, CNG, and fuels from renewable sources).

Source: "Annual Report 2003", www.orlen.pl

Annexure 5: Key Elements of the Value Based Management (VBM) System in PKN ORLEN

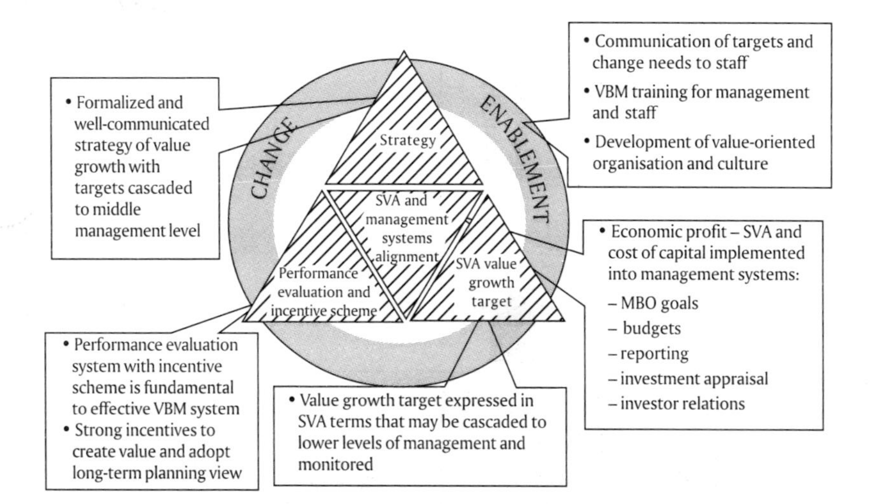

Complex Actions to Double Economic Value by 2006

Advantage

Prime location in the CEE, the potential and size of the market, and our strong position, gives us the opportunity to be one of the most profitable companies in the region

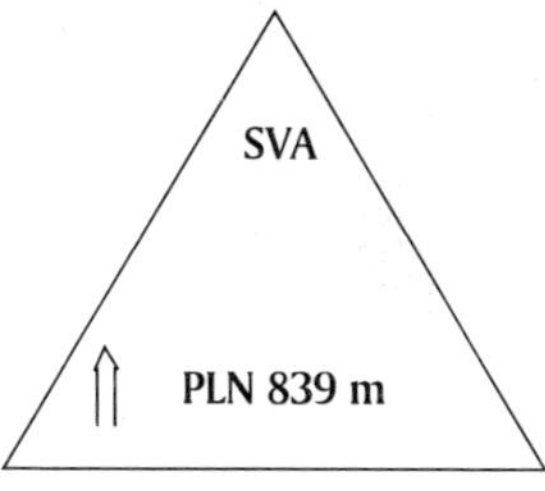

Upside

Doubling economic value by 2006 mainly due to:

- PLN 800 m (complex) cost-cutting programme to 2005
- Synergies between refining and doubled pet-chem production
- Focus on retail

Risk

Active hedging in margin optimization process to cope with volatile market conditions

State of the art technology and reorganization of the retail network to meet future EU regulations

SVA – Shareholder Value Added, SVA = (ROACE – WACC) x Invested Capital

ROACE = EBIT after actual tax rate/average (equity + net debt) CE = EBIT after actual tax rate/average (equity + net debt) – ratio

Source: "PKN Orlen – Equity Story", www.orlen.pl

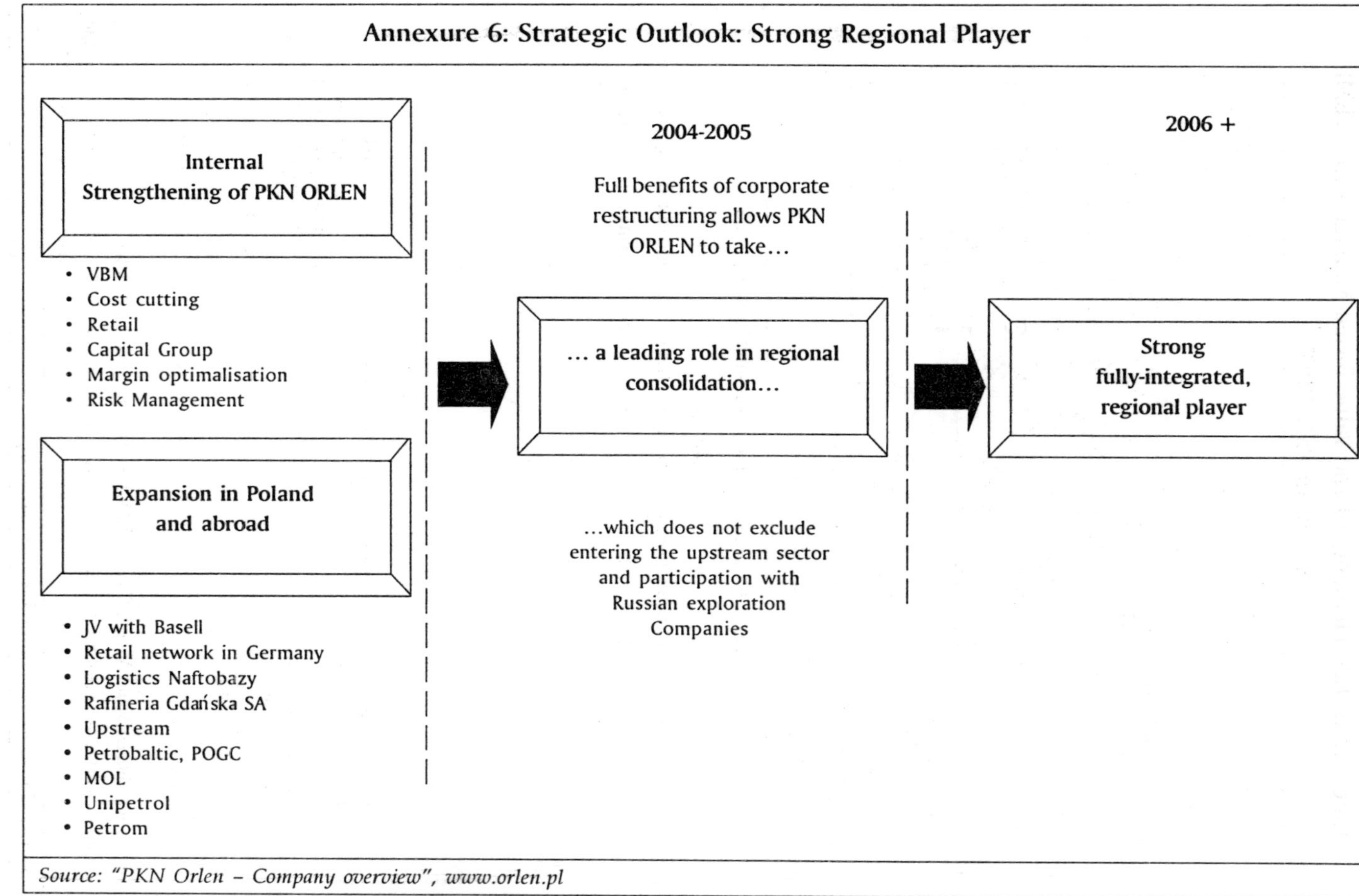

Source: "PKN Orlen – Company overview", www.orlen.pl

12

Shareholder Value Creation of Microsoft and GE*

Pablo Fernández

In this paper, we will define and analyze shareholder value creation. To help us understand this concept better, we will use the example of two listed companies, General Electric and Microsoft, between 1992 and 2003.

To obtain the created shareholder value, we must first define the increase of equity market value, the shareholder value added, the shareholder return, and the required return to equity. A company creates value for the shareholders when the shareholder return exceeds the required return to equity (Ke). In other words, a company creates value when it outperforms expectations. The created shareholder value is quantified as follows: Created shareholder value = Equity market value x ***(Shareholder return – Ke). The created shareholder value can also be calculated as follows: Created shareholder value = Shareholder value added – (Equity market value*** x ***Ke). We also calculate the created shareholder value of 400 American companies during the eleven-year period 1992-2003.***

* Another version of this paper may be found in chapters 1 and 13 of the author's book, "Valuation Methods and Shareholder Value Creation", 2002 Academic Press, San Diego, CA.

On 31st December 1992, General Electric had 854.04 million shares outstanding and the price of each share on the stock market was 85.49 dollars. On 31st December 2003, General Electric had 10,063.12 million shares outstanding and the price of each share on the stock market was 30.98 dollars[1]. Consequently, General Electric's equity market value[2] increased from 73.02 billion dollars in December 1992 to 311.06 billion dollars in December 2003[3]. The increase of equity market value during this period was 238.05 billion dollars. However, this is not General Electric's created shareholder value during those years.

On 31 December 1992, Microsoft had 275.06 million shares outstanding and the price of each share was 85.37 dollars. On 31st December 2003, Microsoft had 10,812.47 million shares outstanding and the price of each share on the stock market was 27.37 dollars[4]. Consequently, Microsoft equity market value increased from 23.48 billion dollars in December 1992 to 295.94 billion dollars in December 2003. The increase of equity market value during this period was 272.45 billion dollars.

To obtain the created shareholder value, we must first define the increase of equity market value, the shareholder value added, the shareholder return, and the required return to equity. It is important not to confuse the created shareholder value with any of the other concepts we have mentioned. All of these concepts will be explained in this paper.

Figure 1 shows that between December 1992 and December 2003, General Electric's equity market value increased 238.05 billion dollars, the shareholder value added was 289.89 billion dollars, and the created shareholder value was 197.93 billion dollars.

---

1 GE had three stock splits in between: 2 x 1 in May 13, 1994, 2 x 1 in May 9, 1997 and 3 x 1 in May 5, 2000.

2 The equity market value is the value of all of the company's shares.

3 On December 31, 2003: 10,063.12 million shares x 30.98 dollars/share = 311.06 billion dollars.

4 Microsoft had five 2 x 1 stock splits in between: May 20, 1994, December 6, 1996, February 20, 1998, March 26, 1999, and February 14, 2003.

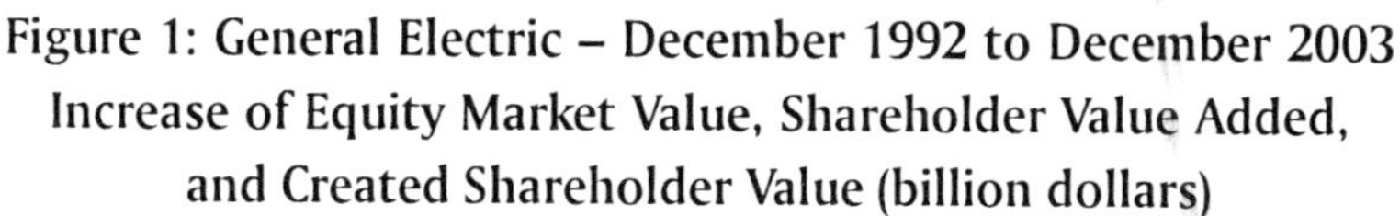

Figure 1: General Electric – December 1992 to December 2003 Increase of Equity Market Value, Shareholder Value Added, and Created Shareholder Value (billion dollars)

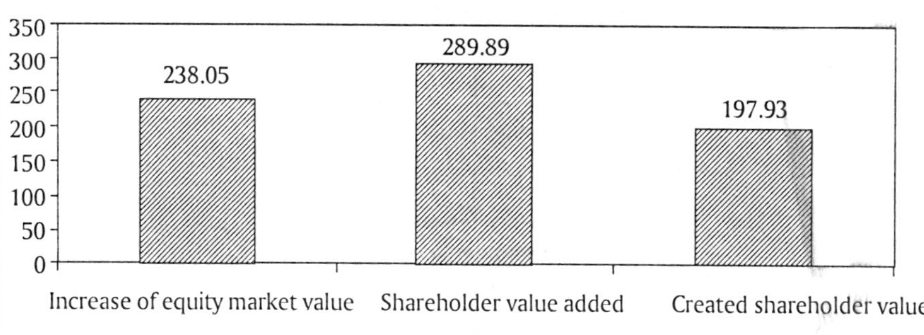

Figure 2: Microsoft – December 1992 to December 2003 Increase of Equity Market Value, Shareholder Value Added, and Created Shareholder Value (billion dollars)

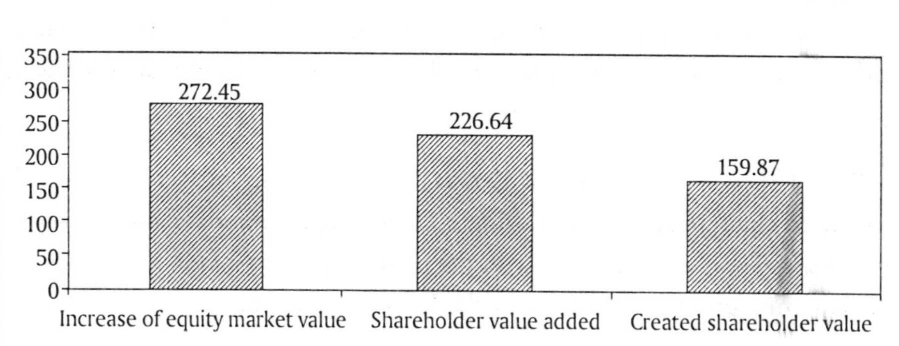

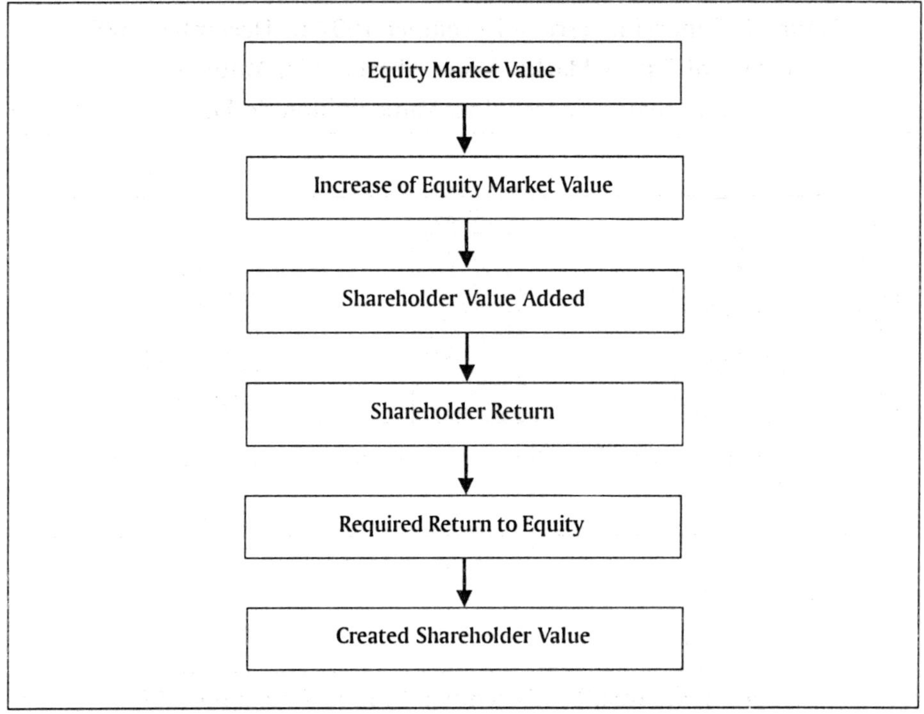

1. Increase of Equity Market Value

The equity market value of a listed company is the company's market value, that is, each share's price multiplied by the number of shares. The increase of equity market value in one year is the equity market value at the end of that year less the equity market value at the end of the previous year.

Table 1 shows the evolution of General Electric's equity market value and the increase of equity market value during each year. It is important not to confuse *the increase of equity market value* with the *shareholder value added*, as they are two different concepts, as we shall see in the following section.

2. Shareholder Value Added

Shareholder value added is the term used for the difference between the wealth held by the shareholders at the end of a given year and the wealth they held the previous year. The *increase of equity market value* is not the *shareholder value added*.

Table 1: General Electric and Microsoft – Equity Market Value and Increase of Equity Market Value During Each Year (billion dollars)

General Electric	1993	1994	1995	1996	1997	1998	1999	2000	2001	2002	2003	Sum
Number of shares (million)	853	1.710	1.670	1.646	3.273	3.277	3.278	9.909	9.927	9.949	10.063	
Equity market value	89,45	87,19	120,26	162,79	240,14	334,24	507,22	475,00	397,89	242,27	311,07	
Increase of equity market value	16,43	-2,26	33,07	42,53	77,35	94,10	172,98	-32,21	-77,11	-155,62	68,80	238,05
Microsoft	**1993**	**1994**	**1995**	**1996**	**1997**	**1998**	**1999**	**2000**	**2001**	**2002**	**2003**	**Sum**
Number of shares (million)	284	582	592	1.195	1.207	2.494	5.160	5.332	5.386	5.351	10.812	
Equity market value	22,88	35,60	51,97	98,75	155,96	345,83	602,43	231,29	356,81	276,63	295,94	
Increase of equity market value	-0,60	12,72	16,38	46,78	57,21	189,86	256,61	-371,14	125,52	-80,18	19,31	272,45

There is an increase in the equity market value, but not shareholder value added when:

- Shareholders subscribe to new shares of the company paying money,
- A conversion of convertible debentures takes place.

There is a decrease of the equity market value, but not a decrease of shareholder value[5] when:

- The company pays money to all of the shareholders: dividends,
- The company buys shares on the market (share buy-backs)

The shareholder value added is calculated as follows:

Shareholder value added =	Increase of equity market value + Dividends paid during the year – Outlays for capital increases + Other payments to shareholders (discounts on par value, share buy-backs....) – Conversion of convertible debentures

Table 2 shows the calculation of the shareholder value added for the period 1993-2003. The shareholder value added has exceeded the increase of equity market value every year. This is because the dividends and other payments to shareholders exceeded the outlays the shareholders had to make.

However, the *shareholder value added* is not the *created shareholder value.* For value to be created during a period, the shareholder return must exceed the required return to equity.

3. Shareholder Return

The *shareholder return* is the shareholder value added in one year, divided by the equity market value at the beginning of the year.

Shareholder return = Shareholder value added / Equity market value

5 When the company pays dividends to the shareholders, they receive money, but the company's equity market value (and the price per share) also decreases by a similar amount.

Table 2: General Electric and Microsoft – Increase of Equity Market Value and Shareholder Value Added Each Year (billion dollars)

General Electric	1993	1994	1995	1996	1997	1998	1999	2000	2001	2002	2003	Total
Increase of equity market value	16,43	–2,26	33,07	42,53	77,35	94,10	172,98	–32,21	–77,11	–155,62	68,80	238,05
+ Dividends	2,15	2,46	2,77	3,05	3,41	3,91	4,58	5,40	6,36	7,16	7,64	48,89
+ Other payments to shareholders	0,84	0,74	3,51	2,86	2,18	2,82	1,46	0,00	2,44	0,99	0,00	17,84
– Outlays by shareholders	0,41	0,77	0,00	0,00	0,00	2,39	0,00	3,58	3,25	2,56	1,94	14,90
– Convertible debentures converted	0	0	0	0	0	0	0	0	0	0	0	0,00
Shareholder value added	19,02	0,18	39,35	48,44	82,93	98,44	179,02	–30,39	–71,57	–150,03	74,50	289,89
Microsoft	**1993**	**1994**	**1995**	**1996**	**1997**	**1998**	**1999**	**2000**	**2001**	**2002**	**2003**	**Total**
Increase of equity market value	–0,60	12,71	16,38	46,78	57,21	189,86	256,61	–371,14	125,52	–80,18	19,31	272,45
+ Dividends	0	0	0	0	0	0	0	0	0	0	0,86	0,86
+ Other payments to shareholders	0,25	0,35	0,65	1,26	3,10	2,50	2,98	4,91	7,44	3,31	0,80	27,55
– Outlays by shareholders	0,96	1,25	1,52	2,14	4,59	13,62	23,17	12,39	10,98	1,50	2,12	74,22
Convertible debentures converted	0	0	0	0	0	0	0	0	0	0	0	0,00
Shareholder value added	–1,31	11,81	15,51	45,90	55,73	178,74	236,42	–378,62	121,98	–78,36	18,84	226,64

For example, as Table 3 shows, General Electric's shareholder return in 1998 was 41%: the shareholder value added in 1998 (98.44 billion dollars) divided by the equity market value at the end of 1997 (240.14 billion dollars).

Table 3: Shareholder Return of Microsoft and General Electric

	1993	1994	1995	1996	1997	1998	1999	2000	2001	2002	2003	Average
Microsoft	-6%	52%	44%	88%	56%	115%	68%	-63%	53%	-22%	7%	24%
General Electric	26%	0%	45%	40%	51%	41%	54%	-6%	-15%	-38%	31%	17%

One way to calculate the shareholder return is: increase in the share's price plus dividends, rights and other payments (discounts on par value, special payments...) divided by the share's price at the start of the year.

4. Required Return to Equity

The *required return to equity* (Ke, also called cost of equity) is the return that shareholders expect to obtain in order to feel sufficiently remunerated. The required return to equity depends on the interest rates of long-term Treasury bonds and the company's risk. Let us look at an example. On December 2002, the return provided by 10-year Treasury bonds was 3.79%. A shareholder would therefore demand a return on his investment that was higher than the 3.79% he could get risk-free. How much higher? That depends on the company's risk. Obviously, he would require a higher return on an investment in shares of a high-risk company than on an investment in shares of a lower-risk company.

The required return is the sum of the interest rate of long-term Treasury bonds plus a quantity that is usually called the company's *risk premium* and which depends on its risk.

Required return to equity = Return of long-term treasury bonds + Risk premium

Ke is the term used for the required return to equity (return on the investment required by the shareholder), also known as the equity cost.

If the one-year, risk-free interest rate is 12%, this means that one million dollars to be paid in one year's time with the guarantee of the State (this is what we mean with the expression "risk-free") today has a value of 1,000,000/1.12 = 892,857 dollars. The value today of obtaining a million dollars in one year's time, as a result of an investment in a company's shares, will be less because that million has more risk (we have less certainty of obtaining it). For the value today of our investment in the company to be less than 892,857 dollars, we must divide the million we expect to obtain by a quantity greater than 1.12. If we give our investment in the company a value of 833,333 dollars (1,000,000/1.20 = 833,333), this means that we are restating at 20% less the million we expect to obtain in one year's time.

Another way of saying this is that the return we require on an investment guaranteed by the State is 12% (the risk-free interest rate) and the required return on an investment in the company is 20%. The difference between 20% and 12% is due to the risk perceived in a company and is usually called the company's risk premium.

Stating this idea as an equation, we could say that the required return on the investment in the company's shares (Ke) is equal to the risk-free rate plus the company's risk premium. The company's risk premium is a function of the company's perceived risk[6]:

Ke = return of treasury bonds + company's risk premium

Table 4 shows the evolution of 10-year Treasury bonds and the required return to equity of General Electric and Microsoft.

Table 4: Yield of 10-year Treasury Bonds and Required Return to Equity of General Electric and Microsoft (data corresponding to December 31)

	1993	1994	1995	1996	1997	1998	1999	2000	2001	2002	2003	Average
10-year treasury bonds (t -1)	6.68%	5.80%	7.84%	5.58%	6.42%	5.74%	4.65%	6.43%	5.10%	5.04%	3.79%	5.73%
Required return to equity (Ke) General Electric	10,7%	9,5%	11,8%	9,0%	10,1%	8,9%	7,4%	9,8%	8,3%	8,2%	7,0%	9,1%
Required return to equity (Ke) Microsoft	11.7%	10.2%	12.7%	9.5%	10.9%	9.5%	8.1%	11.1%	9.7%	9.4%	8.0%	10.1%

6 If, instead of investing in a single company's shares, we were to invest in all companies' shares (in a diversified portfolio), we would then require a return which is the following: Ke = return of Treasury bonds + market risk premium. By way of reference, in 2003 and 2000, most market analysts used a market risk premium around 4%.

5. Created Shareholder Value

A company creates value for the shareholders when the shareholder return exceeds the share cost (the required return to equity). In other words, a company creates value in one year when it outperforms expectations.

The created shareholder value is quantified as follows:

Created shareholder value = Equity market value x (Shareholder return – Ke)

As we already saw that the shareholder return is equal to the shareholder value added divided by the equity market value, the created value can also be calculated as follows:

Created shareholder value = Shareholder value added – (Equity market value x Ke)

Consequently, the value created is the shareholder value added above expectations, which are reflected in the required return to equity.

Table 5 shows the created shareholder value of General Electric. General Electric created value for its shareholders every year except the years 1994, 2000, 2001 and 2002. Microsoft was a value destroyer in the years 1993, 2000, 2002 and 2003.

Table 6 shows in simplified form the relationship between three variables, which are sometimes confused: increase of equity market value, shareholder value added, and created shareholder value.

6. The ROE is Not the Shareholder Return

ROE means Return on Equity. However, it is not true that the ROE, which is calculated by dividing the net income by the shares' book value, is the shareholder return. In Section 3, we already defined the shareholder return as the shareholder value added divided by the equity market value and this is not the ROE. Table 7, which shows General Electric's ROE and shareholder return prove this for each year. We can see that the ROE follows a different course from the shareholder return.

Table 5: General Electric and Microsoft – Evolution of the Increase of Equity Market Value, Shareholder Value Added, and Created Shareholder Value (billion dollars)

General Electric	1993	1994	1995	1996	1997	1998	1999	2000	2001	2002	2003	Total
Increase of equity market value	16.43	–2.26	33.07	42.53	77.35	94.10	172.98	–32.21	–77.11	–155.62	68.80	238.05
Shareholder value added	19.02	0.18	39.35	48.44	82.93	98.44	179.02	–30.39	–71.57	–150.03	74.50	289.89
Created shareholder value	11.22	-8.29	29.04	37.60	66.50	77.17	154.13	–80.07	–111.02	–182.82	57.57	51.01
Created shareholder value in 2003 $	26.55	–17.93	56.13	66.67	107.10	114.17	212.25	–100.43	–128.56	–195.59	57.57	197.93
Microsoft	**1993**	**1994**	**1995**	**1996**	**1997**	**1998**	**1999**	**2000**	**2001**	**2002**	**2003**	**Total**
Increase of equity market value	–0.60	12.72	16.38	46.78	57.21	189.86	256.61	–371.14	125.52	–80.18	19.31	272.45
Shareholder value added	–1.31	11.81	15.51	45.90	55.73	178.74	236.42	–378.62	121.98	–78.36	18.84	226.64
Created shareholder value	–4.06	9.48	10.99	40.97	44.95	163.96	208.40	–445.32	99.51	–111.89	–3.29	13.71
Created shareholder value in 2003 $	–10.42	22.10	22.73	77.42	76.59	255.19	300.04	–577.23	117.57	–120.84	–3.29	159.87

Table 6: Increase of Equity Market Value, Shareholder Value Added, and Created Shareholder Value	
Increase of equity market value	Equity market $value_t$ – Equity market $value_{t-1}$ ↓
Shareholder value added	Increase of equity market value – payments from shareholders + dividends + repurchases – conversions. ↓
Created shareholder value	Shareholder value added – (Equity market value x Ke)

Table 7: General Electric's and Microsoft's ROE and Shareholder Return

General Electric	1993	1994	1995	1996	1997	1998	1999	2000	2001	2002	2003
Shareholder return	26%	0%	45%	40%	51%	41%	54%	–6%	–15%	–38%	31%
ROE	18%	17%	23%	22%	24%	24%	25%	27%	25%	25%	23%
Microsoft	1993	1994	1995	1996	1997	1998	1999	2000	2001	2002	2003
Shareholder return	–6%	52%	44%	88%	56%	115%	68%	–63%	53%	–22%	7%
ROE	43%	35%	33%	41%	50%	46%	50%	34%	19%	17%	19%

7. Comparison of General Electric with other Companies

Table 8 shows the created shareholder value, shareholder value added, shareholder return and market capitalization of selected American companies during the ten-year period 1993-2003. General Electric was the third biggest company in equity market value in 1992, and the biggest in 2003. Microsoft was the nineteenth biggest company in equity market value in 1992, and the second in 2003. The table is ordered by capitalization in 1992.

8. What Should the Shareholder Return be Compared With?

In section 5, we saw that the company creates value if the shareholder return exceeds the required return (and it destroys value in the opposite case).

Table 8: Created Shareholder Value, Shareholder Value Added, Shareholder Return and Market Capitalization of Selected American Companies (million dollars)

		Market Capitalization		Shareholder Return	Shareholder Value Added	Shareholder Value Creation ($ of 2003)
S No	$ million	1992	2003	1993–2003	1993–2003	1993–2003
1	Exxon Mobil	75,917	271,002	277.4%	182,803	56,994
2	Wal Mart Stores	73,560	229,589	254.5%	175,959	59,858
3	General Electric	73,020	311,066	446.5%	289,889	197,930
4	Altria GP.	68,854	110,536	269.6%	115,127	31,173
5	AT & T	68,116	16,034	–19.7%	–7,801	–113,698
6	Coca Cola	54,852	124,414	181.7%	93,546	17,638
7	Merck &.Co.	49,751	102,795	189.6%	99,061	31,838
8	Procter & Gamble	36,449	129,517	361.0%	118,283	69,840
9	Bristol Myers Squibb	34,968	55,464	154.6%	52,347	10,154
10	Johnson & Johnson	33,063	153,334	389.6%	118,945	66,271
11	Pepsico	33,048	80,035	187.5%	53,109	6,971
12	DU Pont E I DE Nemours	31,785	45,742	167.9%	44,759	11,141
13	Intl.Bus.Mach.	28,770	159,449	726.3%	176,771	150,999
14	Abbott Labs.	25,422	72,852	283.1%	60,892	27,501
15	Bellsouth	25,360	52,302	211.5%	50,299	21,072
16	American Intl.Gp.	24,541	172,855	461.5%	104,406	53,458
17	Pfizer	23,901	269,622	596.7%	104,890	43,527
18	Chevrontexaco	23,693	92,331	264.7%	52,762	19,047
19	Microsoft	23,483	295,937	934.9%	226,642	159,867
20	General Motors	22,743	29,944	197.2%	41,945	17,052
21	Walt Disney	22,541	47,718	77.3%	17,481	–26,928
22	Home Depot	22,337	80,747	230.4%	56,077	14,852
23	Verizon Comms.	22,187	96,875	110.8%	9,783	–50,087

Contd...

Contd...						
24	SBC Communications	22,174	86,309	100.7%	–8,511	–79,534
25	3M	22,049	66,579	365.9%	59,914	32,907
26	Wyeth	21,048	56,535	237.5%	44,133	14,715
27	Ford Motor	20,928	28,163	208.4%	59,351	47,708
28	Fannie Mae	20,849	72,933	396.6%	73,062	46,729
29	Intel	18,109	209,350	1112.7%	194,760	158,227
30	Lilly Eli	17,777	78,974	497.6%	73,676	51,327
31	McDonald's	17,740	31,513	122.8%	21,301	–3,804
32	Hewlett-Packard	17,588	70,039	281.6%	60,995	34,769
33	Anheuser-Busch Cos.	16,189	42,922	364.6%	42,852	23,143
34	Kellogg	15,950	15,542	53.9%	6,249	–15,192
35	Sears Roebuck &.Co.	15,711	11,546	250.8%	24,168	22,010
36	Dow Chemicals	15,624	38,267	233.8%	28,569	9,883
37	Sara Lee	14,392	17,158	90.6%	12,155	–7,624
38	PG &.E	14,121	11,518	30.7%	2,937	–15,441
39	Motorola	13,990	32,589	76.5%	8,128	–23,056
40	Schlumberger	13,841	32,035	155.3%	20,593	–933
41	Boeing	13,616	33,721	151.8%	19,109	–7,925
42	Eastman Kodak	13,171	7,356	15.0%	6,131	–6,531
43	Schering-Plough	12,664	25,553	174.1%	22,004	6,320
44	Bank of America	12,536	119,503	354.0%	72,634	21,368
45	Gillette	12,498	37,161	205.3%	22,777	–2,164
46	Emerson Electric	12,335	27,247	208.5%	22,802	6,296
47	Bank One	12,296	50,965	103.4%	3,533	25,000
48	Southern	12,184	22,149	366.1%	29,198	15,643
49	Union Pacific	11,894	17,730	120.3%	11,686	–3,217
50	American Express	11,891	62,037	691.9%	64,067	51,639
51	Toys R US Holdings Co.	11,681	2,698	–68.5%	–7,533	–28,386
52	Gen. Mills	11,223	16,980	123.2%	8,773	–5,185
53	Heinz HJ	11,159	12,819	103.1%	9,449	–5,245
						Contd...

Contd...						
54	Campbell Soup	10,580	11,017	72.7%	9,393	–3,229
55	Edison Intl.	9,850	7,145	51.2%	3,845	–7,857
56	Limited Brands	9,782	9,316	77.4%	4,091	–10,562
57	Amgen	9,551	79,209	600.0%	57,807	38,799
58	JP Morgan Chase &.Co.	9,507	74,804	308.3%	36,696	6,722
59	Kimberly-Clark	9,469	29,808	167.1%	19,948	–866
60	TXU	9,236	7,683	7.0%	1,241	–11,416
61	Penney JC	9,107	7,175	2.3%	77	–13,796
62	Baxter Intl.	9,021	18,626	177.4%	13,671	1,675
63	Colgate-Palm.	8,901	26,889	336.9%	25,621	14,420
64	May Dept. Stores	8,737	8,389	83.9%	6,845	–3,749
65	Freddie Mac	8,710	40,469	467.0%	37,836	25,065
66	Archer-Danls.-Midl.	8,652	9,842	52.1%	3,994	–8,545
67	Norfolk Southern	8,616	9,233	53.8%	4,051	–7,213
68	ITT Industries	8,590	6,847	592.8%	12,597	12,110
69	Honeywell Intl.	8,569	28,818	169.4%	9,060	–9,405
70	Novell	8,505	3,932	–63.1%	–5,169	–28,274
71	Fortune Brands	8,210	10,428	311.1%	11,256	3,850
72	Intl. Paper	8,154	20,713	68.5%	5,091	–11,890
73	Conagra	8,136	14,169	121.4%	9,003	–2,824
74	PNC FINL.SVS.GP.	7,999	15,175	195.8%	13,468	2,946
75	Loews	7,820	9,170	87.2%	5,280	–5,467
76	Chubb	7,771	12,788	93.4%	6,706	–4,518
77	Cons. Edison	7,632	9,675	155.6%	7,975	–1,001
78	Xerox	7,521	10,928	29.1%	2,934	–11,350
79	Weyerhaeuser	7,519	14,068	143.7%	8,587	–2,593
80	Automatic Data Proc.	7,470	23,546	230.5%	17,075	4,652
81	Duke Energy	7,401	18,559	82.8%	5,476	–9,073
82	Gannett	7,316	24,168	324.5%	20,263	10,227
83	Corning	7,298	13,869	14.2%	–4,211	–22,387
						Contd...

Contd...						
84	PUB. SER. ENTER. GP.	7,236	10,300	191.1%	8,765	572
85	CSX	7,085	7,692	35.6%	2,229	–8,512
86	Apple Computers	7,067	7,858	–25.7%	–3,106	–20,963
87	PPG Industries	6,990	10,879	165.7%	9,065	906
88	Raytheon 'B'	6,909	12,503	48.4%	3,697	–6,243
89	Electronic Data Systems	6,779	11,788	–12.2%	–4,537	–28,423
90	Albertsons	6,677	8,311	11.9%	104	–11,250
91	UST	6,665	5,919	101.2%	3,977	–4,407
92	Marsh & Mclennan	6,653	25,393	328.5%	20,629	9,928
93	FPL Group	6,586	12,034	192.2%	9,952	1,819
94	Conocophillips	6,538	44,638	266.9%	21,247	10,571
95	Dominion Res.	6,440	20,707	202.5%	10,731	1,166
96	Rockwell Automation	6,416	6,637	549.6%	14,621	10,092
97	Pitney-Bowes	6,260	9,489	177.7%	9,397	1,848
98	SLM	6,233	16,987	606.9%	17,236	9,953
99	Alcoa	6,137	32,883	423.6%	25,229	14,559
100	Unocal	6,131	9,537	88.9%	5,049	–3,865
101	Merrill Lynch &.Co.	6,115	55,272	836.1%	40,356	29,937
102	AMER. ELEC. PWR.	6,113	12,052	83.1%	3,447	–5,181
103	Wells Fargo &.Co	6,040	99,644	617.4%	63,922	35,987
104	United Technologies	5,953	44,430	870.0%	43,518	36,316
105	Center point EN.	5,941	2,966	0.8%	1,004	–6,583
106	Winn-Dixie Strs.	5,886	1,409	–64.5%	–2,929	–12,221
107	Entergy	5,780	12,899	200.9%	10,265	1,789
108	Exelon	5,757	21,623	316.9%	11,868	2,726
109	Wachovia	5,748	61,872	218.4%	24,054	–4,239
110	Medtronic	5,673	58,919	770.5%	44,961	32,018
111	Sprint	5,612	14,843	152.0%	8,753	–2,287
112	CVS	5,554	14,265	88.0%	3,580	–8,057
113	Georgia Pacific	5,500	7,794	75.7%	4,060	–4,106
						Contd...

Contd...						
114	Suntrust Banks	5,476	20,129	323.3%	14,908	6,423
115	Caterpillar	5,413	28,828	689.5%	29,929	23,721
116	Target	5,400	35,000	600.3%	30,152	21,574
117	Cooper Inds.	5,370	5,408	75.0%	2,473	–5,218
118	Walgreen	5,369	37,286	637.2%	32,198	23,786
119	Citigroup	5,313	250,402	1412.1%	176,740	128,875
120	Air PRDS. & Chems.	5,297	12,006	179.7%	8,421	464
121	Burlington Res.	5,239	11,001	60.2%	4,153	–5,925
122	Dillards 'A'	5,149	1,305	–64.4%	–3,396	–12,698
123	Occidental Ptl.	5,144	16,268	298.8%	12,986	5,524
124	Donnelley R R	5,092	3,426	24.7%	959	–6,005
125	Sysco	4,942	24,093	559.4%	22,493	15,744
126	Marathon Oil	4,938	10,266	177.0%	7,388	138
127	Gt. Lakes Chm.	4,937	1,376	–50.1%	–2,009	–9,098
128	Goodyear Tire	4,899	1,378	–69.8%	–2,995	–11,518
129	DTE Energy	4,814	6,631	131.9%	4,441	–1,473
130	Cisco Systems	4,791	167,268	2118.7%	115,900	78,164
131	GAP	4,748	20,792	413.1%	18,692	11,445
132	Masco	4,507	12,695	137.4%	6,557	–1,815
133	Progress EN.	4,460	11,018	192.9%	6,677	888
134	Bank Of New York	4,331	24,098	548.6%	25,293	19,171
135	Amerada Hess	4,259	4,779	34.2%	1,459	–5,026
136	Alltel	4,216	14,536	166.9%	5,146	–4,360
137	H & R Block	4,211	9,871	265.7%	7,855	1,717
138	Cigna	4,206	8,078	289.3%	14,533	11,283
139	Intl.Flav.& Frag.	4,188	3,271	33.3%	1,201	–4,285
140	Torchmark	4,141	5,154	92.2%	2,865	–3,280
141	PPL	4,133	7,758	193.2%	5,042	–145
142	Nike 'B'	4,033	11,797	271.9%	9,458	2,751
143	Fleetboston Finl.	4,030	46,032	298.5%	25,679	9,124
						Contd...

Contd...

144	Oracle	3,983	69,161	1788.1%	74,562	67,574
145	Avon Products	3,975	15,962	521.3%	15,446	10,236
146	Deluxe	3,922	2,089	83.7%	1,560	–3,770
147	Unitedhealth Gp.	3,904	34,131	723.1%	32,728	23,323
148	NAT.City	3,896	20,614	324.6%	12,612	2,680
149	Genuine Parts	3,893	5,776	113.8%	3,875	–1,724
150	Textron	3,886	7,761	230.5%	7,987	3,473
151	Texas Insts.	3,841	50,846	984.2%	38,922	27,258
152	Burl.Nthn.Santa Fe C	3,825	12,009	170.9%	7,466	–2,247
153	Wrigley William Jr.	3,817	10,324	317.1%	9,991	5,549
154	First Data	3,781	29,947	389.5%	23,856	11,597
155	Keycorp	3,733	12,289	186.3%	11,872	5,065
156	Carnival	3,685	25,013	461.1%	18,022	9,506
157	Illinois Tool Wks.	3,649	25,855	488.4%	19,221	11,815
158	Comerica	3,648	9,831	279.8%	8,352	3,759
159	Rohm & Haas	3,613	9,510	209.9%	6,302	723
160	Safeco	3,596	5,394	95.1%	2,674	–2,588
161	Unumprovident	3,573	4,669	–26.5%	–1,965	–9,501
162	Firstenergy	3,528	11,610	191.4%	6,030	225
163	AON	3,525	7,508	103.4%	3,558	–2,229
164	Hershey Foods	3,521	7,676	307.2%	8,137	4,511
165	Liz Claiborne	3,437	3,870	95.7%	1,661	–3,932
166	Sun Microsystems	3,422	14,602	325.4%	4,383	–5,584
167	Phelps Dodge	3,403	6,798	107.1%	3,559	–1,469
168	Providian Finl.	3,402	3,378	134.7%	5,373	3,009
169	Nucor	3,396	4,384	59.7%	1,810	–3,940
170	Computer Assocs. Intl.	3,394	15,832	370.4%	12,861	5,651
171	Constellation En.	3,359	6,536	188.2%	5,034	882
172	Deere & Co.	3,339	15,893	472.0%	14,726	9,909
173	State Street	3,281	17,406	440.7%	14,322	8,728

Contd...

Contd...						
174	LNA. Pacific	3,260	1,893	–24.5%	–898	–6,684
175	Humana	3,249	3,681	218.5%	5,649	7,855
176	St. Paul	3,234	9,046	186.6%	6,247	964
177	Fifth Third Bancorp	3,228	33,629	567.4%	20,934	12,451
178	Bausch & Lomb	3,202	2,695	20.8%	312	–4,880
179	Knight-Ridder	3,180	6,182	230.4%	5,129	1,277
180	Newell Rubbermaid	3,180	6,248	43.8%	1,040	–5,134
181	Nordstrom	3,173	4,714	104.8%	2,811	–2,595
182	Grainger W W	3,151	4,325	84.8%	2,390	–2,178
183	V F	3,134	4,684	113.1%	3,251	–1,417
184	Tribune	3,123	16,112	397.1%	11,334	6,331
185	Whirlpool	3,119	5,061	111.4%	3,125	–1,771
186	Lincoln Nat.	3,105	7,185	216.0%	6,758	2,061
187	Halliburton	3,080	11,390	136.7%	3,492	–5,287
188	Gen. Dynamics	3,073	17,873	630.6%	14,687	11,127
189	Reebo K Intl.	3,056	2,316	20.3%	577	–4,212
190	Cincinnati Fin.	3,052	6,698	187.4%	5,122	702
191	Ingersoll-Rand	3,043	11,776	319.3%	9,205	4,168
192	McGraw-Hill Co.	3,014	13,397	489.6%	12,681	8,752
193	Becton Dickinson &.Co.	2,983	10,447	381.2%	9,061	5,384
194	Sunoco	2,976	3,951	177.7%	2,901	–560
195	Intl. Game Tech.	2,960	12,360	487.4%	9,839	4,224
196	Fedex	2,950	20,141	398.5%	13,833	6,745
197	Sigma Aldrich	2,862	3,965	118.0%	2,672	–1,691
198	Mellon Finl.	2,859	13,815	398.2%	16,745	12,698
199	Temple Inland	2,840	3,401	57.9%	1,421	–2,902
200	Cooper Tire Rub.	2,838	1,579	–22.2%	–779	–5,597
201	Hasbro	2,833	3,713	63.5%	1,444	–3,343
202	Aflac	2,832	18,554	772.0%	18,077	14,377
203	Eaton	2,823	8,206	296.0%	7,094	3,077
						Contd...

Contd...

204	Newmont Mining	2,803	17,801	61.3%	8,640	650
205	Viacom 'B'	2,800	71,702	112.6%	11,790	–16,195
206	Hercules	2,766	1,353	–29.1%	587	–2,185
207	Golden West Finl.	2,758	15,677	660.8%	14,731	10,637
208	Sempra EN.	2,744	6,801	138.5%	3,440	–1,137
209	Autozone	2,743	7,436	334.2%	7,535	2,796
210	Dow Jones &.Co	2,731	3,032	135.5%	3,328	494
211	Baker Hughes	2,731	10,769	96.8%	4,947	–1,967
212	Frank. Res.	2,730	12,936	382.2%	10,521	5,145
213	Southwest Airlines	2,726	12,705	321.6%	9,280	3,948
214	Allegheny En.	2,718	1,620	–5.2%	456	–2,927
215	Xcel Energy	2,706	6,772	49.2%	–34	–5,288
216	Sherwin-Williams	2,702	5,064	178.5%	4,003	211
217	MBIA	2,649	8,537	230.9%	6,031	1,405
218	Dover	2,622	8,050	319.1%	7,615	4,441
219	Interpublic GP.	2,613	6,119	53.1%	–769	–6,364
220	Clorox	2,540	10,248	445.7%	9,331	5,716
221	Delta Air Lines	2,528	1,458	–52.0%	–1,371	–6,669
222	Federated Dept. Strs.	2,489	8,521	140.8%	5,055	–1,308
223	MBNA	2,456	31,750	1287.1%	28,786	24,567
224	Circuit City Stores	2,438	2,133	20.1%	115	–5,429
225	Jefferson Pilot	2,433	7,144	373.5%	7,326	4,385
226	Mattel	2,431	8,284	67.3%	2,960	–3,852
227	Mccormick &.Co NV.	2,426	3,731	151.8%	2,322	–1,209
228	Teco Energy	2,391	2,546	24.3%	701	–2,648
229	EOG Res.	2,350	5,314	233.5%	4,109	218
230	Pall	2,327	3,373	73.1%	1,540	–2,178
231	Engelhard	2,307	3,757	138.3%	2,474	–980
232	Meadwestvaco	2,245	5,967	102.0%	2,644	–606
233	Supervalu	2,215	3,834	151.2%	2,505	–515

Contd...

Contd...						
234	Nthn. Trust	2,193	10,198	423.7%	9,143	5,898
235	Praxair	2,183	12,422	425.9%	9,871	5,601
236	Kerr-Mcgee	2,173	4,688	48.2%	657	–3,442
237	Dana	2,156	2,727	8.1%	–1,009	–5,921
238	Boston Scientific	2,125	30,112	604.2%	22,392	13,238
239	Hilton Hotels	2,065	6,499	196.3%	3,653	–1,013
240	Ryder System	2,065	2,190	84.7%	1,150	–1,513
241	Tenet Hlthcr.	2,054	7,460	101.5%	974	–5,927
242	New York Times 'A'	2,039	7,078	328.2%	7,223	4,012
243	US. Steel	2,023	3,617	43.1%	1,042	–3,434
244	Office Depot	2,005	5,233	66.5%	–85	–6,835
245	St. Jude Med.	1,994	10,585	348.2%	8,002	3,903
246	TJX Cos.	1,977	11,097	617.4%	11,420	7,778
247	Cendant	1,967	22,564	159.2%	637	–18,667
248	Progressive Ohio	1,942	18,055	794.2%	16,211	12,303
249	Paccar	1,936	9,932	747.7%	9,688	7,096
250	Stanley Works	1,934	3,070	144.3%	2,334	–382
251	Radioshack	1,878	5,035	365.3%	5,674	3,286
252	Stryker	1,869	16,958	790.0%	14,814	11,253
253	BMC Software	1,868	4,220	105.8%	–50	–5,857
254	Biomet	1,865	9,266	419.1%	7,623	4,157
255	Harrahs Entm.	1,862	5,498	299.6%	4,688	2,317
256	Vulcan Materials	1,826	4,838	282.1%	4,104	1,783
257	Bear Stearns	1,817	7,971	692.9%	8,763	6,799
258	Williams Cos.	1,802	5,089	111.3%	–598	–5,839
259	Johnson Controls	1,798	10,487	550.8%	9,061	6,372
260	Avery Dennison	1,784	6,189	404.8%	5,823	3,632
261	Pinnacle West Cap.	1,774	3,653	191.7%	2,945	429
262	Nisource	1,768	5,758	177.9%	2,360	–246
263	Lowe's Companies	1,760	43,556	1825.5%	38,442	33,384
						Contd...

Contd...						
264	Huntington Bcsh.	1,756	5,150	235.1%	4,052	788
265	Dell	1,756	87,003	4430.7%	89,956	88,349
266	Bard C R	1,750	4,193	202.0%	3,047	311
267	Allergan	1,749	10,312	609.0%	9,384	6,794
268	Chiron Corp	1,724	10,696	303.4%	7,185	2,067
269	Amer. Greetings 'A'	1,689	1,342	10.4%	233	–2,334
270	Forest Labs.	1,679	22,596	1128.3%	19,493	16,153
271	Dynegy 'A'	1,674	1,199	–46.4%	–5,186	–9,492
272	Unisys	1,638	4,907	46.6%	–1,596	–8,665
273	Anadarko Petroleum	1,625	12,798	271.3%	2,393	–3,245
274	Northrop Grumman	1,610	17,507	268.0%	4,173	–433
275	Advd. Micro Devc.	1,589	5,194	64.5%	1,428	–4,802
276	Maytag	1,585	2,188	144.0%	2,389	570
277	Coca Cola Ents.	1,584	9,949	467.6%	7,205	3,963
278	Ashland	1,581	3,023	142.8%	1,921	–652
279	Equifax	1,562	3,407	316.6%	4,590	2,469
280	Brunswick	1,546	2,913	150.4%	1,928	–659
281	Black &.Decker	1,512	3,834	215.2%	3,196	691
282	Ambac Financial	1,511	7,415	434.7%	6,140	3,839
283	MGIC Invt	1,476	5,609	361.2%	5,197	3,019
284	CMS Energy	1,469	1,228	–29.6%	–837	–3,613
285	Parker-Hannifin	1,434	7,055	453.4%	5,999	3,749
286	Brown-Forman 'B'	1,401	3,015	343.4%	3,246	1,672
287	Nicor	1,384	1,499	124.8%	1,353	–194
288	Centurytel	1,377	4,704	181.3%	2,929	213
289	Parametric Tech.	1,358	1,049	–40.5%	–1,256	–5,577
290	Worthington Inds.	1,358	1,558	75.0%	736	–1,321
291	Marshall & Ilsley	1,355	8,661	357.1%	6,399	3,531
292	Harley-Davidson	1,353	14,400	958.1%	13,338	10,897
293	Cummins	1,343	2,070	63.9%	762	–1,986
						Contd...

Contd...

294	Snap-On	1,330	1,878	111.9%	1,316	–426
295	Kroger	1,321	13,790	406.3%	7,050	1,456
296	Family $.Strs.	1,316	6,176	442.6%	5,207	2,918
297	Amsouth Banc.	1,308	8,601	289.4%	5,799	2,484
298	Applied Mats.	1,296	37,732	2027.7%	30,786	25,104
299	Leggett & Platt	1,293	4,152	210.3%	2,930	412
300	Countrywide Finl.	1,291	13,966	618.3%	10,523	7,373
301	Computer Scis.	1,286	8,285	239.2%	3,093	–1,587
302	Bemis	1,285	2,656	157.4%	1,834	–135
303	Safeway	1,283	9,678	573.8%	8,661	5,309
304	Thermo Electron	1,267	4,103	187.6%	2,713	–79
305	Goodrich	1,251	3,492	87.5%	1,257	–1,473
306	Cintas	1,249	8,570	488.4%	6,395	3,745
307	Wendy's Intl.	1,244	4,471	252.6%	3,322	1,011
308	Thomas &.Betts	1,229	1,338	–6.7%	–332	–2,774
309	AES	1,224	5,850	116.7%	–3,310	–9,354
310	Amer.Power Conv.	1,220	4,865	252.9%	3,359	137
311	Regions Finl.	1,206	8,265	223.8%	3,697	–688
312	Southtrust	1,179	10,864	697.2%	9,971	7,385
313	Omnicom GP.	1,177	16,593	899.5%	13,479	10,519
314	El Paso	1,156	4,909	–26.6%	–13,850	–20,495
315	Ecolab	1,156	7,052	603.6%	6,516	4,862
316	Applera Appd. Bios.	1,156	4,308	200.9%	3,024	276
317	Allegheny Techs.	1,144	1,066	–44.1%	–2,040	–6,043
318	National Semicon.	1,132	7,017	270.9%	4,226	–250
319	Autodesk	1,109	2,773	132.0%	1,519	–908
320	Perkinelmer	1,103	2,165	125.9%	392	–1,480
321	Kohls	1,051	15,280	1098.3%	12,594	10,198
322	US Bancorp	1,048	57,438	915.7%	23,036	10,229
323	Peoples Energy	1,047	1,491	159.2%	1,223	–65

Contd...

Contd...

324	First Ten. Nat.	1,034	5,535	580.6%	5,724	4,352
325	Millipore	1,000	2,101	207.1%	1,653	366
326	Genzyme	987	11,048	359.8%	6,038	2,589
327	Charles Schwab	986	16,062	1355.2%	10,582	6,817
328	Nextel Comms. A	983	29,852	203.4%	10,124	–1,281
329	Centex	976	6,691	619.9%	5,638	3,842
330	Keyspan	965	5,853	191.2%	2,764	146
331	Jones Apparel Group	961	4,451	271.5%	2,868	808
332	Washington Mutual	944	36,081	448.0%	19,434	6,510
333	Staples	935	13,518	653.6%	8,302	4,298
334	Ball	928	3,357	368.5%	2,749	1,383
335	Electronic Arts	928	14,202	824.7%	11,112	8,364
336	EMC	910	31,033	1704.9%	14,544	5,262
337	Compuware	902	2,320	87.7%	445	–2,414
338	Scientific Atlanta	900	4,145	342.7%	3,162	792
339	Linear Tech.	900	13,143	1288.7%	11,993	9,891
340	Apache	880	13,141	446.8%	8,584	5,056
341	Synovus Finl.	874	8,727	687.1%	7,529	5,592
342	Tyco Intl.	850	52,976	565.8%	–7,436	–35,216
343	Molex	838	3,503	309.4%	2,578	1,054
344	Big Lots	828	1,661	23.5%	–69	–2,586
345	Pulte Homes	823	5,767	565.8%	4,371	2,859
346	Boise Cascade	802	1,961	93.7%	793	–969
347	Analog Devices	780	16,973	1586.8%	13,630	10,610
348	Comcast 'A'	764	44,485	454.9%	14,888	12,598
349	Danaher	738	14,052	1342.3%	11,305	9,371
350	Dollar General	724	7,074	832.5%	6,143	4,556
351	Micron Tech.	724	8,215	622.2%	1,589	–3,513
352	Crane	720	1,827	276.0%	1,672	734
353	Adobe Sys.	712	9,145	950.8%	8,696	5,922

Contd...

Contd...						
354	Paychex	697	14,044	1884.6%	13,573	12,242
355	Trowe Price Gp.	652	5,904	888.0%	5,426	4,316
356	Citizens Comms.	638	3,533	15.9%	922	–1,256
357	ADC Telecom.	628	2,390	105.5%	–3,184	–6,939
358	Bed Bath &.Beyond	624	12,935	1775.0%	11,558	10,287
359	Solectron	614	4,943	153.0%	–6,092	–12,888
360	Tektronix	603	2,678	431.6%	2,437	1,199
361	Plum Creek Timber	601	5,572	373.9%	2,589	1,312
362	Adolph Coors 'B'	598	1,971	322.8%	1,731	870
363	Rowan Cos.	576	2,179	197.0%	1,215	–319
364	Cardinal Health	574	26,479	771.0%	15,211	8,208
365	Navistar Intl.	572	3,300	113.5%	1,510	–1,460
366	Xilinx	571	13,225	1735.6%	10,204	7,838
367	Fiserv	569	7,663	692.6%	5,896	4,219
368	HCA	550	20,385	211.5%	10,645	–8,438
369	Tiffany & Co	541	6,628	1019.6%	5,806	4,590
370	Manor Care	533	3,082	219.4%	1,288	–706
371	Qualcomm	503	43,148	3566.0%	12,581	–4,960
372	Teradyne	500	4,870	562.1%	3,213	1,077
373	BB & T	495	21,121	449.1%	9,656	4,611
374	LSI Logic	484	3,362	230.1%	29	–3,342
375	Starbucks	484	13,061	1333.9%	10,853	8,951
376	Sealed Air	483	4,601	331.0%	1,849	–493
377	KB Home	477	3,361	420.8%	2,824	1,765
378	Zions Bancorp.	466	5,512	691.7%	3,650	2,124
379	Sungard Data Systems	453	7,961	645.2%	5,006	3,100
380	Best Buy Co.	438	16,961	2323.5%	14,641	12,131
381	Alberto Culver 'B'	428	3,781	448.3%	1,758	1,098
382	Meredith	420	1,965	715.5%	2,149	1,937
383	Union Planters	404	5,938	200.2%	2,633	–804
						Contd...

Contd...						
384	Maxim Integrated Prds.	398	16,292	2604.3%	12,108	9,995
385	Andrew	394	1,835	140.7%	559	–378
386	Nabors Inds.	380	6,083	538.5%	3,313	1,106
387	Charter One Finl.	377	7,692	544.1%	5,780	3,494
388	Health Man. As. A	352	5,827	956.8%	5,010	3,677
389	Tellabs	339	3,509	736.6%	603	–1,639
390	Symantec	316	10,628	912.7%	8,462	6,491
391	Concord EFS	309	6,902	1045.8%	2,401	228
392	Medimmune	306	6,282	562.1%	1,847	–419
393	Symbol Techs.	304	3,876	903.2%	2,866	1,880
394	Peoplesoft	283	8,545	1210.4%	3,567	1,056
395	Kinder Morgan Kans	274	7,283	517.7%	5,081	3,546
396	Altera	259	8,579	2714.6%	7,797	6,554
397	KLA Tencor	229	11,398	1811.2%	8,467	5,920
398	Clear Chl. Comms.	187	28,828	2786.8%	3,059	–6,842
399	Time Warner	164	78,105	7775.8%	–28,439	–66,238
400	Biogen Idec	80	12,023	2416.7%	3,359	2,307
		2,409,199	9,144,622		6,285,445	2,050,471

However, the shareholder return is often compared with other benchmarks[7]. The most common benchmarks are:

a) *Zero.* If the shareholder return is positive (above zero), the shareholders have more money in nominal terms than at the beginning of the year.

b) *The return of treasury bonds.* If the shareholder return exceeds that of investing in Treasury bonds, the shareholders have obtained an additional return for bearing more risk (the additional risk of investing in the company instead of investing in Treasury bonds).

c) *Required return to equity.* If the shareholder return exceeds the expected return, the company has created value: the shareholders have obtained a return that is greater than that required to compensate the additional risk of investing in the company instead of investing in Treasury bonds.

7 Comparing different benchmarks enables different questions to be answered.

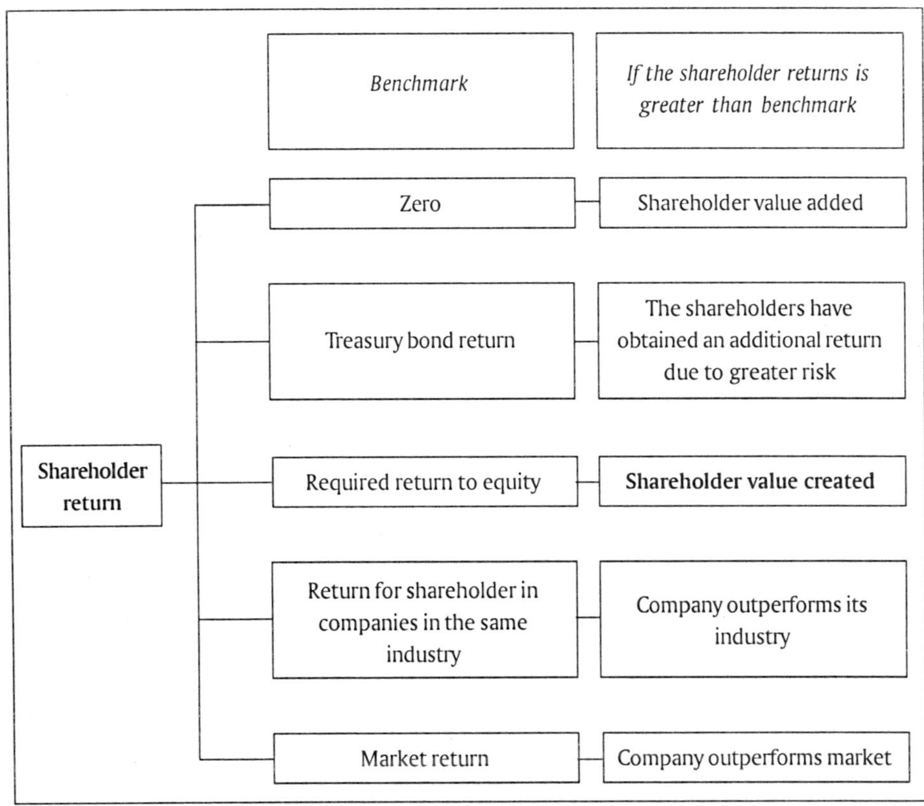

d) *Shareholder return of companies in the same industry.* If the shareholder return exceeds the shareholder return of companies in the same industry, the company has created more value than the other companies in its industry (for an equal investment and risk).

e) *Return of the stock market index.* If the shareholder return exceeds the return of the stock market index, the company has outperformed the market as a whole.

(Pablo Fernández, PricewaterhouseCoopers, Professor of Corporate Finance, IESE Business School, Spain. The author can be reached at fernandezpa@iese.edu).

Index

D

E

F

G

H

I